厦门社科丛书

中共厦门市委宣传部
厦门市社会科学界联合会 编

希望的国度

晚清西人看中国

[英] 仁信（James Johnston）◎著
周维江 黄秀君 ◎译

China and Its Future

In the Light of the Antecedents of
the Empire, Its People, and Their Institutions

厦门大学出版社　国家一级出版社
XIAMEN UNIVERSITY PRESS　全国百佳图书出版单位

图书在版编目(CIP)数据

希望的国度:晚清西人看中国/(英)仁信(James Johnston)著;周维江,黄秀君译. --厦门:厦门大学出版社,2024.5
(厦门社科丛书)
ISBN 978-7-5615-9121-5

Ⅰ. ①希… Ⅱ. ①仁… ②周… ③黄… Ⅲ. ①中华文化-研究 Ⅳ. ①K203

中国国家版本馆CIP数据核字(2023)第184185号

责任编辑	章木良
美术编辑	蒋卓群
技术编辑	朱 楷

出版发行 厦门大学出版社
社　　址 厦门市软件园二期望海路39号
邮政编码 361008
总　　机 0592-2181111　0592-2181406(传真)
营销中心 0592-2184458　0592-2181365
网　　址 http://www.xmupress.com
邮　　箱 xmup@xmupress.com
印　　刷 厦门集大印刷有限公司

开本　720 mm×1 000 mm　1/16
印张　12.75
插页　4
字数　200千字
版次　2024年5月第1版
印次　2024年5月第1次印刷
定价　56.00元

本书如有印装质量问题请直接寄承印厂调换

厦门大学出版社
微信二维码

厦门大学出版社
微博二维码

厦门社科丛书

总 编 辑：中共厦门市委宣传部
　　　　　厦门市社会科学界联合会
执行编辑：厦门市社会科学院

编委会

主　　任：吴子东
副 主 任：潘少銮
委　　员：彭心安　郑尚定　李晓燕　林奕田　苏秋华
　　　　　徐祥清　施琦婷　陈艺萍　吴文祥　方　颖
　　　　　王丽霞　洪文建　方晓冬　官　威　李包明
　　　　　李　桢　徐　隆

编辑部

主　　编：潘少銮
副 主 编：陈艺萍　吴文祥　王彦龙　李　桢　徐　隆
编　　辑：陈戈铮

希望的曙光
——译者序

这本书的英文原著出版于1899年。一个82岁高龄的英国老人，在面对积贫积弱的中国屡屡战败和欧洲列强跃跃欲试瓜分中国的危局之时，在看到欧洲暴发户国家和日本因打了几场胜仗，便在幅员辽阔、历史悠久的中华帝国面前矫揉造作地摆出一副高人一等的架势之时，在自古以来西人眼中的东方帝国神话肥皂泡般破灭、洋人唱衰中国、中国人也开始自我怀疑自我否定之时，他禁不住拍案而起，把他亲身了解和长期研究的中国介绍给当时的西方读者。他呼吁西方列强持公正和大度的态度对待中国，尊重中国的统一与独立；他还告诉欧洲暴发户国家，在中华文明已走过了几千年后，他们的国家才刚刚从野蛮之中摆脱出来；他恳请英国政府停止鸦片贸易，停止给中国人民造成的灾难。

在这本名副其实的写给未来的书中，他还大胆地预测，中国不会亡国灭种，中国是充满希望的国度，它只是刚刚从长久的酣睡中被惊醒，可大象一旦真正醒来怎么是猴子可相比拟的，其体量巨大、潜力无限，中国的崛起势在必行；中国拥有未来，不在于洋人的怜悯，而只要给它公平竞争的机会即可；能够拯救中国的是中国自己，那根植于国情与文化中的一切：它在于中国的幅员辽阔、资源丰富，在于民为本君为轻、以德治国的理念，在于儒家的个人德行与社会道德的思想，在于道家的天人合一思想，在于中国人的宗教信仰，在于其文化传承，在于中国固有的一切优秀传统、制度与文化之中。

他还强调，"尽管火药最早是中国人发明的，却只是用来鸣放礼炮向朋友致敬的"，不是用来制造炮弹杀人的，这不是西方人可以理解的思维方式。类似地，指南针是中国人发明的，是用来环球航行，到远方的国度表达善意的，不是全球殖民、血腥掠夺用的；造纸术和印刷术是中国人发明的，是用来印刷文字，传播知识、文化与文明的，不是用来签订不平等条约的。在中华民族最黑暗、最悲惨、最迷茫的历史时刻，他能够秉持公正之心，扶正扬善，基于自己对中国的研究，出于或朴素的善意或历史的洞见或政治家的远见，敢于为中国发声，对中华民族的快速觉醒、未来崛起充满信心，给国人的制度自惭、道路踌躇、文化自卑带来安慰并为国人指引方向：中国要学习西方的科学与技术，但也不要丢弃自身优势，要固本创新。

这个对中华文明充满赞许，坚定地相信中国拥有未来与希望的英国人叫詹姆斯·约翰斯顿（James Johnston），中文名仁信。

仁信1817年出生，1905年去世①，享年88岁；曾作为英国长老会牧师于1853—1855年间在厦门传教。妻子名为埃伦·B. 约翰斯顿（E. B. Johnston）；有3个女儿，分别名为仁力西（Jessie）、米塔（Meta）和莉娜（Lena）。

作为厦门三大外国公会之一，英国长老会来华传教比美国归正教会（1842）和伦敦

仁　信

公会（1844）稍晚。1845年，英国长老会召集宣教士前往中国宣教，但两年过去了，应者寥寥，且难堪大任。差会于是考虑取消中国宣教的计划，但是意外地得到宾为霖（William Chalmers Burns）的申请加入。宾为霖于1847年出发，在东南亚一带活动，随后在香港结识了于1850年5月先期抵达厦门的用雅各（James Young）医生；1851年二人结伴到广州，然后到达厦门。用雅各医生开设诊所，同时宣教；宾为霖刻苦学习闽南话，并到白水营和马坪开展教务。

1853年4月22日，在英国长老会曼彻斯特教务议事会上，仁信被按立为牧师，接受委派赴厦门传教，是继宾为霖之后的第二人。此时长老会抱有的想法是建立某种带有教育性质的传教团，就像达夫博士（Dr. Duff）在印度建立的那样。仁信被指派前往格拉斯哥，在自由教会的师范学院里进行数月的教学方法学习，并于赴华途中转道印度马德拉斯邦，花费两个月的时间，天天在自由教会的学校里上课，并参访当地教会学校或公立学校。

仁信先坐船到香港、广州，然后在厦门短暂停留，接着继续旅行去上海考察，广泛接触，打算在开放的口岸寻找建立教育机构的机会。他最后得出结论：英语在中国的地位太过卑微，当时的中国不具备创建教育体系所需或借此营利的条件，而这在印度却很成功；等到中国人开始学习西方科技，愿意请英语教师时才是恰当的时机。他提议给皈依基督教的中国人的子女授课，并未获得广泛认可。后来，英国长老会同意放弃建立教育机构的任务。正是这次旅行，让仁信见到了真实的中国华南和华东地区。仁信于1853年12月初②从上海返回厦门，开始学习汉语，负责打理白水营等宣教点的收支。1854年8月，用雅各医生病重，因海外服务年限和宣教理念的缘故，宾为霖成为陪同用雅各回国休养的最佳人选。此时的仁信汉语还不过关，无法全面接手当地教务，幸好有美国归正教会的罗帝（Elihu Doty）和打马字（John Van Nest Talmage）相助。不巧，仁信于此时患病，其中一种病是痢疾，不得不卧床工作数月。1855年初，仁信健康状况恶化，医生建议他返回英国治疗和休养。1855年5月，仁信坐船经由红海返英。接替而来的杜嘉德牧师（Carstairs Douglas）因船舶绕行好望角于8月抵达厦门，与仁信错过。

回国后，仁信为在厦门建立一所学校成功募集到2500英镑。他的病情未能如医生预料的那样很快痊愈，因此，一年之后长老会拒绝批准他的返华申请。他只好延长休养期，去法国南部住了一年。他一直打算返回中国却未果。杜嘉德在1857年4月8日写给母亲的信中还提到仁信的事情，"您特别询问的唯一事情就是我的房子。首先，我要说这不是我的房子，它是仁信的，我一直期望他能够回来居住。它共有三层……"③仁信的健康状况不允许他返华，英格兰又没有职位空缺，进退两难之中，仁信接受了格拉斯哥圣詹姆斯自由教会多年前就发出的邀请，在格拉斯哥安定下来。仁信还一直是英国长老会下属的苏格兰公会的名誉秘书长。

1877年，仁信退休之后，举家从格拉斯哥迁居到苏格兰中部斯特林地区的艾伦桥镇。1880年，又搬到伦敦东南部的上诺伍德居住。1905年10月15日，仁信于伦敦辞世。

仁信未竟的返华心愿，由他的女儿仁力西得以完成。1885年12月，24岁的仁力西抵达厦门，开始了她20多年无法割舍的中国情缘，传教、兴办女学、管理弃儿堂。1904年因感染登革热和胸膜炎高位截瘫，被护送回国，1907年病逝于伦敦。1885—1904年间，仁力西主理鼓浪屿上的乌埭女学，1910年新校舍启用后为纪念她而更名为"怀仁女学"。

仁信在晚年，写作完成了关于中国的两本书，即《英国长老会在中国大陆与台湾》（1897），以及现在这本《希望的国度：晚清西人看中国》，又译《中国及其未来》（1899）。这是一本写给外国人了解中国用的通俗读物，内容安排上涉及国土、疆域、人民、工业和艺术、贸易和商业、农业、习惯和举止、妇女和儿童的地位、历史、政府、行政、教育和文学、四书五经、宗教等方方面面。尽管广度有余，在深度上却显得不足。但是作者在序言中也有所说明，他原本准备写成大部头，但鉴于中国国内、国际形势逼人，迫不得已仓促成书，为中国发声。

最后，需要说明的是，仁信在谈及中国的许多历史事件的时间、事物的数据时，经常使用约数，并非我们习惯上的精确数字；另外，也存在一些史实错误或知识性错误。对此，译者在文中试图一一加注说明，若有疏漏与不妥之处，还请方家指正。

【注 释】

① 关于仁信的个人背景，除了几本著作和几封信件外，现在能够找到的资料不多，尤其是在他来中国之前的信息无从查得。经过笔者考证和推算，仁信的出生年份应该是1817年，去世日期为1905年10月15日。他的女儿仁力西（Jessie M. Johnston）在日记中写道："（1905年）10月4日——父亲病得很厉害。他的年龄正好是我两倍，医生说，我们俩都有着'强大的恢复力'！"仁力西出生于1861年10月8日，1905年时是44岁，那么当时仁信应该是88岁，由此推出仁信的出生年份为1817年。他去世的日期，仁力西有明确记载："（1905年）10月16日——父亲归天了。他昨晚非常平静地离开了我们。"参见黄秀君、周维江译：《仁力西：厦门生活忆略》，厦门：厦门大学出版社，2019年，第149页。

② 仁信返厦具体日期应该为12月2日午后或3日上午。宾为霖在1854年1月16日的一封信中写道，"用雅各医生娘萨拉在仁信从上海返回厦门的14小时后去世"。而用雅各医生娘萨拉（Mrs. Sarah Harnett Young）于1853年12月3日逝世，故有此推算。萨拉原为伦敦公会的夏蜜姑娘，1851年与用雅各医生结婚，1853年因难产母婴双亡，享年37岁。参见叶克豪：《鼓浪屿内厝澳崎仔尾传教士公墓文献考证》，《鼓浪屿研究（第八辑）》，

北京：社会科学文献出版社，2018年，第196页。

③ John M. Douglas, *Memorials of Rev. Carstairs Douglas, Missionary of the Presbyterian Church of England at Amoy, China*, London: Waterlow & Sons Limited Printers, London Wall, 1877, pp.29-30.

序 言
Preface

中国正处于危急关头，欧洲列强气势汹汹，这迫使我迅速出版了这本通俗读物。本书的素材原本很大程度上是为卷帙浩繁的大部头而准备的。我担心，仓促付梓会给人留下急就章的印象，但我相信，在此形势紧迫之际，纰漏谬误虽存，唯良好之意愿堪为托词。我所言之实皆有理有据，所发之论皆深思熟虑。某些主题的论述时有重复，系本书之过，但我相信，因其对本书欲达成之目的意义重大，故而即便不值得称许，却也情有可原。

我对中国的过去与未来的说法和判断，不是仰仗在华小住的几年，而是依靠我对亚洲，尤其对中国问题长及一生的兴趣与关切。在中国住上几年的时间，即使

The present critical state of China, and the attitude of European Powers, compel me to issue at once this popular form of a work meant to be of more pretentious proportions, for which the materials were in a large measure prepared. If rapidity of production has, as I fear, left signs of haste in composition, I trust that, in the circumstances, good intentions will be an excuse for imperfect performance. No statement of fact has been made without good authority, nor opinion expressed without careful thought. There are some subjects on which there are repetitions in statement of facts or expressions of opinion, which are a fault in composition, but which I trust will be pardoned, if not approved of, on account of their importance in their bearing on the object of the work.

I do not rest my claim to be heard, regarding either the past or future of China, on a brief residence of a few years in that country—only long enough to impress a thoughtful student with the difficulties of the subject—but on a lifelong interest in Asiatic questions, especially those connected with China.

To one who has pored over the records of the history of China, covering a period of 4000 or 5000 years, and studied its institutions—the nearest, in a continuous and living form, to those of the earliest known inhabitants of our world—it is impossible to read with philosophic calmness the pretensions of the upstart nations of Europe to carve out for themselves, from that vast and venerable empire, provinces larger and with populations more numerous than their own territories and people—and that in the name of civilization of an empire which was civilized thousands of years before these nations had emerged from barbarism.

While I admit the superiority of Western civilization in many of its aspects, I may ask, in the strong language of a distinguished American writer: Is China to be civilized by France, "whose common sailors in a shipwreck clubbed drowning women and children who tried to get into the lifeboats? whose Parisian gentlemen trampled underfoot

对一个细心的学者来说，也仅仅只能对中国话题的困难程度产生初步印象。

中国的历史纵横四五千年，而其制度近乎是人们所知的世界上最早的生民的制度，且连绵不断，生生不息。因此，对一个曾经研读过中国历史典籍，并研究过其典章制度的人来说，当他看到欧洲暴发户国家在幅员辽阔、历史悠久的中华帝国面前摆出妄自尊大的架势时，他不可能泰然处之，而是拍案而起。要知道，中国的一个省都要比欧洲国家的面积更为广阔、人口更为众多，而且在其文明进程已走过了几千年后，欧洲的国家才刚刚从野蛮之中摆脱出来。

尽管我承认西方现代文明在许多方面有其优越性，但我可以借用一位美国名作家的激烈措辞问一问："法国的水手在一次海难中用棍棒击打试图爬上救生艇的溺水妇女和儿童；法国巴黎的绅士们把这片土地上最高贵、最优秀的女人踩在脚下，让她们在燃烧着的街头火焰中毁灭；法国拥有骑士风范的将军们将一个无辜而又勇敢的战友当作重罪犯判刑，为的却是法国军队的'荣誉'。"中国要由这样的法国来"开化"吗？我再补充一句，在"开化"中国的"伟大事业"中，德国能够帮上忙吗？德国商人不是用像松节油一样灼热有毒的烈酒毒害非洲土著吗？德国最伟大的政治家不是因为用欺骗行为把他的三流王国提升为一流帝国而得意扬扬吗？德国皇帝①不是一边因为一名基督教传教士的死索要赔偿而攫取中国的一个港口，并企图占领一个省，而另一边却将"邪恶至极的土耳其人"用来称他的好友②，他自己的手上却也沾满了成千上万基督徒的鲜血吗？俄国，一个目前正处于过渡状态的国家——开始摆脱农奴制、制止鞭打女人裸背、禁止在国内对犹太人和史敦达派③教徒加以迫害和驱逐，能够对中华文明有所助益吗？中国才一直是一个完全没有宗教迫害精神的国度。

甚至是我们自己偏爱的英国，也必须与鸦片贸易断绝一切官方联系，并竭尽全力停止它曾给中国造成的灾难。我们必须努力消除战争造成的伤害——战争削弱了中国政府的实力，扰乱了国家行政；而西方政治家只能用看起来似是而非的诡辩术

the highest and best ladies in the land, leaving them to perish in the flames of a burning bazaar? and whose chivalrous generals condemn an innocent and brave companion in arms to the life and death of a felon, for the honour of the French army?". I may add, is Germany to assist in this good work, whose merchants poison the natives of Africa with spirits fiery and noxious like turpentine? whose greatest statesman gloried in the acts of deception by which he raised his third-rate kingdom to a first-rate empire? And whose Emperor seizes a harbour and attempts to grasp a province of China as a solatium for the murder of a Christian missionary, while he claims as his dear friend the "unspeakable Turk," though his hands are dripping with the blood of thousands of Christians? Is Russia, only now in a state of transition from the serfdom or slavery of her subjects, and the use of the lash for the bare backs of women, persecuting and banishing Jews and Stundists at home, to aid in the civilization of China?—A land that has been singularly free from the spirit of religious persecution.

Even our own favoured country must wash her hands of all official connection with the opium trade, and do her best to arrest the evil it has inflicted on China. We must strive to undo the mischief caused by wars which have weakened the Government and disorganized the administration of the country—wars which the Christian politician can only defend by the use of what looks very like sophistry to soothe his conscience, which appears to the heathen a mere excuse for acts of high-handed cruelty and injustice....

The fair, though favourable, description of the Chinese Empire is also designed to appeal to the just and generous sentiments of those who talk lightly of the partition of China among the Powers of Europe, as if it were the abode of barbarous tribes or of a bankrupt civilization. China is still capable of great things if the people are allowed fair play. They are only now awaking from the sleep of centuries. They are slow to move, but will have a momentum proportioned to their vast numbers. If broken up, they may inundate the lands of their conquerors with their swarming population, disorganizing the labour markets, and upsetting the costly enterprise of Western commerce by their industry, economy, and intelligence.

...Great Britain—the Power which first broke down the wall of exclusiveness, behind which the people had lived for untold ages in contented security and comparative comfort. I would earnestly appeal to the conscience of my fellow-countrymen... to their heart, that they may act generously toward a nation we have injured, while benefiting ourselves; to their imagination, that they may be tender in their treatment of an empire so ancient and venerable, and withal afflicted with not a few of

来辩护才能抚慰自己的良心，但这诡辩术不过是为自己霸道、残酷、邪恶的战争行径寻找的借口。

我对中华帝国的描述尽管充满赞许，却是不偏不倚，也旨在呼吁那些轻描淡写地谈论在欧洲列强之间瓜分中国的人，持公正和大度的态度，因为在这些人眼里，中国仿佛是野蛮部落或没落文明的居所。如果允许中国人参与公平竞争，中国还是有能力做成大事的。他们现在从几个世纪的沉睡中刚刚醒来，此刻行动缓慢，但终将获得与他们庞大数量相称的动力。如果中国被瓜分了，中国的人口可能会蜂拥而至，淹没征服者的土地，扰乱西方劳动力市场，并因其产业、经济和智慧之长而扰乱成本高昂的西方商业。

正是英国率先打破清政府闭关锁国的围墙，而围墙之内，无数年来，中国人民过着满足、安宁、相对舒适的生活。对我的同胞们，我真诚地呼唤他们的仁慈之心，请他们慷慨地对待一个我们伤害过并从中获利的国家；呼唤他们的想象力，请他们温柔地对待一个如此古老、可敬，且又因年老体衰等可以原谅的原因受着不小折磨的，但仍具有极强恢复能力的帝国。④

the excusable infirmities of age, but still possessed of great recuperative power.

【注　释】

① 德国皇帝：德皇威廉二世，德意志帝国末代皇帝和普鲁士王国末代国王（1888年6月15日至1918年11月9日在位）。1897年11月14日，德国借口2名传教士在山东曹州巨野被杀，派远东舰队强占了胶州湾，夺取青岛炮台。1898年3月6日，李鸿章代表清政府与德国公使签订了《胶澳租界条约》。通过这个条约，德国在"租借"的名义下，强占了胶州湾，并把山东变成了德国的势力范围，从而开启了帝国主义瓜分中国的先河。——译者注

② 此处"邪恶至极的土耳其人"指的是阿卜杜勒·哈米德二世，奥斯曼帝国的苏丹和哈里发（1876—1909年在位）。其统治时期，奥斯曼帝国继续受到欧洲列强的侵略和宰割。在法国1881年夺取奥斯曼帝国在北非名义上的藩属国突尼斯，英国1882年占领奥斯曼帝国在北非名义上的藩属国埃及后，他寻求新即位的德国皇帝威廉二世的支持。作为报酬，他允许德国修建巴格达铁路（1899）。——译者注

③ 史敦达派：19世纪后半叶东正教派别之一。流行于俄国和乌克兰农民中，受基督教新教影响。——译者注

④ 这本小书只是个引子，对于任何希望继续研究中国话题的读者，我们推荐如下书目：柯乐洪（A. R. Colquhoun）的《转变中的中国》（China in Transformation）、寇松（G. N. Curzon）的《远东问题》（Problems of the Far East）、丁韪良（Dr. William Alexander Parsons Martin）的《花甲忆记》（A Cycle of Cathay）、密迪乐（T. Meadows）的《中国人及其叛乱》（The Chinese and Their Rebellions）、明恩溥（A. H. Smith）的《中国人的性格》（Chinese Characteristics）和卫三畏（S. Wells Williams）的《中国总论》（The Middle Kingdom）。——原注

目录 Contents

第一章　国家概况　　1

有趣的研究 / 别称众多 / 古代对中国的描述 / 关于中国的浪漫幻想 / 资源与自足性 / 地理环境特征 / 中国的河流 / 山脉 / 湖泊和湖畔诗人 / 司马光《独乐园记》/ 中国植物区系 / 动物区系 / 矿产资源 / 建筑丰碑的缺失 / 丰碑下的奴役 / 长城 / 大运河 / 自然环境和宗教形式

第二章　人民及其追求　　31

衡量的标准 / 特色品质 / 人口 / 养活人口的方法 / 工业与技艺 / 越古老越值钱 / 停滞 / 早期的发明 / 早期的商业和贸易 / 国内贸易 / 中国的城市 / 推崇农业 / 土地所有权 / 耕作制度 / 田赋收入 / 文明的习惯 / 礼仪和习俗 / 子女侍奉之责 / 餐桌礼仪 / 有用的礼仪规范

第三章　妇女和儿童的地位　　57

妇女的地位 / 孟母 / 婚姻 / 同姓不婚 / 离婚 / 婚俗 / 幸福的婚姻 / 妇女的救赎 / 孝顺 / 儿童教育

第四章　中国的历史、政府和行政管理　　69

中国人的"历史感" / 过度谨慎 / 二十六次起义，一次大变革 / 中国的早期历史 / 水利工程师——大禹 / 一条先于摩西的律法 / 夏商两朝 / 诸子百家 / 中国的一个大变革王朝 / 焚书坑儒 / 汉朝 / 印刷术的发明 / 哲学与批判的

兴起 / 大运河 / 明朝 / 在19世纪衰败的原因 / 西方国家之过 / 对专制的限制 / 腐败的行政人员 /《大清律例》/ 法律面前人人平等 / 联结的纽带 / 日本的胜利 / 以德治国 / 文官占上风 / 希望尚存 / 灾难的原因

第五章　教育和文学　　　　　　　　　　　96

国民教育 / 文职人员的最高回报 / 科举考试 / 鼓励读书 / 结果难料 / 文字起源 / 复杂且不便 / 汉语的声调 / 书面语与口语 / 教育体制 / 经典 / 原汁原味 / 四书五经 / 巨大的影响 / 孔子的影响 / 孔子的长相 /《尚书》/ 起义的权利 / 禹的品德 /《诗经》/ 诗的概念 / 诗歌示例 /《易经》的性质 /《礼记》/《春秋》/ 四书 / 中国的博斯韦尔 / 孔子语录 / 藏书阁 / 类书和字典 / 中国文学全盛时期

第六章　中国的宗教　　　　　　　　　　　138

原生性宗教 / 同一个宗教 / 儒学非儒教 / 孔子的功业 / 历史的开端 / 彼时之宗教 / 中国的古今宗教 / 著名的"道教创始人" / 老子的探索 / 佛教——一个外来宗教 / 儒道佛三者的相互关系 / 宗法性宗教的保存 / 中国经典 / 中国宗教的包容性 / 中国择一神教 / 神性 / 皇帝，上帝唯一的祭司 / 祭典的仪式 / 牺牲和祭坛 / 祭典 / 皇帝祭天祝文 / 祭天颂歌 / 远离血腥淫佚的典礼

第七章　中国的未来　　　　　　　　　　　159

中国的境况 / 中国觉醒 / 教育改革 / 甲午战争的影响 / 现已无法重新沉睡 / 中国的疆域和统一 / 历史激起希望 / 不因奢侈而萎靡 / 身体素质 / 智慧 / 神的品质 / 道德的标准 / 与日本人比较 / 展望未来 / 毫无根据的悲观主义 / 戈登的错误 / 强制入拜上帝会 / 对立的政府理论

附录　中国的人口　　　　　　　　　　　　176

译后记　　　　　　　　　　　　　　　　　184

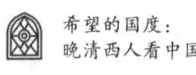

Contents

Chapter I The Country

An Interesting Study / Many Names / Ancient Description of China / Romantic Fancies about China / Resources and Independence / Physical Features / Rivers of China / Mountains / Lakes and Lake Poets / The Garden of Sse-Ma-Kouang / Flora of China / The Fauna / Mineral Resources / Absence of Architectural Monuments / Monument Slavery / The Great Wall / The Grand Canal / Physical Geography and Form of Religion

.... pp.1-30

Chapter II The People and Their Pursuits

Standard to Measure by / Characteristic Qualities / Population / How Supported / Industries and Arts / The Older Specimens the Bets / Arrested Progress / Early Inventions / Early Trade and Commerce / Home Trade / Cities in China / Agriculture Honoured / Tenure of Land / System of Farming / Revenue from Land / Civilized Habits / Manners and Customs / Duties of Children / Manners at Table / Forms Useful

.... pp.31-56

Chapter III The Position of Women and Children

The Place of Women / The Mother of Mencius / Marriage / Prohibited Degrees / Divorce / Marriage Customs / Happy Marriages / The Redeeming of Womanhood / Filial Obedience / Education of Children

.... pp.57-68

Chapter IV The History, Government, and Administration of the Chinese

Chinese "Historic Sense" / Excess of Caution / Twenty-Six Rebellions, One Revolution / Early History of China / The Engineer Yu / A Mosaic Law Anticipated / The Hea and Shang Dynasties / Its Illustrious Men / China's One Revolutionary Dynasty / Slaughter of Literati / The Han Dynasty / Discovery of the Art of Printing / Rise of Philosophy and Criticism / The Grand Canal / The Ming Dynasty / Causes of Deterioration in the Nineteenth Century / Responsibility of Civilization / Limitations on Autocracy / A Corrupt Executive / The Criminal Code / All Equal in the Eye of the Law / Bonds of Unity / Japanese Triumph / Government by Moral Force / Civil Power Predominates / There Still Is Hope / Causes of Disaster
.... pp.69-95

Chapter V Education and Literature

National Education / Highest Reward in the Civil Service / Examination for Office / Talent Only Encouraged / Doubtful Results / Origins of Letters / Complex and Inconvenient / The Tone in Chinese / Written and Spoken Language / The System of Education / The Sacred Books / Genuine and Authentic / The Four Books and Five Classics / Their Great Influence / Influence of Confucius / Description of Confucius / The "Shoo King," or History / The Right of Insurrection / The Character of Yu / The "Shii King," or Book of Odes / Notions of Poetry / Specimens of Poetry / Nature of The Book of Changes / The Book of Rites / The "Chun-Tseu" / The "Four Books" / Chinese Boswells / The Sayings of Confucius / Chinese Libraries / Encyclopedias and Dictionaries / China's Augustan Age
.... pp.96-137

Chapter VI The Religion of China

Primitive Religion / The One Religion of China / Not Confucianism /

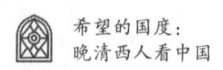

Confucius' Work / Commencement of History / What the Religion Was / Present and Past Religion of China / The Reputed Founder of Taoism / Laotsze's Speculations / Buddhism, a Foreign Religion / Mutual Relations of the Three Religions / Preservation of the Patriarchal Religion / The Chinese Canon / Tolerance of Chinese Religion / Chinese Henotheism / The Divine Attributes / The Emperor, the Only Priest and Worshiper of Shang-Ti / Form of Worship / The Victims and Temple / A Solemn Rite / A Prayer Said by the Emperor / Hymns from the Chinese Liturgy / Free from Cruel and Licentious Rites
.... *pp.138-158*

Chapter VII The Future of China

China's Position / China Awakening / Education Movement / Effect of the Japanese War / Sleep Now Impossible / Extent and Unity of China / The Past Inspires Hope / Not Enervated by Luxury / Physical Stamina / Intellectual Power / Character of Their Gods / The Standard of Morality / Compared with the Japanese / Hope for the Future / Groundless Pessimism / Gordon's Mistake / Compulsory Conversions / Adverse Theories of Government
.... *pp.159-175*

Appendix The Population of China
.... *pp.176-183*

Afterword
.... *pp.184*

插图目录
List of Illustrations

庐山牯岭 / The Kuling Valley in the Lu Mountains 8
牯岭 / Kuling Valley 13
老虎陷阱 / A Tiger Trap 18
路边客栈 / A Wayside Inn 27
从平台上捕鱼 / Fishing with a Net from a Platform 36
切割花岗岩 / Hewing Granite 38
弹棉花 / Cleaning Cotton 40
走街串巷的修鞋匠 / An Itinerant Cobbler 42
在家织布 / Weaving at Home 44
收割水稻 / The Rice Harvest 50
福建的山涧及拱桥 / Mountain Stream and Arched Bridge in Fuh Kien 73
下冲式水车和上射式水车 / Under-and Over-Shot Wheels 75
一位官员视察弓箭手 / A Mandarin Reviewing Archers 90
一队省级驻军 / A Sample of a Provincial Army 117

第一章　国家概况
Chapter I　The Country

有趣的研究

无论一位学者研究的是神圣史还是世俗史，中国总能引起他的兴趣，这是其他任何或古老或现代的帝国无法比拟的。就疆域、时间跨度以及孤立于世界之外等方面而言，中国独一无二。世界上的现代帝国没有中国那般可以追溯到最远古的过去的历史。许多古老的帝国已经消逝，我们只能通过其不确定的传统、靠不住的文献或正在变得破败的废墟来研究它们。但是中国就在我们的眼前，活灵活现，与它数千年前一个模样。欧洲现存的帝国皆历史短暂，鲜有长达几百年的统治，而中国则长达几千年。甚至已经灭亡的古希腊和古

An Interesting Study

China has an interest for every student of history, either sacred or profane, which no other empire, ancient or modern, can claim. It is unique in its extent, duration and isolation from the rest of the world. Modern empires have no past history like that of China, stretching away into the remotest antiquity. Ancient empires have disappeared, and we can only study them in uncertain traditions, or doubtful documents, or mouldering ruins; but China lives before our eyes, much the same as she was thousands of years ago. The existing empires of Europe are of yesterday, and can scarcely boast of as many centuries of dominion as the Chinese can of millenniums. Even the extinct empires of Greece and

Rome are modern compared with the origin of the Chinese Empire. The ancient empires of Egypt and Babylon cannot claim an antiquity greater than that of China, while their dominion perished more than 2000 years ago; but China, though old as they, still exists with an unbroken record of independent government—the oldest, the largest, the most populous, of any empire in the world, either ancient or modern.

Many Names

During its long history China has borne many names in foreign lands, none of them the same as that by which it designates itself. In ancient times it was called in the East Sin or Since, or Seres, or Chin, or, as in Isaiah, Sinim; and in the Middle Ages it was called by the Persian name of Cathay, or that by which it is still known in Russia, Kitai. The Chinese themselves from the twelfth century B.C. have called their country Chung Koh, or the Middle Kingdom; but other names have been used at different times, from the name of some powerful or favourite dynasty, such as Tsin in the second century B.C., imposed by the despot who united the small States into a united empire, and in later times after the illustrious Han dynasty. In their pride they speak of their country as Thien Hia—All under heaven; or Sz Hai—All within the four seas; or in terms of affection they call it the Flowery Land.

罗马帝国，与中华帝国的起源相比，也是很新近的。尽管古埃及和古巴比伦的统治在两千年前就消亡了，但不能宣称它们拥有比中国更加古老的历史。而中国虽然历史悠久，却仍然绝世独立，有着延续不断的独立政府的记录，成为世界上不论古老还是现代的帝国中历史最悠久、疆域最辽阔、人口最众多的一个。

别称众多

在其漫长的历史中，中国在外国有很多称呼，可没有一个别称与本名的意思相同。古时，中国被称为"震旦"①，或者"丝国"②，或者"秦"，而古希伯来圣经《旧约·以赛亚书》用"希尼"（Sinim）来称呼拉丁语化的"秦"；在中世纪，波斯语称中国为"契丹"，今日俄国依然在使用这一称呼。从公元前12世纪起，中国人就把自己的国家称为"中国"，即"中央王国"；但在不同时期也使用过其他名字，名字取自某个强大或最受欢迎的王朝名，如公元前2世纪③统一诸国的秦朝以及后来辉煌的汉朝。他们骄傲地称自己的国家为"天下",或者"四海",或者更喜欢称其为"花国"。

古代对中国的描述

最近,一位作者仔细分析了古人关于中国诸多称呼的观点后,在《不列颠百科全书》中评论说:"如果我们去掉反常的记述和明显的杜撰成分,而将丝国人及其领土所在古国融合为一,会得出如下结论:'丝国人居住的地区是一个幅员辽阔、人口众多的国家,东临大洋和可居住的世界的极限,向西延伸到高加索山脉④和巴克特里亚王国⑤的边界。其人民文明、温和、公正、节俭,不与邻人发生冲突,甚至不愿与人亲密交往,但不反对出售自己的产品,其中以生丝为主打,但也包括丝绸、精美的毛皮和品质卓越的铁器。'这显然是对中国人的定义。"

把上述古人的描述同中世纪的描述,并同今天所看到的现实相比较,我们就会被这么长久以来存在的惊人一致性震撼。中国人在托勒密时代使用的语言在我们这个时代依旧可以非常得体地使用。13世纪

Ancient Description of China

A recent writer in the "Encyclopedia Britannica," after a careful analysis of the opinions of the ancients regarding China under its many names, says: "If we infuse into one the ancient nation of the Ceres and their country, omitting anomalous statements and manifest fables, the result will be something like the following—'The region of the Ceres is a vast and populous country, touching on the east the ocean and the limits of the habitable world, and extending west to Imaus and the confines of Bactria. The people are civilized, mild, just, and frugal, eschewing collisions with their neighbours, and shy even of close intercourse, but not averse to dispose of their own products, of which raw silk is the staple, but which includes also silk stuffs, fine furs, and iron of remarkable quality.' That is manifestly a definition of the Chinese."

Comparing the description given above by the ancients with those of the Middle Ages, and with what we find them in our own day, we are struck with the marvellous uniformity which has existed for such a length of time. The language of Ptolemy might be used in our day with perfect propriety, and in the thirteenth century Carpini writes of them thus: "Now, these Kitai are heathen men, and have a written language of their own.... They seem, indeed, to be kindly and polished folks enough. They have no beards, and in character of countenance have a considerable resemblance to the Mongols, but are not so broad in the face. They have a peculiar language. Their betters as craftsmen, in every art practised by man, are not to be found in the whole world. Their country is very rich in corn, in wine, in gold, in silver, in silk, and in every kind of produce tending to the support of mankind." The notice of Rubruk, of the same period, shrewder and more graphic, runs thus: "Further on is great Cathay, which I take to be the country which was anciently called the land of the Ceres. For the best silk is still got from them...The sea lies between it and India...The common money of Cathay consists of pieces of cotton-paper, about a palm in length and breadth, on which certain lines are printed resembling the seal of Mangu Khan. They do their writing with a pencil such as painters use, and a single character of theirs comprehends several letters so as to form a word."

Romantic Fancies about China

Owing to its great extent and comparatively high civilization, China at a very early period took hold of the imagination of the world. The distance from

时，柏朗嘉宾⑥这样写道："现在，这些中国人是异教徒，拥有自己的书面语言。他们看起来很和蔼，很有教养，事实也是如此。他们不蓄胡须，面貌特征与蒙古人非常相似，但脸庞没那么宽阔。他们的语言很独特。在人类从事的每一种技艺中，能胜过他们的工匠全世界也找不到。中国盛产谷物、酒、黄金、白银、丝绸，以及各种有助于人类生存的农产品。"同一时期的鲁布鲁克⑦的观察更敏锐、更生动，他是这样记述的："再往前是伟大的中国，我认为它就是古时被称为丝国的国家。因为最上乘的丝绸仍然来自它……中国与印度隔大海相望……中国通用货币是纸币，由棉纸制成，长宽约为一巴掌大小，上面印有象征蒙哥汗⑧玺印的几行印文。他们写字用的是类似画家的画笔，单单一个方块字就由几个偏旁部首组合而成。"

关于中国的浪漫幻想

由于地域广袤、文明程度较高，中国在很早以前就抓住了世界的想象力。与西方文明国家距离遥远，更平添了中国的迷人魅力，以及一丝神秘感，进而增加了它的影响力。早期作家详细描述了中国的宏大与富饶，把它描绘成一个群山环抱、空间开阔、充满欢乐的山谷；早期的旅行者渴望去探访它，商人则急于分享它的财富。它刺激哥伦布通过更短、更容易的水路抵达中国海岸，而不是经由波斯帝国、青藏高原的不毛之地或戈壁沙漠的陆路。哥伦布在未知海域向西航行的目的是抵达"中国及附近岛国日本"。现在由于有铁路横穿他误打误撞发现的大陆，一条从欧洲到中国的交通要道开辟出来。我们可以引用的最高权威之一——乔治·斯当东爵士⑨冷静地评估过古人关于中国的猜测，证明古人的猜测并没有太离谱。他说："在任何一个帝国的藩篱之内，就幅员、富饶和资源而言，现在没有、也从未有过哪个国家可以与中国相比。"

资源与自足性

中国的资源丰富若此，可以为其境内四亿庞大的人口提供所有的必需品和舒适的生活。其他帝国没有哪个能够如此自给

the civilized nations of the West lent it enchantment, and a sense of mystery which increased its influence. Early writers expatiated on its grandeur and wealth, and described it as a spacious and happy valley surrounded by mountains; early travellers were ambitious to visit it, and traders were anxious to share its riches. It stimulated Columbus to reach its shores by a shorter and easier passage than by the overland route through Persia, and the inhospitable region of Tibet or the desert of Gobi. He tells us his object in sailing to the west, over unknown seas, was to reach "Cathay and its outlying island of Zipangu," or Japan, and now by the facilities of railway transit across the great continent which he discovered by mistake, a highway is opened up from Europe to China. That the ancients were not far wrong in their guesses about China is shown by the calm estimate of Sir George Staunton, one of the highest authorities we can quote. He says: "Within an imperial ring-fence there is not, nor has there ever been, a country to be compared with China, in extent, fertility, and resources."

Resources and Independence

The resources of China are so great that its vast population of 400000000 can find all the necessaries and comforts of life within its borders. No other empire is so self-contained and independent of other countries, which accounts for its long isolation and its reluctance to trade with foreigners. It has no need for their products, and feels little desire to part with its own, for which there is abundant demand at home. Besides, those representatives of foreign nations who first sought commercial relations had acted so much like pirates or invaders that they and their countrymen were naturally looked on as barbarians, with whom intercourse was by no means desired by a civilized and peace-loving people.

Physical Features

Since the character of a people, and their history as a nation, are largely influenced by the physical characteristics of the country they live in, we shall give a brief outline of the leading features of China. The geographical conformation of China proper is varied and interesting, and from its great fertility and boundless resources it can support its immense population. There are vast alluvial plains in the north, and rich fertile valleys scattered over the whole land; there is varied scenery of hill and dale in the east, and grand views amid the mountain ranges of the west and north.

Rivers of China

Its river systems are marvellously distributed. There are two rivers of the first class, the Yang-tze-Kiang and Hwang-ho, the former the third longest river in the world, and, if its tributaries

自足，独立于其他国家之外，这也是中国长期与世隔绝，不愿与外国人通商的原因。中国不需要别国的产品，也不欲舍弃那些在国内的需求量就很大的产品。此外，最初来华寻求商贸关系的外国代表，他们的行径非常像海盗或侵略者，因此他们及其同胞自然被视为野蛮人，文明而又爱好和平的中国人绝不希望与之交往。

地理环境特征

由于一个民族的性格及历史，在很大程度上受到他们居住地的自然环境影响，我们将简要地概述一下中国主要的地理环境。中国的地理结构多样而有趣，凭借其肥沃的土地和无尽的资源，可以供养庞大的人口。北部有广袤的冲积平原，遍布肥沃的河谷；东部的丘陵和山谷景色各异；西部和北部的山脉景色壮丽。

中国的河流

中国水系分布绝佳。有两条第一等的河流，长江和黄河。长江是世界第三长的河流，如果算上其支流，在灌溉、排涝和内河航运方面,它给流经国带来的益处远远超过其竞争对手密西西比河、亚马孙河。

如果管理得当,黄河能够造福无限,但由于政府重视不足、河道变迁无常,它赢得了"中国之殇"的名号;但是,中国沿岸生态系统的辉煌不在于河流的长度,而在于河流的数量及分布。河流把整个国家的积水迅速排掉,且让土壤变得肥沃,从来没有哪个国家的人能像中国人那样对河流带给自己的特殊恩惠进行钻研探究。中国人利用河流做内陆运输;在大大小小的平原各处开挖河渠进行灌溉;把河水注入运河,运河又成为灌溉的水源和便利村庄与农田的交通方式,这对农业具有双重好处,而我们拟议的轻便铁路仅能充当半个替代品。中国的这些河流,无论大小,都是它独自占有的;河道从源头到入海口,都在这个紧凑而辽阔的国家境内。

山 脉

华夏地区的山脉很大程度上是西藏地区和印度之间山系的延伸。它们主要从西

be included, of far greater advantage to the country than its rivals, the Mississippi and Amazon, for irrigation, drainage, and inland navigation.

The Hwang-ho, which might under proper management be the source of unmeasured blessing, has by the neglect of the Government and its erratic course earned the name of "China's sorrow"; but the glory of the Chinese riparian systems does not lie in the great length of the rivers, but in their number and distribution. The whole country is at once drained and fertilized by them, and no people have ever turned to account their water privileges as the Chinese have. They use them for transit all over the interior; they tap them for irrigation on every level plain, large or small; they drain them into canals, which again are made sources of irrigation and means of transit for the convenience of villages and farms, a double advantage to agriculture, for which our proposed light railways will be but half a substitute. These rivers of China are her own, great and small; their courses from fountain-head to their mouths on her own coasts are all within the limits of the compact but vast country.

Mountains

The mountain ranges of China proper are to a great extent the continuation of

庐山牯岭
The Kuling Valley in the Lu Mountains

南向东北方向延伸,自喜马拉雅山脉终年积雪区域向下,高度逐渐降低,到达东海岸时海拔只剩下几百英尺⑩高。山脉向东延伸时,南北走向分支出许多侧脊,除此之外,还有一些独立源头的山脉沿不同方向上升隆起。山脉的分布极大地改变了气候和降水。中国总体上气候良好、降水充足,这对中国来说大有裨益。

湖泊和湖畔诗人

中国的湖泊数量并不众多,面积也不太大,但有些却以美丽著称,其中以湖北与湖南的为主。点缀着美丽岛屿的太湖,是中国人眼中的天堂,自古以来,在其湖畔产生了一批湖畔诗人,这比英国湖畔诗人华兹华斯⑪定居格拉斯米尔湖畔早了上千年。我们从古伯察⑫《中华帝国纪行》一书中引用一首诗,是11世纪司马光晚年时写的。尽管翻译过来的作品有种种缺点,但它对自然的欣赏在当时很了不起,作者不愧为中国最伟大的政治家之一。结尾的句子所表达的除了他为国家实际做出的牺牲外,别无他者。我们自作主张,将散文

those of Tibet and India. They stretch across the country chiefly from south-west to north-east, gradually diminishing in height as they leave the region of eternal snow in the Himalayas until they have only an elevation of a few hundred feet on the eastern shore. They send off many spurs to the north and south, besides which there are ranges of independent origin rising in different directions. The climate and rainfall are greatly modified by their distribution, much to the advantage of the country, which is, on the whole, healthful and well watered.

Lakes and Lake Poets

The lakes of China are not numerous or large, but some of them are celebrated for their beauty, those of Hu-peh and Hu-nan being the chief. The Tai Lake, studded with beautiful islands, is the paradise of Chinamen, and from time immemorial has produced its school of lake poets thousands of years before Wordsworth took up his abode on the shores of Grasmere. We quote from Huc's "Chinese Empire" a poem of a later date by Sse-ma-Kouang, written about the end of the eleventh century of our era. With all the disadvantages of a translation, its appreciation of Nature is remarkable for the period, and worthy of one of the greatest statesmen of China. The closing sentences express no more than the sacrifice he actually made for his country. We have taken the liberty of turning the prose into blank verse, which claims no merit except fidelity to the translation:

The Garden of Sse-Ma-Kouang

　　Their stately palaces let others build
　　To hide their cares, or to display their pride;
　　Enough for me, a twenty acre plot,
　　To amuse my leisure, and converse with friends.
　　In midst of this a spacious hall I built
　　To hold my treasure of five thousand books.
　　In this I hold communion with the wise,
　　And talk with ancient sages in their works.
　　A small pavilion, built with modest taste,
　　Stands in the midst of water to the south,
　　Fed by a streamlet from the western hills,
　　Which plunges headlong from the mountain's side.
　　Here it has formed a basin, out of which
　　Five streams flow out like claws of spotted pard.
　　The graceful swans swim on its placid breast,
　　And in large numbers sport upon its banks.
　　On the border of the first, which

翻译成无韵诗，别无可取之处，唯有忠实于原文[13]：

司马光《独乐园记》

尊贤坊巍峨，

隐人之忧，显人之傲；

于其关外，迁叟买田二十亩，

自娱、晤友，足矣。

其中为堂，

聚书五千卷。

于此，上师圣人，

下友古贤。

堂南沼中，有一亭，素朴之风，

沼中兀立，

洛城龙门山，坡上溪水跌落，

西山水自来。

溪流注此沼中，

疏水为五派，若虎爪；

沼中天鹅凫静水，

众鹅嬉戏于岸。

自沼北伏流出北阶，

悬注庭中，

悬石若象鼻；

石顶矗立见山台，

清新空气，自由呼吸，

观红日初升，灿若宝石。

疏水伏流分渠有二，

绕双层梯田步廊，

接壤玫瑰圃、石榴园。

北渠曲曲，状美若弓，

丛竹如幕蔽天，

散布沙子、贝壳各色；

岛上植竹，

另有渔人之茅庐——钓鱼庵；

另外两渠时合时分，

嬉戏向下，流过青草坡地，

途中缀满欢快花朵，渠水缓行，

过浅滩，成水洼，

如碧岸嵌玉玦。

少顷，过草地，向下而出；

流水拍岸岩，

搅动于狭窄河床，泛起泡沫，

银波翻滚，

经蜿蜒渠道，一路前行。

书堂沼北横屋六楹，

散落山坡，

plunges down

    Frequent cascades, there overhangs a rock

    Curved like the trunk of a huge elephant;

    Upon its summit stands a pleasure-house,

    Where I can freely breathe the bracing air,

    And see the rubies deck the rising sun.

    The second branches into two canals,

    Around which winds a double terraced walk,

    Bordered with roses and with pomegranates.

    The northern branch bends like the graceful bow,

    And forms a little isle with sheltered bower,

    Strewn round with sand and shells of varied hue;

    One half is planted out with evergreens,

    On the other side the fishers' rude thatched huts;

    The other two seem to approach and shun

    Each other playfully, as down the sloping meads,

    Enamelled with gay flowers, they slowly glide,

    Then leave their shallow beds to form small pools

    Of purest pearl in emerald borders framed.

    Anon they leave the meadows and descend;

    The waters dash against opposing rocks,

第一章　国家概况　　　　　　　　　　　　　　　　　　　　　　Chapter I　The Country

Fretting and foaming in their straitened beds,
Then rolling off in silver waves, they flow
Through winding channels, lengthening their course.
To north of the huge hall are sundry cots,
Scattered at random up and down the hill,
Nestling in narrow gorges half concealed.
The gravel pathways intersect the hills,
Shaded by tufted grooves of the bamboo,
So that the sun's fierce rays may not pass through.

After a lengthened description of all parts of the garden and surrounding scenery, for which we cannot find space, and should only spoil by condensation, the poet goes on:

When tired with writing and composing books,
I leave the hall and step into a boat,
In which I row myself from point to point
To seek fresh pleasures in my garden plot.
Sometimes I land upon the fishing isle,
Where with a broad straw hat upon my head,
To guard me from the sun's too ardent rays,
I wile the fishes with my tempting bait,
And muse on human passions like to theirs.

半隐半掩，栖息狭窄谷中。
砾石小路贯穿山丘，
丛竹遮蔽，
以御烈日。

之后，司马光细述花园各部及周围风景，但是本书篇幅有限，缩写又只会破坏整体意境，故略去。诗人接着写道：

每每志倦体疲，
出书堂，入小船，
渠中泛舟，花园寻乐。
时有踏足池岛，
头戴斗笠，
以御烈日，
以饵诱鱼，
感悟世人趋死，莫不如是。
间或，背负矢箙，
手握弯弓，缘崎岖岩石而上，
似叛逃者匍匐、潜藏，
静待野兔出洞，
箭出，兔中矢而亡。
呜呼！人类之愚甚于兔也；
待兔谋其拙，屠龙艺亦虚。
花园现斜阳，

牯岭
Kuling Valley

At other times, with quiver at my back,
And bow in hand, I climb the rugged rocks,
And thus like traitor lie, stealthily in wait,
Watching for conies creeping from their holes,
And with my fatal arrows pierce them through.
Alas ! we men more foolish are than they;
They fly from danger, we do sport with it.
The setting sun still finds me in my garden,
Watching in silence swallows in their flight,
Tenderly anxious for their little ones,
Or stratagems of hawks to catch their prey.
The moon arising gives an added joy;
The murmuring waters and the rustling leaves,
The beauty rare of heaven bright with star,
Plunge me in rev'rie, speaking to my soul.
Wandering about I listen silently,
And night has reached the middle of its course
Ere I have reached the threshold of my door.
My learned friends sometimes invade my home
And listen to my works, or read me theirs,
Our frugal meal enlivened by good wine,
And seasoned by philosophy. At court
Men seek voluptuous pleasures, forging lies,
Fostering calumny, and laying snares;
While we're invoking Wisdom

静看燕子飞，

雏燕待哺向巢归，

或觑鹰隼猜。

明月时至，增欢；

叶沙沙，水潺潺，

天空何美，星光璀璨，

敬由心生，唯意所适。

逍遥相羊，无语静听，

寻幽不思返，

坐啸夕阳偏。

群贤时集堂中，

窥仁义之源，探礼乐之绪，

佳酿蔬食鲜，

格致味道增。

庙堂之上，

人骄纵，用谗佞，

佞人臣，明争暗斗，

栽赃诬蔑，钩心斗角；

自未始有形之前，

暨四达无穷之外。

事物之理，举集目前；

斯文在兹！

奈猛风过后，

闭门常独居，独乐斯园。

所言为何？

当言否？

身为人夫，又为人父，

英名愧终贾，高节谢巢由——

都人心望幸，注目不离东。

别了，独乐园！别了！

属意尊亲爱国，

服从都人召唤。

复纵乐一日，

行无所牵，止无所框，

耳目肺肠，悉为己有。踽踽焉，洋洋焉。

中国植物区系

很少有国家能像中国这样拥有如此丰富多样的植物区系。假如列出一长串在中国发现的所有植物，对作者来说枯燥乏味，对读者来说也无益处；但是列举一些更常见、更有用的植物可能比较有意思。

中国有着英国也有的林木，其中橡树、松树、雪松、栗子、柳树、灌木和其他树

at her gates,
And offering her the homage of our hearts.
My eyes are constantly upon her set;
On me, alas! her rays come through thick clouds;
But let them be dispersed, though by a storm,
And then this solitude will be to me
The temple of felicity and truth.
What do I say? Shall I? A husband, father,
Citizen, and man of lettered fame—
My life is not my own, but to the State
By twice ten thousand duties I am bound.
Adieu, dear garden! once again, adieu!
Me love of kindred and of country claims,
The city calls me, and I must obey.
Then keep thy pleasures for some other day,
They may anon dispel some carking cares,
And save my virtue from temptation's snares.

Flora of China

Few countries, if any, can boast of so rich and varied a flora as China. To give a long list of all the trees and plants that have been discovered on its soil would be a task tedious to the writer and unprofitable to the reader of these pages; but a few names of the more common and useful of the different kinds of plants may be interesting.

Of our own forest trees, the oak, the pine, the cedar, the chestnut, the willow, the thorn, and others, are found in abundance; of those strangers to our climate, the banyan extends its perennial shade over a vast area from its original root, with rootlets descending from its spreading branches—as much a village favourite as the oak and elm of our country. The camphor-tree grows to a large size, and the bread-fruit-tree with its blue blossoms is an attractive object; the betel-nut rises gracefully to the height of 50 feet; the rattan spreads its branches like the vine, and the variegated leaves of the castor-oil plant add beauty to the foreground.

There are few fruit-trees with which we are familiar in this country which are not found in China, such as the pear, the plum, the peach, and the fig, but they differ much in fruit and flavour from those of England. Of their own fruit-trees there is great variety and abundance. Their Chinese names would be meaningless; but those of the banana, the orange, the lime, the lychi, and pineapple are well known.

Vegetables of all kinds are abundant; we need only name melons, onions, leeks, cabbages, turnips, peas, beans, spinach, celery, and the sweet potato. The tea plant, by the cultivation of which China has laid the civilized world under obligation, introducing a cheering and refresh-

种，数量较多；还有那些不适宜英国气候生长的树木，其中，榕树从主根长起，蔓延的枝条上延伸出许多气生根，树冠巨大，遮天蔽日，常年带来阴凉，它在乡村受人喜爱，就像橡树和榆树受英国人喜爱一样。樟树长得很大；面包果树开蓝色花朵，很吸引人；槟榔树舒展地向上长到50英尺的高度；白藤像葡萄藤一样蔓延开来；蓖麻叶子色彩斑驳，平添美感。

英国人熟悉的果树，没有哪个是中国没有的，例如梨树、李子树、桃树和无花果树，但它们的果实和味道都与英格兰的大不相同。中国的果树种类繁多，数量丰富。提及果树的中文名意义不大；但是香蕉、橙子、青柠、荔枝和菠萝的中文名却广为人知。

蔬菜品种丰富，应有尽有；我们只需提及一些菜名便可，瓜、洋葱、韭菜、卷心菜、萝卜、豌豆、四季豆、菠菜、芹菜还有红薯。茶树是土生土长的植物，中国以茶树种植给了文明世界一份恩惠，传给我们一种愉悦、提神的饮料，相对来说又不成瘾。可悲且可羞的事实是，我们以怨报德，把鸦片这一最具诱惑、最有害的毒药输入中国，鸦片损害了中国的繁荣，玷污了英国的荣誉。中国所有的物产中，最重要的是大米，对于中国人来说，大米是主食，没有大米的日子是不可想象的。当中国人得知英国种不出大米时，一下子就"恍然明了"，原来这就是英国人如此乐意离开自己那悲惨的国家，如此急切地想要进入上等的大米可以让人吃个够的中国的原因。当一个中国人遇到朋友，首先就会提出请客，用厦门方言说是"呷饭"（chia pung），意思是"吃米饭"。米饭即等同于"饭"。

  中国的花卉如此多样和丰富，不胜枚举，中国不愧被称为"花国"。许多生长在田野和路边的野花，在英国已被栽培成最受欢迎的品种。花中的皇后——玫瑰花，与杜鹃花和玉兰一样，自然地生长在山坡上。小径旁，万寿菊生长；大树上，爬满旋花花叶，优美茂盛，金银花与之争奇斗艳，美丽芬芳；林地中，紫罗兰与风铃草把身藏。

ing beverage, comparatively free from abuse, is indigenous to the soil. It is a sad and humbling fact that we have repaid our obligations by introducing into that country the most seductive and pernicious of poisons—opium—a blight on the prosperity of China and the Honour of England. But chief of all the productions of China is its rice, the staff of life to a Chinaman, who cannot conceive of people living without it. When he learns that rice won't grow in England, it at once explains to him why we are so willing to leave such a miserable country, and are so anxious to get access to China, where we can eat our fill of its choice food. The first invitation when a Chinaman meets a friend is, in the Amoy dialect, "chia pung" "eat rice." It is equivalent to "food."

  We cannot describe the flowers of China—so varied and abundant as to entitle it to assume the name of the Flowery Land. Many of those which grow wild in the fields and roadsides have been acclimatized as favorites in our own country. That queen of flowers, the rose, grows wild on the hillsides in China, along with the azalea and magnolia. The marigold grows by the footpaths, and the convolvulus covers large trees with its graceful flower and leaf; honeysuckle vies with it in luxuriance, and adds fragrance to its beauty, while violets and bluebells hide in the woodlands.

老虎陷阱
A Tiger Trap

动物区系

由于人口密度和充分的开垦情况，中国的动物区系相对于植物区系来说比较有限；尽管有些害兽被捕食，但害兽数量却还是很多。在北方有熊，熊掌被认为是餐桌上的美味，导致熊被大肆杀戮，否则熊的数量将会更多。鹿、豹数量不多。在厦门附近的山上，时有猛虎被打死，不幸的是，在老虎与当地人的博弈中，往往是老虎成功地杀死当地人。在家畜之中，猫和狗在许多意义上都是最受欢迎的；它们不仅被当作宠物来看待，有些品种的狗更可能被做成狗肉饼。中国有猴子，按照达尔文进化论，传闻山东的猴子已经进化到相当高的程度，如果茶树生长在人手无法触及的陡峭之处，猴子可以替人类采摘茶叶。不幸的是，理论上说，山东并不生长茶树。中国某些地区会饲养一些小黄牛，水牛则随处可见，一脸沉郁，或拉着犁铧或在沟渠里吃草，常见的情景是"牧童归去横牛背，短笛无腔信口吹"。绵羊和山羊在中国大部分地区都很稀少，而猪作为一种经济型的养殖家畜，在人们罕有的动物性食品

The Fauna

From the density of population and the high cultivation of the country, the fauna of China is limited, compared with its flora; there is more than enough of vermin, though even some of these are killed for food. In the north, bears are found, and would be more numerous, were it not that their paws are considered a delicacy of the table, which leads to their destruction. Deer and leopards are not numerous, and in the mountains around Amoy the royal tiger is sometimes killed, but unhappily is more frequently successful in this sport, at which two can play, by killing the natives. Of domestic animals the cat and dog are favorites in more senses than one; they are not only prized as pets, but some species of dogs are more highly prized in the form of puppy-pies. Monkeys are found, and those in Shantung were said to have reached such a point of Darwinian evolution as to be employed in picking leaves from tea-plants that grew in precipitous places beyond the reach of human hands. Unfortunately for the theory, the tea-plant does not grow in Shantung. A few small oxen are reared in some parts, and the water-buffalo, with his subdued pessimistic look, is seen everywhere, dragging the plough or feeding in the ditches, often with his herd—a little boy—seated on his back and playing on a primitive Pan-pipe.

Sheep and goats are scarce in most parts of the country, but the pig, being an economical feeder, forms the chief item in the rare animal food of the people.

Horses are small but hardy, like our Shetland ponies. Ignorance of this fact in natural history led to a ridiculous fiasco when Lord Macartney went in great state, with a magnificent retinue, as Ambassador to Peking in 1792. To make a great impression on the minds of the Emperor and his people, his lordship took out with him a grand state-coach, and, as he could not take his own large carriage horses, he took their gold-mounted harness and trappings, with his powdered coachman in state livery. The Emperor graciously promised to lend him horses, and did his best; but when the diminutive ponies in shaggy coats arrived, the coachman, who had never before sat behind such specimens of "horseflesh," rushed into his master's presence, and, in tones of horror, exclaimed, "My Lord, they have sent us four cats!" The Ambassador had to content himself with a sedan-chair, followed by his powdered servants on foot.

Mineral Resources

China is as rich in treasures hid in the bowels of the earth as in the fertility of its soil, and can supply all her own wants out of her own mines. All the common minerals, except platinum,

中占据了首要地位。

中国马体型小，但很强壮，类似英国的设得兰矮种马。1792年，马戛尔尼[14]作为英国全权大使，率领宏大使团出访大清帝国，次年进入北京。他在博物学方面对中国马匹的无知导致了一场荒唐的惨败。为了给乾隆皇帝和他的子民留下深刻的印象，马戛尔尼随行带了一辆恢宏的皇家马车，同时，由于无法从国内带来曳车的高头大马，他就带上了嵌金的马具和饰物，他的马车夫也搽上粉，穿上盛装。乾隆皇帝恩许借马给他，且鼎力相助；但是当长毛厚皮的小矮马赶来时，马车夫因为从未坐在这种标本般的小马身后赶过马车，便急忙冲到主人跟前，用惊恐的声音喊道："大人，他们给我们送来了四只猫！"结果，大使不得不坐上轿子，而他那些搽粉的仆从则跟在后面步行。

矿产资源

中国地表土壤肥沃，地下宝藏同样丰富，矿藏可以自足。除铂金外，所有常见矿物不仅仅存在于样品中，而且是可供开采的，开采成本表明其储量是多么丰富。在陕西、新疆和西藏都有金矿开采，但黄金只用作饰品，不用作钱币。白银分布在63个不同的地区，并且与铜一起作为货币流通。铁矿资源丰富，质量上乘；煤是动力和文明进步的基本条件，在内地十八省都有。煤炭在74个地区开采。在群山间悬崖峭壁而过的长江上游，也有煤矿。这些矿井是通过河床上方数百英尺的高处开采的。煤炭装在篮子里，在用两根绷紧的粗绳构成的像铁轨一样的索道上运送，斜斜地拉向河岸。煤炭可以在矿坑里买，每吨大约3~6先令⑮。

中国乃福泽之地，土地肥沃、资源丰富，这些事实很大程度上解释了中国早期文明的形成，资源使其不受对外贸易约束，并培养了绝世独立和不爱对外交往的精神。这些特点由于第一批到访中国口岸的外国人而得以强化，因为这些外国人举止粗鲁、行为不端。葡萄牙人和荷兰人的所作所为就像海盗一样，并且英国人也好不到哪里去，初期的英国商人傲慢地恫吓中国，要求通商，还肆无忌惮地走私鸦片。

ire not only found in samples, but produced at a price which shows they are abundant. Gold-mines are worked in the province of Shen-si, and the dependencies of Illi and Tibet, but gold is only used for ornament, not for currency. Silver is found in sixty-three different districts, and, along with copper, is the medium of exchange. Iron is found in abundance, and of the finest quality, and coal, that essential condition of power and progressive civilization, is found in each of the eighteen provinces of China. It is worked in seventy-four different districts. It is also found in the upper reaches of the Yang-tze-Kiang, cropping out of the face of the mountains through which the river has worn a passage. The mines are worked from a height of hundreds of feet above the bed of the river. The coal is lowered in baskets running on two thick ropes, like rails, stretched tightly at an incline to the river's bank. It can be bought "at the pit," at from about three to six shillings the ton.

These facts respecting the fertility and resources of that highly-favoured land account in a large measure for the early civilization of China, rendering it independent of external commerce, and have fostered the spirit of isolation and aversion to foreign intercourse. Their feelings have been strengthened by the rude manners and unrighteous conduct of the first foreigners who visited her shores. The Portuguese and Dutch acted like pirates, and our first English traders were little better, with their arrogant and blustering demands for trade, and their unprincipled smuggling of opium.

Absence of Architectural Monuments

Travellers frequently complain that the features of Chinese scenery are not adorned with castles and with stately mansions, like those of Europe, and that their old towns contain no venerable monuments of their ancient greatness, like the Pyramids of Egypt, nor remains of architectural beauty, like the public buildings of Rome, the temples and tombs of India, or the grand old cathedrals of Europe. It must be admitted that the Porcelain Tower, the Great Wall, the Grand Canal, and a few second-rate temples and monasteries, are nearly all the works that can be pointed out. But is this to the credit or the disgrace of China? It is spoken of in a deprecatory tone by artistic travellers, who contrast this old civilization with the interesting ruins and splendid monuments of other lands.

Monument Slavery

To our mind, the absence of these old monuments from the cities and scenery of China is the highest proof of the superiority of China to these fallen empires of the West. For of what are the remains of these great works the proof? Look lower down than the outward show, and what do we find—beneath the display of genius in a few architects and engineers—but the evidence of tyranny, oppression and cruelty of

建筑丰碑的缺失

外国旅行者常常抱怨说，中国风景的特色，不像欧洲那般是由城堡和高堂广厦来装点的，而且中国古城既没有埃及金字塔那样古老、伟大、令人肃然起敬的丰碑，也没有像罗马的公共建筑、印度的庙宇和陵墓，或欧洲古老宏的伟大教堂那样的富有建筑美的遗迹。必须承认，琉璃塔⑯、长城、大运河以及一些二流的寺庙和寺院几乎是可圈可点的全部丰碑了。但这于中国是荣耀还是耻辱？爱好艺术的旅行者总是以贬低的口吻谈论起这一点，他们将中国古老的文明与其他国家引人入胜的废墟和辉煌壮观的丰碑进行对比。

丰碑下的奴役

在我们看来，中国的城市和风景中缺乏古老的丰碑，是中国比那些西方失落的帝国优越的最高证明。那些伟大丰碑的遗迹证明了什么？透过外表看本质，丰碑除了展现几位建筑师和工程师的天赋之外，便是少数人对被役使为奴隶的多数人实施暴政、压迫和残酷虐待的证据，除了把脑海中美好的愿景变成石砌的实物建筑之外,我们还能看到什么?剥去我们面对金字塔和印度教庙宇时产生的敬畏感和惊奇感,超越我们在凝视古希腊罗马的废墟以及印度穆斯林征服者的陵墓时怀有的那份崇敬和美感,我们是否知道这些丰碑的代价是什么?那是饱受摧残、被压迫、被奴役的人的眼泪、呻吟与鲜血!

埃及金字塔使数百万人民遭受长期苦难和残酷的压迫。据说,为了在吉萨⑰建造胡夫大金字塔,每年要驱使10万人工作3个月,历时18年,而这座金字塔的建造算是所有工程中对人民来说压迫最少的。泰姬陵,最精美的艺术品,"大理石写就的诗",却是恐怖和残酷之作;它饱含着生命摧残、残酷死亡,不是上千,而是上万无辜受害者,他们背井离乡,只为建造一座陵墓,以满足某个暴君的骄傲,抚慰他失去爱妃的伤痛。谢天谢地,中国没有这样的丰碑!中国的帝王从来没有尝试这样做,人民也从来没有成为专制的工具而被奴役和压榨。

印度的大寺庙和欧洲中世纪的大教堂

the few over the many who were employed as slaves to turn the exquisite ideal of the brain into the material structure of stone? Strip them of the sense of awe and wonder with which we look on the Pyramids and Hindoo temples; get behind the sentiment of veneration and aesthetic feeling with which we gaze upon the ruins of Greece and Rome, and the mausoleums of the Mohammedan conquerors of India, and of what do we find them the price? The tears, groans and blood of a down-trodden, crushed and enslaved population!

The Pyramids of Egypt cost the prolonged misery and cruel oppression of millions of the people. It is said that 100000 men were made to work three months in the year for eighteen years to build the Great Pyramid of Ghizeh, and that seems to have been constructed with the least of oppression to the people of any. The Taj-ma-hall, the most exquisite work of art—"a poem in marble"—was the work of horrid cruelty; it was steeped in the blasted lives and cruel deaths of tens, if not hundreds, of thousands of innocent men, torn from their homes and families to rear a tomb to gratify the pride and soothe the feelings of a despot for the loss of one of his favourite wives. Thank God, China has no such monuments! Her kings never attempted such works as these, and the people were never such tools of despotism as to be thus enslaved and crushed.

What are even the great temples of India and the grand cathedrals of medieval Europe a proof of? We cannot help admiring their architectural magnificence, and we feel the sense of power or the soul of beauty so lovingly displayed in the genius and skill with which the wonderful effects are planned, and the minute care with which every detail has been worked out by master minds; but we cannot help reflecting on the painful fact that many of the grandest of these buildings, reared at infinite cost for the worship of the gods of India or the God of the Christian, were built through the spiritual tyranny—the most degrading of all forms of tyranny—of a despotic priesthood, working on the superstitious fears of a guilty conscience, by which the people were enslaved and oppressed. We are happy to say China never was deprived of religious liberty through the power of priestcraft... These opinions will appear worthy of a Goth or Vandal, but a defence of the civilization of the most ancient empire in the world demanded their utterance, as an explanation of an admitted fact—the absence of aesthetic monuments in China.

The Great Wall

It is characteristic of the Chinese people, and creditable to their common-sense and independence of spirit, that the only great monuments they can boast of are the Grand Canal and the Great Wall, both of them really great as engineering works, especially when we take into consideration

都能证明什么？我们不禁赞叹它们在建筑上的雄伟，从中体会到力量感或美的化身，力量与美精心展现于古迹设计的天分与技巧之中，还展现于工匠大师巧饬中一丝不苟的执着；但是，我们也不禁反思这一痛苦的事实，即许多最宏伟的丰碑是为崇拜印度诸神或基督教上帝而耗费无限，并通过专制的祭司集团的精神暴政——所有暴政形式中最有辱人格的一种——来建造而成的，祭司们利用人们对罪恶感的盲目恐惧，对人们实施奴役和压迫。我们很高兴地说，中国从来没有因为祭司的权力而被剥夺宗教自由。这些无视宏伟丰碑意义的观点看似与哥特人⑱或汪达尔人⑲相媲美，但若要捍卫世界上最古老的中华帝国文明，便需要这些话语，来解释中国缺乏美学意义上的丰碑这一公认的事实。

长　城

在中国人中很典型的思维是，（同时要记住，中国人的常识和独立精神也是很值得称道的，）他们自我夸耀的仅有的伟大丰碑是大运河与长城，这是两项真正伟大的工程奇迹，尤其是考虑到它们修建的时间之早。公元前200年[20]，始皇帝将彼此交战不断的列国征服，建立了一个庞大的帝国，下令修建这项伟大的工程，以抵御北方匈奴的入侵，长城在许多世纪里一直为中原提供有效保护。它构成了北部边界，从东到西，穿过河流，翻过高山，穿过深谷，绵延1255英里[21]。它最初的规格是20英尺高，底部25英尺宽，顶部15英尺宽，两辆战车可以在护墙内轻松通过；全程大约每100码处就有一座塔楼，几乎是城墙高度的两倍。300年后罗马帝国时代修建的著名的哈德良长城[22]，从泰恩河到索尔威河，长约60英里，将它与长城相比，我们就可以推断出长城的伟大之处。中国长城自东向西绵延1500英里，偶尔因地势原因有所曲折，长度是哈德良长城的25倍，而且更高、更宽。

大运河

大运河，又称"闸河"[23]，比长城更能代表中国的和平，以及中国人的商业魄力与宏伟构想，因为长城是征服者秦始皇旨

the early date of their construction. The Great Wall was built by the Emperor Chi hwang ti 200 B.C., the man who reduced the many small independent kingdoms, which were at constant war among themselves, into one vast empire, and planned and extended this great work as a defence against the Tartar barbarians on the north, from whom it was for many centuries an effectual protection. It forms the northern boundary of China proper, and runs from east to west, across rivers, over lofty mountains, and through deep valleys, in an unbroken line of 1255 miles. In its original form it was 20 feet high, 25 feet wide at the base, and 15 feet at the top, on which two chariots could pass with ease within the parapets; there are towers nearly twice the height of the walls at about every hundred yards of the entire length. Some idea of the greatness of this work may be gathered by a comparison with the famous Roman Wall from the Tyne to the Solway, a distance of about sixty miles, built some 300 years later. The Chinese Wall, allowing for necessary deviations from the straight line, is 1500 miles long, twenty-five times the length of the Roman Wall, besides being much higher and broader.

The Grand Canal

The Grand Canal, or "River of floodgates" or "locks" as it is well called, is more characteristic of Chinese peaceful industry, and their grand conception of commercial enterprise, than the Great Wall—a military scheme of the conqueror Tsin Chi, meant for the preservation of peace. By this canal, and taking advantage of rivers on its route, the chief cities on the north and south of China, Peking and Canton, were connected by unbroken water communication, and access obtained to the world outside by sea at the two extremities. This gave a stretch of 1200 miles in what may be called a straight line. Of this water-way, between 600 and 700 miles are real Canal, in many places 200 feet broad, and so laid down as to make it a highway to the capital from all parts of the Middle Kingdom by means of the rivers and smaller canals throughout the greater part of the empire. The commencement of the work is involved in remote obscurity, but it was completed by Kublai Khan, who deepened and extended it in the beginning of the thirteenth century, as we are told by the traveller Marco Polo, who resided at his Court and described the work.

Such works as these are more worthy of a great and free people than Egyptian pyramids as tombs for the dead, Indian temples for the superstitions of the living, and Roman amphitheatres for the slaughter of men and beasts to amuse a cruel and depraved race.

Physical Geography and Form of Religion

The geographical features of China must have exerted an influence favourable to the

在维护和平而修建的军事工程。通过这条运河，并利用其沿线的河流，中国南方的广州与北方的北京之间的主要城市由接续不断的水路贯通，在南北两端通过海路与外部世界相通。它绵延1200英里。这条水道有600~700英里的河段是真正的运河，许多河段宽达200英尺，如此一来它就成了一条水上大道，通过遍布帝国大部分地区的河流与较小的运河把首都与帝国各个地区联通起来。运河开凿的开端遥不可查，但竣工是在忽必烈时期，他在13世纪初[24]加深并延长了它，正如旅行家马可·波罗对运河加以描述的那样，他当时居留在忽必烈的宫廷中。

埃及金字塔系死者的坟墓，印度寺庙系活人的迷信，罗马圆形剧场系屠杀人类与野兽以娱乐某个残酷、堕落民族之所，与此相比，大运河与长城更配得上一个伟大和自由的民族。

自然环境和宗教形式

正如我们所见，中国的地理特征一定对维系中国温和、理性的宗教形式产生了

路边客栈
A Wayside Inn

maintenance of a moderate and rational form of religion, such as we find it. The blending of mountain and plain in due proportions under one race and one form of government saved it from the extremes which a great preponderance of mountain or plain tend to develop. …The religion, like the social and political institutions of the country, developed itself into a mild and moral system …

有利的影响。在同一个种族和同一种政府形式之下，山地与平原按适当比例混杂，使中国避免因单一山地或平原的巨大优势而走向极端。中国的宗教，就像其社会制度和政治制度一样，发展成为一种温和的富有道德的体系。

【注　释】

① 震旦：古代印度人对中国的称呼，音译自梵文，又译作真丹、旃丹、指难等。——译者注

② 丝国：古希腊和古罗马地理学家、历史学家对与丝绸相关的国家和民族的称呼，一般认为指当时的中国或中国附近地区，又译作赛里斯。——译者注

③ 秦始皇统一六国的时间为公元前221年，应为公元前3世纪。原文有误。——译者注

④ 高加索山脉：原文"Imaus"，即意貌山。该词常出现于西方地理文献中，现代学界对其地望的认识主要有三种（帕米尔高原、喜马拉雅山、阿尔泰山），但其更重要的含义是曾为西方的亚洲地理体系中一座虚构的山脉。古典文献所记载的意貌山最初只是模糊地表示喜马拉雅山，并被视作横贯亚洲东西的陶鲁斯（高加索）山脉最东段，托勒密则又将其描绘成中分亚洲北部斯基泰的南北向山脉。后世地理著作、地图便继承了这两种真实与想象杂糅的意貌山概念，来华传教士中文世界地图中还为调和中西文化而对其位置略有改动。随着亚洲北部主要轮廓被初步探察清楚，这一历史地名自17世纪末便逐渐消失。——译者注

⑤ 巴克特里亚王国：中亚古国，相当于现代阿富汗北部，是公元前3—前2世纪一个强大的希腊化奴隶制王国。——译者注

⑥ 柏朗嘉宾（John of Plano Carpini, 1180—1252）：小兄弟会（方济各会）的创始人之一，曾被教皇英诺森四世派往蒙古，成为13、14世纪东西方交往热潮的先行者。柏朗嘉宾回欧洲后，将他在沿途的见闻记录下来，写成了《柏朗嘉宾蒙古行纪》。该书分

九章，详细介绍蒙古的地理概况、衣食住行、宗教信仰、民间习俗、大汗王室、战略战术、征服地区情况以及深入探讨抵御蒙古入侵的战术等内容，对研究东西方文化交流有很高的价值。——译者注

⑦ 鲁布鲁克（William of Rubruck）：法国方济各会修士。1253年奉罗马教皇英诺森四世和法王路易九世之命出使蒙古。写有出使蒙古记行，1839年和1900年分别用法文和英文刊行，有中译本《鲁布鲁克东行纪》。——译者注

⑧ 蒙哥汗：元宪宗孛儿只斤·蒙哥（1209—1259），蒙古可汗。1251年7月1日至1259年8月11日在位。为元太祖成吉思汗之孙、拖雷长子，其四弟即元世祖忽必烈。——译者注

⑨ 乔治·斯当东爵士（Sir George Staunton, 1st Baronet, 1737—1801）：英国探险家、植物学家。1793年，斯当东成为英国访华使团的副使（正使为马戛尔尼），他将沿途的所见所闻详细记载下来，写成《英使谒见乾隆纪实》一书。该书以一个西方人的视角看盛世时期的清朝，是研究清朝中期历史的重要史料。1801年1月14日，斯当东逝世，其从男爵爵位由独子乔治·托马斯·斯当东（即小斯当东，George Thomas Staunton）继承。——译者注

⑩ 1英尺约为0.3048米，以此换算。下同。——译者注

⑪ 华兹华斯（William Wordsworth, 1770—1850）：英国诗人，其许多作品的灵感均来自湖泊地区。他与柯尔律治（Samuel Taylor Coleridge）一道写就的，包括《丁登寺》在内的《抒情歌谣集》（1798）是浪漫主义的里程碑；其他代表作品有《咏水仙》（1804）和《序曲》（1805）。1843年被封为桂冠诗人。1799—1808年，华兹华斯和妹妹多萝西·华兹华斯（Dorothy Wordsworth）曾在格拉斯米尔湖畔定居。——译者注

⑫ 古伯察（Evariste Regis Huc, 1813—1860）：法国入华遣使会会士。1839年3月24日赴中国，之后进行了一次环中国的长途旅行。他还是第一个进入西藏的法国人。撰有《中华帝国纪行》等著作。——译者注

⑬ 英文原作者声称忠实于司马光的原作，故而翻译成英文无韵诗的形式。但是，其实际效果与原文相去甚远，因此，译者在将英文回译成汉语时，基本无法对应司马光《独乐园记》的原句。所以，翻译时采用散文体意译，不同于司马光原作。——译者注

⑭ 马戛尔尼（George Macartney, 1737—1806）：英国近代著名政治家，曾率领使团以给乾隆皇帝祝寿为名，于1793年抵达中国，欲通过谈判打开中国市场，却无功而返。这是中西交往史上的一件大事。——译者注

⑮ 先令：英国的一种旧货币单位，20先令等于1英镑。——译者注

⑯ 著名的琉璃塔被太平天国起义军出于战略目的摧毁了。据说琉璃塔能够影响当地的守护神，进而可保南京城坚不可摧。——原注

⑰ 吉萨：位于开罗西南，尼罗河西岸，是金字塔和狮身人面像所在地。——译者注

⑱ 哥特人：日耳曼人的一支，3—5世纪从东方入侵罗马帝国；东哥特人在意大利建立王国，而西哥特人在西班牙建立王国。——译者注

⑲ 汪达尔人：日耳曼人的一支，于4世纪和5世纪进入高卢、西班牙和北非，并于455年占领罗马，并大肆破坏。——译者注

⑳ 秦始皇统一六国后，即开始北筑长城，时间应为公元前221年。原文有误。——译者注

㉑ 1英里约为1609米，以此换算。原作者叙述的长城长度不对，两处分别提到的是1255英里（相当于2019千米）、1500英里（约2414千米），而国家文物局2012年宣布中国历代长城总长度为21196.18千米。——译者注

㉒ 哈德良长城：罗马城墙的一部分。罗马城墙指罗马帝国时代罗马人在罗马、意大利或其他殖民地修建的保护性城墙，对于英国人来说，哈德良长城最为熟悉。哈德良长城横穿英格兰北部，西起索尔威湾，东至泰恩河口，长118.3千米（73.5英里，原文有误）。它的一些残垣断壁保留至今。——译者注

㉓ 闸河：大运河上船闸众多，因此获此别称。船闸设置的目的主要是解决水源补给问题，便利船只通行。——译者注

㉔ 忽必烈在综合南北方经济发展需要以及对南方实施有效控制等因素后，于至元十二年（1276）批准丞相伯颜的奏折，下令修建和整治南北运河各段，于是大运河迎来了它的第三个阶段——京杭大运河时期。原文时间"13世纪初"有误。——译者注

第二章　人民及其追求
Chapter II The People and Their Pursuits

衡量的标准

凡是在中国生活过、逐渐了解中国人，并因其所拥有的良好品质而对其产生善意和兴趣的人，会痛苦地发现，中国人有一种强烈的倾向，即对自己的缺点老是念念不忘，或者把自己的天真无邪当作嘲弄的对象。大多数中国人习惯于以基督教般具有教化作用的最高标准来衡量自己，而且不是以我们100年前的，而是现在的标准来衡量。

特色品质

若因为中国人的礼仪和风俗与英国不同，就把他们当作轻蔑和嘲弄的对象，实

Standard to Measure by

To anyone who has lived in China, and has learned to know the people, and to feel a kindly interest in them for the good qualities which they do possess, it is painful to find in this country so strong a tendency to dwell on their faults, or turn their innocent peculiarities to ridicule. It is the custom of most to measure them by the high level of the Christian standard, and that, not of what we were even a hundred years ago, but by our attainments at the close of the present century, with all its humanizing influences…

Characteristic Qualities

It is still more unreasonable to speak of the Chinese as objects of contemptuous ridicule because their manners and customs are different from ours. A clever traveller who has spent a month or two in the country, will tell, amidst the laughter of his audience, how the Chinaman wears a long "pigtail" hanging from the crown of his head, and will put his chief guest on his left hand as the place of honour, while he mounts his horse on the off side; how he actually writes from right to left of the page in lines running from the top to the bottom, and begins to read at the wrong end of a book; that he orders his servant to whiten his shoes, and wears white for mourning, while a dutiful son presents his father with a handsome coffin as a birthday present; how mothers bind the feet of their daughters until they can wear a shoe $2\frac{1}{2}$ inches in length, and poets indite verses, not to ladies' eyes, but to their little feet, which they call "golden lilies," and praise their graceful walk, which they declare to be as elegant as the waddling of a duck. One of our poets tells the visitor to China that he will be waited on by smart young men about Canton in nankeen tights and "pigtail", handing you conserves of snails,

 With many rare and dreadful dainties:
  Kitten cutlets, puppy pies,
  Bird's-nest soup, which, so convenient,
  Every bush around supplies.

在是荒谬。一个头脑灵光的旅行者在中国待了一两个月,便在他听众的哄笑声中讲述中国人是如何在脑瓜顶上垂下一条长长的辫子;他们还请主客左手就座,因为左为尊,而他们上马时则从右侧上;书写时依照竖排自右向左行的顺序,书则是左翻的;他们去祭奠时命仆人把鞋子擦白,并穿着白色,而孝子在父亲生日时献上考究的棺材作为礼物;母亲给女儿缠足,直到她们能穿上两英寸①半的小鞋为止,文人骚客留下诸多诗赋,不写女人的明眸,而专门写女人的小脚,他们称之为"金莲",赞颂她们莲步娉婷,楚楚可怜。一位英国诗人告诉赴华的旅行者,在广州一带,机灵的年轻伙计留着辫子,穿着土布紧身衣在一旁服侍,递给你一些蜗牛制品②:

  佳肴稀奇又可怖:
  猫肉丸子狗肉饼,
  燕窝汤,最便当,
  鸟巢盏盏煲羹汤。

人 口

诗人用破格的修辞法夸大了中国人表面的特点,毋庸赘言,以此来评判一个民族是愚蠢的做法,因为同样地,中国人在英国的风俗习惯中同样可以发现许多可嘲弄的东西。在所有民族中,中国人是最不应该被嘲弄的。他们是一个审慎、真诚、勤勉、节俭、吃苦耐劳的民族,他们的算术、工业、商业、文学、历史、文字等方面的成就要求每一个细心的学者怀着敬意对其加以研究。

中国的人口是世界奇迹之一。中国人口达到4亿人,这数字是最称职的行家认可的。中国的帝王们就已习惯了对国民进行人口普查,把它当成一种神圣的职责,比欧洲早了2000多年,当时的欧洲想都没想到这事。自古以来,在每年的祭天大典上,皇帝都会把人口数呈献给最高统治者——上帝,如果国家人口增长了,就会感谢天恩,如果人口减少了,就会哀叹和自责。

减去边地2000万人口,华夏地区就剩下3亿8000万人,供养在150万平方英里

Population

We need not say it is folly to judge of a people by such superficial characteristics, exaggerated by poetic license, when the Chinaman can find as much to laugh at in our own habits and customs as we do in his. Of all nations, the Chinese are the last to be laughed at. They are a sensible, earnest, industrious, economical, hard-working people; their numbers, industries, commerce, literature, history, and character demand the respectful study of every thoughtful student.

The population of China is one of the wonders of the world. That it numbers with its dependencies about 400000000 of people is allowed by the most competent judges. The Emperors of China had been in the habit of keeping a census of their people 2000 years before such a thing was dreamt of in Europe; it was regarded as a sacred duty. The number of the people has been presented by the Emperor to Shang-ti—the Supreme Ruler—from time immemorial at the great annual sacrifice, with grateful thanks if there was an increase, and with lamentation and self-reproaches if there was a decrease in the population.

Deducting 20000000 for the dependencies would leave 380000000 for China proper, supported on a compact territory of 1500000 square miles, making about 280 to the square mile, a number not so great as that supported on many a small country like Belgium and England, but very great when spread over so large an area, including bare hills and the many barren regions which are inevitable in a country half as large as Europe, where the population is only on an average of ninety-one to the square mile, a third of the average over the whole of China. There is great diversity in the density of the population in different provinces. A large portion in the east and south has a population of only about 150 to the square mile, while the great plains on the northeast have an average of 450, and the province of Shantung has as many as 600 or 700 to the square mile. It would be unfair to compare provinces in China with European kingdoms in respect of density, for most of the latter are largely dependent on foreign countries for their food supplies. China, with a few exceptions, provides for her population from her own internal resources.

How Supported

But it may be asked, How can the land support so great a population? The answer is simple enough. First of all, the people live almost entirely on vegetable diet and fish. To rear a sheep for food requires, we are told, as much land as would support a man,

的地势平坦的狭小土地上，每平方英里约280人。这个数字没有比利时、英国等许多小国的数字那么大，但是如果把半个欧洲视作一个国家的面积，光秃秃的山丘和许多不可避免的贫瘠地区都算在内，那么每平方英里只有91人，是华夏地区的1/3。不同省份的人口密度差异很大。东部和南部大部分地区每平方英里仅有约150人，而东北的大平原地区每平方英里有450人，山东省的人口则每平方英里达六七百人之多。将中国各省的人口密度与欧洲国家的进行比较是不公平的，因为欧洲大部分国家的粮食供应很大程度上依赖外国，而中国，除了个别地区例外，都是靠自己国内的资源养活国人的。③

养活人口的方法

但可能有人会问，中国的土地怎么能养活这么多人口？答案很简单。首先，人们几乎完全以蔬菜和鱼类为生。据说，养一只肉羊所需的土地足以养活一口人，而养一头肉牛所需的土地足以养活八口人或两个家庭。其次，气候和土壤允许一年种两季庄稼，有时种三季。再次，中国人从海洋和河流中大量收获各种鱼类。平坦海岸或河口的浅水区用来繁殖和饲养鱼类，就像土地用来繁育或饲养牛羊一样，河流也被用来放养鱼类，适于随时捕捞。最后，人民是节俭、勤劳和出色的土地耕作者。他们庄稼轮作、施肥、灌溉的用地和养地结合的耕作方式令人钦佩。他们有效发挥、充分利用每一小块可播种的土地，正如汉密尔顿博士所说："中国人把种子播到人们认为只有鸟儿才能收割得了的地方。"

工业与技艺

如果考虑到中国是靠着自己的聪明才智发明和制造所有产品的话，那么中国工业很了不得。他们无法从邻国借鉴到什么，因为中国遥遥领先。他们也无法从欧洲学到什么东西，因为中国离古希腊、古罗马或古埃及太过遥远了。他们很有可能从人类的发源地带走了四五千年前就存在的促成文明的一些较朴素的元素。

and an ox takes as much as would support eight men or two families. Then, the climate and soil admit of two crops, sometimes three, to be grown on the same land in one year. Third, Chinamen reap a great harvest of fishes of all kinds from both sea and rivers. Shallow water on a flat shore or estuary is farmed for the breeding and rearing of fishes, as land is in this country for the breeding or rearing of sheep and oxen, and the rivers are kept stocked with fish, which are caught by all kinds of expedients. Fourth, the people are frugal, industrious, and excellent cultivators of the soil. Their system of rotation of crops and manuring and watering the soil is admirable. They turn everything to the best account, and take advantage of every little plot of ground they can plant a seed on; as Dr. Hamilton said, "They sow where one would think none but the birds could reap the harvest."

Industries and Arts

The industries of China are wonderful, when we consider that they are all the product of their own intelligence and invention. They could borrow nothing from their neighbours, for they were far ahead of them. They could learn nothing from Europe, they were too remote from Greece, Rome, or Egypt. It is more than possible that they carried from the original seat of the human race some of the simpler elements of civilization as they existed 4000 or 5000 years ago.

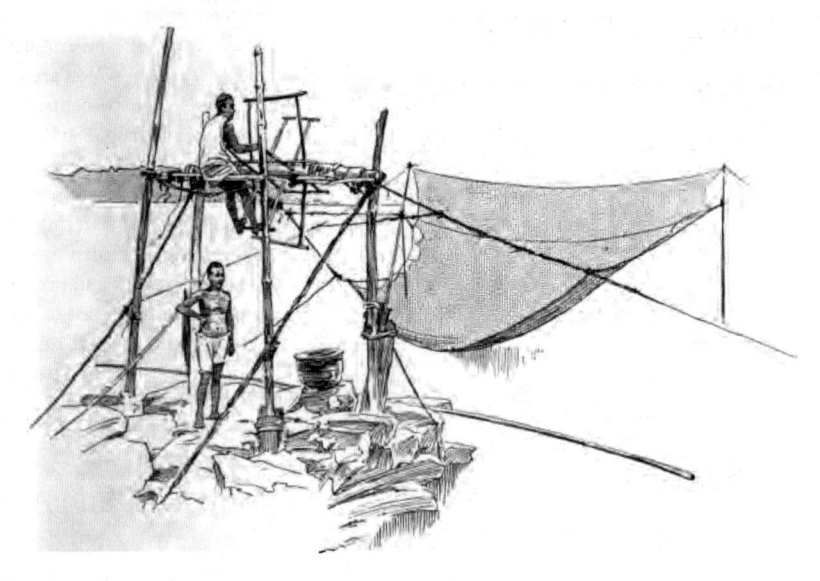

从平台上捕鱼
Fishing with a Net from a Platform

越古老越值钱

中国的工业与技艺有着自己的兴趣点。它们不仅得到了高度的发展，而且有自己的证据，证明它们在很早的时候就达到了现在所占据的崇高地位。中国的工业与技艺有着自己的兴趣点。它们不仅得到了高度的发展：拥有自己现在所占据的崇高地位的证据，这已经为很早时期的中国历史所主张，并为早期旅行者的独立证词所证实；而其陶瓷制品，在时间上早于、技艺上领先于所有其他国家，因而陶工最精美的作品被以中国的名字命名，即"china"（瓷器）。陶瓷制造的高级技艺现已失传，你可能会在欧洲所有的大集市上遇到中国人，那里有最好的瓷器古董出售，中国人以高价购买其中的上品，然后带回中国，再以惊人的价格卖给中国的富贾、王公。中国古玩收藏家在伦敦、巴黎、维也纳或莫斯科购买最好的瓷器，回来就可以夸耀一番。这与他们最好的珠宝、木头和象牙雕刻作品大体相同。

最好的瓷器都是古旧物件，稍次者也

The Older Specimens the Bets

The arts and industries of China have an interest altogether their own. They have not only attained a high development: they bear their own evidence that they had reached the high position they now occupy at the very early date claimed for them in Chinese history, and confirmed by the independent testimony of early travellers, the ceramic manufactures, in which China anticipated and excelled all other nations, giving the name of china to the finest forms of the work of the potter. The higher forms of that manufacture are now lost, and you may meet with Chinamen in every great European mart, where the finest antiquities in china-ware are on sale, buying the best of them at enormous cost, to be taken back to China and sold at fabulous prices to the wealthy merchants and princes of their own country. Chinese collectors of bric-à-brac can boast of the finest specimens of their own china-ware as purchased in London, Paris, Vienna, or Moscow. It is much the same with their finest works in jewellery, wood, and ivory carving.

The finest specimens are all old, and the next best are not new discoveries in art, but slavish imitations of the old. Even their manufactures in silk, for which they were the first to rear the worms, and to excel in weaving and embroidery,

切割花岗岩
Hewing Granite

不是新烧制的瓷器,而是对古旧物件缺乏创意的仿制品。中国人最早养蚕抽丝,精于织锦、刺绣,不过丝绸制造业也只是通过细心模仿古旧款式和质地来维持,尽管朝廷对丝绸贸易的鼓励程度不亚于对农业的鼓励。每年春天,皇帝扶犁亲耕,天子三推,官员按照他们的官职来推,官职越低,推的次数越多;同时,皇后带着侍从们到桑林采叶喂蚕,其产出的丝被制成皇家贡品。无论在制造业上还是在礼仪上,所有的一切都采用最古老的方法;这两者皆自公元前2300年的尧舜时代延续至今日。

停 滞

一个来自西方的旅行者第一次进入中国时会惊奇地发现,他在工业和技艺方面所看到的一切几乎都与他在自己国家所习惯的相近,但几乎都是以一种更原始、更朴素,显然也很古老的形式存在,一切事物都烙印着发展受阻、停滞不前的印记;然而,中国人凭借最初的发明过得很不错。山坡上有石灰窑和砖厂,砖块的长度、宽度和厚度的比例举国统一。木匠、铁匠、

are only kept up by a careful imitation of the old styles and textures, even though as much encouragement is given to the silk trade as to agriculture. When the Emperor yearly ploughs three furrows in spring with his own imperial hand, and his courtiers a larger number, according to their descending ranks, the Empress at the same time goes out with her attendants to the mulberry groves, and feeds the worms which spin the silk for the imperial offerings. All is done on the oldest methods, in the manufacture and in the ceremony; both are gone through to-day as they were performed by Yao and Shun 2300 years before Christ.

Arrested Progress

In entering China for the first time, a visitor from the West is struck with the resemblance of almost everything he sees, in its arts and industries, to what he has been accustomed to in his own country, but almost all in a ruder or simpler form, evidently old: the stunted form of an arrested growth is stamped on everything; and yet the people get on wonderfully with their primitive inventions. The lime-kilns on the hillside, the brick-works, in which the length, breadth, and depth of the bricks bear the same proportions that they do in this country. The carpenter, blacksmith, weaver, and ploughman go on using tools which bear the same resemblance to ours which the bud bears to the full-blown flower, all bearing the

弹棉花
Cleaning Cotton

织工和农夫继续使用与我们相似的带有古老痕迹的工具，二者就像花蕾和盛开的花朵的关系一样。纸，1世纪由中国发明④，仍然是以同样的方式制造着。冯道⑤于10世纪发明了雕版印刷术，而一个名叫毕昇⑥的刻工在1000年左右发明活字印刷术，比所谓的发明者谷登堡⑦的铅活字印刷术早了500年，但活字印刷直到外国传教士加以完善，并将其首先用于印刷字典、《圣经》和其他基督教书籍之后，才得以广泛应用。老式的活字印刷术继续用于印刷部分帝国法令，马可·波罗很有可能在13世纪见过，并将印刷术带到了欧洲。在专利法出现之前，人们习惯于隐瞒新发明，这就解释了为什么中国没有因印刷术的发明而获得赞誉，也解释了为什么旅行者没有提及这些发明。

早期的发明

我们还可以找出许多其他起源于中国的有用的发明。航海罗盘最初被称为"指南车"，大约公元纪年伊始，中国就在使用了；那时出版的一本辞书把磁石描述为"赋

marks of a hoary antiquity. Paper, which was invented in China in the first century of our era, is still made in the same way. Printing from the written characters engraved on wooden blocks was discovered by Fung tau in the tenth century, and movable types were invented by a blacksmith of the name of Pi-Shing, in the year 1000 A.D., 500 years before the discovery by Gutenberg, the supposed inventor, but never came into general use until the foreign missionaries perfected the system and used it first for printing dictionaries, the Scriptures, and other Christian books. The old types continued in use for printing some of the imperial edicts, and it is quite possible that Marco Polo may have seen them in the thirteenth century, and brought the invention to Europe. The habit of concealing new inventions, before patent laws were thought of, would account for China not getting credit for the discovery, and for the traveller not mentioning it.

Early Inventions

There are many other useful discoveries of which we find the originals in China. The mariner's compass, at first called "the south-pointing chariot," was used in China about the commencement of the Christian era; and a dictionary published at that period describes the loadstone as "that which gives polarity to the needle," as good a definition as could well

走街串巷的修鞋匠
An Itinerant Cobbler

予针以指极性之物"，这和我们在19世纪所能给出的定义一样好。指南针最初是用来穿越大沙漠的，但如今在岸边的每一艘渔船上都挂着它，尽管形态很粗糙。中国发明火药500年后，欧洲才开始了解它，但中国只在欢庆的时刻用它来燃放烟火，向朋友致敬时鸣放礼炮，而不是用来消灭敌人。用火药杀人的"文明形式"正是西方国家教给中国人的，但学生在这方面仍然远远落后于他们的授业导师。

早期的商业和贸易

中国的商业和对外贸易可以追溯到尧舜时代。大禹，伟大的工程师，受命于尧，疏导治理上古大洪水，于公元前2200多年之前，写了一本有趣的书，叫作《禹贡》⑧。这是世界上最古老的关于商业的著作，书中列举了当时中国人与其他国家和地区进行贸易的物产清单。他提及"丝绸、漆器、皮草、夏布、盐、宝石、金、银、其他金属、象牙、手工制品等"⑨。

这些物产的贸易在大禹时代似乎比以后的朝代更为自由，而现在的清朝没有大

be given in this nineteenth century. It was first used for crossing the great deserts, but is now found in rude form, but well hung, in every fishing-boat on the coast. Gunpowder was invented in China 500 years before it was known in Europe, but was used for fireworks on occasions of rejoicing, and for firing salutes in honour of friends, not for the destruction of their enemies. It was Christians who taught them this form of civilization, in which they are still far behind their instructors.

Early Trade and Commerce

The trade and foreign commerce of the Chinese can be traced back to the days of Yao and Shun. The great civil engineer Yu, who was employed by Yao for draining the water of a great flood, wrote an interesting book more than 2200 years before Christ, called "The Tribute-of Yu," the oldest book on commerce in the world, wherein he gives a list of the articles in which the Chinese of that time carried on trade with other nations. Amongst other things he names "silk, lacquer-ware, furs, grass-cloth, salt, gems, gold, silver, and other metals, ivory, and manufactured goods."

The trade in these things seems to have been freer in Yu's time than under later dynasties, and it has not been much promoted by

在家织布
Weaving at Home

力促进贸易，直到国门被坚船利炮打开，被迫开放通商口岸。自此以后，茶叶和丝绸的对外贸易大大扩展。

国内贸易

中国的贸易主要是在其国内进行，其疆域广阔，人口众多，使帝国有足够的力量维持自给自足。与国内贸易相比，对外贸易虽然规模也很大了，但价值很小。据说茶叶和丝绸的国内贸易如此之大，以至于出口贸易对这些商品在中国的价格没有明显的影响。当茶叶和丝绸出口额分别达到每年六百万和五百万英镑的时候，它没有使中国国内的茶叶价格提高一厘一毫，中国人也没有为三尺丝绸多付一分钱。国内贸易的设施很是便利，任何有些规模的城镇都有钱庄，通过钱庄可以把银票发往全国任何地方。当铺数量众多，往往规模很大，据说是最早的银行机构，现在仍然是汇兑的重要方式。

中国的城市

中国城市的数量是其工商业发展的标

their present conquerors, the Tartars, until it was forced upon them at the cannon's mouth. Since then, foreign commerce has been greatly extended in tea and silks.

Home Trade

The chief trade of China is within its own borders, which are large enough and sufficiently populous to develop the energies of the self-contained empire. Compared with this home trade, the external trade, large as it is, is of small value. So great is the home trade in tea and silk, that it is said the export trade has had no appreciable effect on the price of these commodities in China. When tea and silk were exported to the value of £6000000 and £5000000 sterling a year respectively, it did not raise the price of tea one farthing in the pound to the nation, and the people of China did not pay a penny more for a yard of silk. The facilities for internal trade are good, and towns of any considerable size have their banks, by which letters of credit can be sent to any part of the country. Pawnbrokers' shops, which are numerous, and often very large, are said to have been the first banking establishments, and are still an important means for the transmission of money.

Cities in China

The number of cities in China is a sign of the commercial industries of the people;

some of them are of great size, and count their inhabitants by millions. The provincial capital Wu-chang, on the south of the river Yang-tsze, with the cities of Han-yang and Hankow on the north of it, form an aggregate of population such as has never been collected within the same area in any other part of the world, except it be in London with its suburbs.

The tendency to migrate from the country to the city was characteristic of the Chinese as a trading and commercial people from an early period. It may be that mutual protection was a factor in developing this tendency. It is said that there are no fewer than 1700 walled cities in China, the walls of which would extend as much as 6000 miles in length—a fourth part of the circumference of the globe. A good many of their cities contain more than half a million of inhabitants, and a few are much more populous. The confinement within walls has made narrow, ill-ventilated streets a general necessity, and, owing to the filthy habits of the people, they are generally malodorous and dingy. Some, however, can boast of large open spaces, with noble trees and wide streets, often ornamented with handsome monumental structures in wood or granite, elaborately carved or chiselled, to commemorate the virtues of distinguished men or women who have adorned the city by their lives, or by some special meritorious deed.

Agriculture Honoured

It is characteristic of China that the tiller of the soil is held in public esteem as second only to the cultivator of literature. The

志；有的规模很大，居民数以百万计。省会城市长江南岸的武昌，加上北岸的汉阳、汉口所聚集的人口，除了伦敦及其近郊外，世界其他地方都比不上。

从农村向城市迁移的倾向是中国人作为一个很早就从事商业贸易的民族具有的典型特征。公共安全可能是形成这种倾向的一个因素。据说中国有城墙的城市不下1700座，城墙总长达6000英里，相当于地球周长的1/4。许多城市容纳的居民都有50万以上，还有几个城市的人口要多得多。城墙以内空间封闭，不可避免地导致街道普遍狭窄、通风不良，而且由于人们不讲卫生的习惯，这些街道一般都是臭烘烘、脏兮兮的。然而，有些城市却自矜拥有大片宽敞的空间、高大的树木和宽阔的街道，常点缀以漂亮的木质或花岗岩质的功德碑，刻凿精美，以纪念那些以生命或丰功伟绩装饰了这座城市的杰出男女。

推崇农业

中国的一个特色是，农民的地位被公认为仅次于书生。上文提及，皇帝和他的高官每年春天都举行扶犁亲耕仪式，以此作为宗教仪式和人民的榜样，并使人民认识到农业劳动的尊严和重要性。然而，农业虽然重要、光荣，但读书才是最为重要的，正如孔子的格言和榜样所示，在获得尊严与意义方面，修身比耕种重要。

土地所有权

在中国，"溥天之下，莫非王土；率土之滨，莫非王臣"，所以，农民直接从皇帝那里租来土地，虽然更大的部分由他们所属的宗族占有，但并没有封建制度的痕迹。宗族可能有自己的族长为代表，但族长的职位纯粹是推举产生的，他对土地没有个人所有权。该体制很像印度至今仍存在的农村公社，在文明的早期阶段，它或多或少地在世界许多地方盛行。依据中国法律，土地是永佃的，就像摩西律法把土地租赁给巴勒斯坦的犹太人一样。凡在府、州、县之官府登记为土地承租人，并取得了加盖官印的"红契"的人，只要他付田租，其永佃权就不能被合法地剥夺；如果土地被抵押出去，他也可以在三十年内的

Emperor and his highest officers of State, as we have seen, go through the form of holding the plough every spring as a religious ceremony, and an example to the people, and to impress them with the dignity and importance of agricultural labour. But important and honourable though it be, such is the supreme importance of literature, as laid down in the maxims and example of Confucius, that the cultivation of the mind comes before the cultivation of the soil in dignity and importance.

Tenure of Land

The land of China belongs to the Emperor, as the father or representative of the people, and is rented directly from him by the farmers, though larger portions are held by the clans to which they belong, but with no trace of the feudal system. The clan may have a representative of its own, but his office is purely elective, and he has no personal claim on the land. The system is very much like the village communities which are still found in India, and have prevailed less or more over many parts of the world in the earlier stages of civilization. By Chinese law the lease of land is secured in perpetuity, in much the same way as it was secured to the Jews in Palestine by the laws of Moses. The man who has been registered in the Government office of his district as the tenant of land, and has taken what is called a "red deed," bearing direct imperial authority, cannot be legally deprived of it so long as he pays the rent, and in the event of its being mortgaged, he can at any time within thirty years get it back by payment of the mortgage. The forms of registration are simple, but the first expenses are comparatively heavy. These are evaded in case of transfer from one tenant to another by what are called "white deeds," binding the party to pay the land tax or rent. The rent of land, thus taking the form of an imperial tax, is not burdensome, amounting on an average to about six shillings per acre for good land, and from one shilling to two shillings or more for inferior soil. In the case of a tenant reclaiming waste land, he is allowed a number of years, less or more, according to the condition of the ground, free from rent or land-tax.

System of Farming

The system of farming is rude but effective. More depends on hard labour than skill; but experience has taught many practical lessons, which the industrious farmer has not neglected. If his land is light, he dredges the bottom of the nearest river or canal to enrich it; if it is heavy soil, he dredges the sea for shells, which he burns to lime for his fields. To fertilize the fields, all kinds of vegetable refuse, with ashes, soot, bones ground to powder, hair shaved from the heads and beards of the millions of Chinamen, are carefully preserved and sold to the farmer, who collects every unclean thing from animals and men for manure. He has some notion of rotation of crops, and the system of farming is more like that of our gardener.

He hoes or digs the ground by hand labour, or, if the field is large,

任何时候，通过偿还抵押款而赎回土地租赁权。地籍登记形式简单，但首期费用相对较高。如果永佃权从一个佃户转移到另一个，这些费用可以通过"白契"来规避，"白契"用于约束乙方支付田赋或田租。因此，田租是以帝国赋税的形式支付，负担并不沉重，良田平均为每英亩六先令左右，薄田为一至二先令或者更多一些。对于开荒垦田的农户，允许他免田租或田赋耕种，年限长短依据土地的状况而定。

耕作制度

耕作制度原始但有效。耕作更多地依靠辛勤劳作而不是技巧；但历代经验积累下许多实践的教训，勤劳的农民从未忽视。如果土质疏松，就到最近的河流或运河底部挖泥肥田；如果土质黏重，就从大海挖取贝壳并焚烧，施石灰沃土。为了给田地施肥，各种蔬菜垃圾，以及草木灰、煤灰、磨碎的骨粉、从数百万中国人的身上剃下来的头发和胡须，都小心地保存下来，卖给农户，农户也把人畜的粪尿收集起来做成农家肥。农民有作物轮作的概念，其耕作制度更像英国园丁的做法。

农民锄地或翻地靠手工劳作，抑或田地很大，就给耕牛和驴子套上轭具来犁地，或者，在一些蛮荒地区，会把驴和农民的妻子拴在一起犁地，而犁铧比改装的锄头好不了多少。漫着水的稻田用水牛耕种，在丘陵地区，农民还耗费惊人的气力，用人工把农家肥和水运送到山侧的田块上。中国人要想在他们称之为农田的小块土地上勉强维持生计，就得付出所有的耐心和不懈的努力。尽管务农很光荣，利润却很微薄，而且农民普遍较贫穷，但偶尔会遇到肥沃土地上的乡绅，他们神态可敬、自如。然而，财富不外露，除非主人足够强大，可以抵抗强盗的袭击，以及底层执法人员更严苛的勒索。

田赋收入

根据非常粗略和欠充分的数据计算，全部的田赋收入为每年1500万至2000万英镑。其中只有800万至1000万英镑上缴京城；另一半留在各州府，用于供养军队和维持行政运转。朝廷从食盐专营和子口

he ploughs it with the unequal yoke of an ox and ass, or, in some rude districts an ass is harnessed with his wife, the plough being little better than a converted hoe. The flooded rice or paddy field he ploughs with the water-buffalo, and in hilly regions he expends an amazing amount of labour in conveying manure, and even water, by human labour to the cultivated patches on the sides of the mountains. It takes all the patient and untiring industry of a Chinaman to make a modest living out of the small plots which they call farms. Though their occupation is honourable, the profits are small, and farmers are generally poor, but you occasionally come on larger farmers on rich soil, with all the air of respectability and comfort. Anything having the appearance of luxury or wealth is, however, carefully avoided, unless the owners be strong enough to defy the attack of robbers, and the more oppressive exactions of the petty officers of the law.

Revenue from Land

It is computed, from very rough and unsatisfactory data, that the entire revenue from the land tax is from £15000000 to £20000000 a year. Of this only from £8000000 to £10000000 reaches the capital; the half of it is retained in the provinces for the support of the army and administrative purposes. The Central Government derives large sums from a monopoly on salt and transit dues, so that, leaving out the last, the rent of land and profit on trade form the chief source of revenue, both land and salt being Government monopolies.

收割水稻
The Rice Harvest

税中获得了大笔的收入，因此，除去子口税，田赋和贸易带来的利润构成了主要的收入来源，而土地和食盐都由朝廷垄断。

文明的习惯

从西亚和中亚进入中国，可见这些国家当地人的生活习惯和举止差别很大。他们生活在户外，或大门敞开，很容易让人形成偏见。在阿拉伯、锡兰⑩、印度和马六甲海峡，你可以看到穷人坐在地上或茅屋的地板上用手抓饭来吃，他们常常围坐在同一个盆旁，把手伸进去抓着吃。富人的不同之处仅仅在于，他们有地垫或蒲团可坐于其上，有更大的洗手设施，却以同样原始的方式用手抓饭吃。在中国，每个人不论好坏都有个座椅，从穷人的竹凳到富人精心雕花的椅子。每个人都有自己的勺子和筷子，这对生手来说可能有些棘手，但至少优点是卫生干净，而且比用手吃饭的习惯有明显的改进。

过去四千年来，中国人甚至不像东方其他文明国家那样习惯睡在平铺于地板上的席子或软垫之上，而是睡在某种床上；

Civilized Habits

On entering China from Western and Central Asia, the contrast between the habits and manners of the natives of these countries is very marked… Their life in the open air, or with open doors, gives ample opportunity of forming an opinion. In Arabia, Ceylon, India, and the Straits of Malacca, you see the poor sitting on the ground or the floor of their huts eating their food with their fingers, often sitting round the same bowl, and all dipping into the same dish. The rich only differ by having mats or cushions to sit on, and greater facilities for washing their hands while eating in the same primitive fashion. In China…every man has a seat of some kind, from the bamboo stool of the poor to the elaborate carved chair of the rich. Each has his spoon and his chopsticks, which may be awkward to the amateur, but at least have the merit of being cleanly, and a decided advance on the habits of monkeys and kangaroos.

…Instead of lying down on mats or cushions spread on the floor, as is the custom of even the civilized nations of the East, the Chinese for the last 4000 years have slept on beds of some kind; it might be only a board or cane frame on trestles for the poor, while the rich have slept on four-post beds, with silk or satin curtains, from before the Christian era.

Manners and Customs

Asiatics are generally polite even to servility, but the Chinese have elevated politeness into a ritual, tedious and wearisome to an impatient European, but to the leisurely Asiatic sacred and important as a religious duty. Sages in China have devoted their attention to the regulation of the forms of social intercourse, on the principle that the outward forms of courtesy are essential to the cultivation of the feelings of respect and affection, of which they are the natural expressions. The "Book of Rites," which treats chiefly of forms and ceremonies for all occasions sacred and secular, from the highest formalities of the Court and the altar down to the humblest duties of the meanest subjects in the ordinary courtesies of daily life, is one of the most ancient and sacred of the classics. In its original form it was attributed to Confucius, but only as editor or "transmitter." The substance of its leaching is traced back to a period 2300 years before Christ. It gives the minutest details of the duties to be performed to God and man, and of the forms to be gone through, of the dresses to be worn, and even of the manner and expression of the countenance in which the ceremonies are to be performed. The daily forms prescribed for a married son and the younger branches of the family in serving their parents will give some idea of the attentions prescribed in this "Book of Rites." It says:

自公元前开始，穷人可能只是睡在搭起来的一块板或藤条上，而富人却睡在带有丝绸或缎子床帘的四柱床上。

礼仪和习俗

亚洲人总体上讲究礼貌，甚至近乎卑微，但中国人将其提升至某种仪式般的地步，这对缺乏耐心的欧洲人来说显得冗长啰唆，但对从容不迫的亚洲人来说，则像宗教义务般神圣、不可或缺。中国的先贤致力于规范社交礼仪，其指导原则是外显的礼貌形式对于养成敬人、爱人的情感必不可少。《礼记》主要讲述一切神圣和世俗场合需遵循的礼仪，从宫廷和祭坛的最高礼仪，到最底层人民在日常生活的普通礼仪中践行的最微不足道的职责，它是最古老和最神圣的经典之一。《礼记》最初的版本归功于孔子，但他仅仅是编纂者或"传播者"。其体现出的实质可追溯到公元前2300年。它极其细致地说明对神祇和他人应履行的职责、应采取的形式、应着之装，甚至是典礼过程中应持的举止和面部表情。《礼记》为成家了的儿子和家庭中的年轻人制定了侍奉父母的日常礼仪，从中我们可以对它定下的典章制度有所了解。它写道：

子女侍奉之责

子事父母：鸡初鸣，咸盥漱。栉，继，笄，总，拂髦；冠，缕缨；端；韠；绅，搢笏。左右佩用，左佩纷帨、刀、砺、小觿、金燧，右佩玦、捍、管、遰、大觿、木燧。逼，屦，着綦。

媳妇同样梳洗干净，穿戴整齐：

以适父母、舅姑之所。及所，下气怡声，问衣燠寒；疾痛苛痒，而敬抑搔之。……进盥，少者奉槃，长者奉水，请沃盥；盥卒，授巾。问所欲而敬进之，柔色以温之。……父母、舅姑必尝之而后退。

餐桌礼仪

生活中方方面面应遵行的规则也被详尽地确定下来。以下关于餐桌礼仪的忠告，是法国修道院长格鲁贤[11]在自己的著作中引用的，出自一部至少公元前500年的中华

Duties of Children

Men on serving their parents at the first cock-crowing must wash their hands; rinse their mouths; comb their hair; bind it together with a net; fasten it with a bodkin, forming it into a tuft; brush off the dust; put on the hat, tying the strings, ornamented with tassels; also the waistcoat, frock, and girdle, with the note-sticks placed in it, and the indispensables attached on the right and left; bind on the guards; and put on the shoes, tying up the strings.

The wife being dressed with equal care,

They then go to the chambers of their father and mother, and father-in-law and mother-in-law, and having entered, in a low and placid tone, they must inquire whether their covering is too warm or too cold, and ask if they are free from pain and discomfort. In bringing the apparatus for washing, the younger—if there are other sons—must present the bowl, the elder the water, begging them to pour and wash, and after they have washed hand them the towel. In asking, and respectfully presenting what they wish to eat, they must cheer them by their mild manner, and must wait until their father and mother, and father-in-law and mother-in-law, have eaten, and then retire.

Manners at Table

The duties in every relation of life are laid down with like minuteness of detail. The following advice for conduct at the table, quoted by Abbe Grosier, from one of the classics, at least 500 years before Christ, is worthy of that accomplished exquisite of the eighteenth century, Lord Chesterfield:

When you entertain anyone, or

eat at his table, pay the strictest attention to propriety; be careful not to devour your victuals greedily; never drink long draughts; avoid making a noise with your mouth or teeth, and neither gnaw your bones nor throw them to the dogs; never sop up the broth that is left when everyone else is done, nor testify, by external signs, the pleasure you receive from any particular food or wine; neither pick your teeth, blow upon wine which is too warm, nor make a new sauce to whatever is placed before you; take small bits at a time; chew your victuals well, and never let your mouth be too full.

Forms Useful

Chinese ceremonial prescriptions appear to us too elaborate and minute, but if we look back to the long history of this great empire—the longest and largest which has ever existed in freedom and independence, with so large a measure of peace and prosperity—we are constrained to admit that its laws and customs must have been suited to the character and circumstances of the people. To us they seem fitted only to produce a race of formalists or hypocrites. To them they appear to have kept up the spirit of reverence for parents which has been the basis of loyalty to the Emperor, the father of the people, and the security for peaceful submission to "the powers that be."

经典⑫，其中描述的风度完全抵得上18世纪娴于社交的翩翩绅士切斯特菲尔德勋爵⑬。

共食不饱，共饭不泽手。……毋流歠。毋咤食。毋啮骨。毋反鱼肉。毋投与狗骨。……毋嚃羹。毋絮羹。毋刺齿。毋歠醢。……濡肉齿决，干肉不齿决。毋嘬炙。

有用的礼仪规范

中国的礼仪规范在我们看来太过复杂和细致，但如果回顾这个伟大帝国的悠久历史——在自由与独立中存在的最久远、最庞大的帝国，以及如此宏大的和平与繁荣，我们不得不承认其法律和习俗一定适合其国民的性格和环境。在我们看来，这些规范似乎只适合造就因循守旧或伪君子一族；在他们看来，这些规范似乎保持了对父母的敬畏之心，而皇帝乃万民之父，敬畏之心即为忠君爱国的基础，也是平和地屈服于当权者的保障。

【注　释】

① 1英寸约等于2.54厘米，以此换算。下同。——译者注

② 这位诗人如果被请来帮忙准备一顿中餐，会发现"蜗牛"是稀有而昂贵的海参，至于"燕窝汤"，燕窝不是在灌木丛中能随意找到的，而是只有在马来群岛的一些荒岛上才能找到，而且如此稀少，乃至好的品种每磅要花5个几尼。——原注

几尼：旧时英国的一种金币，定值为21先令。——译者注

③ 考虑到人们的生活习性，此处给出的数字没有什么不可置信的。相反，每一个省的人口数字都很有可能是准确的。每个省的生育力与它的平方英里人数相对应，每平方英里七八百人是最大的比例。威尔克斯船长在斐济群岛上发现，每平方英里有一千人居住，在帕劳群岛中某个不如江苏和安徽肥沃的岛上，每半平方英里就有四百人居住。——原注

威尔克斯（Charles Wilkes, 1798—1877）：美国海军军官和探险家，发现南极大陆。南极洲的威尔克斯地就是以他的名字命名的。——译者注

④ 中国在西汉时期就出现了纸。105年，宦官蔡伦改进了造纸技术，从此纸成为主要的书写材料。——译者注

⑤ 冯道（882—954）：字可道，号长乐老，瀛州景城（今河北沧州西北）人，五代十国时期著名宰相。雕版印刷术发明者是谁，一千多年来争论不休，冯道是说法之一。——译者注

⑥ 毕昇（972—1051）：淮南路蕲州蕲水县（今湖北省黄冈市英山县）人，北宋发明家。毕昇创造发明的胶泥活字、木活字排版，是中国印刷术发展中的一个根本性改革，是对中国劳动人民长期实践经验的科学总结，对中国和世界各国的文化交流做出伟大贡献。——译者注

⑦ 谷登堡（Johannes Gutenberg, 1398—1468）：德国发明家，西方活字印刷术的发明人，西方第一位使用活字和印刷机的人。他的发明导致了一次媒体革命，迅速地推动了西方科学和社会的发展。——译者注

⑧ 《禹贡》：中国古代名著，属于《尚书》中的一篇，对其作者说法不一。其地理记载囊括了各地山川、地形、土壤、物产等情况，是中国古代文献中最古老和最有系统性地理观念的著作。——译者注

⑨ 引自卫三畏的《中国总论》。——原注

⑩ 锡兰：斯里兰卡于1972年之前的旧称。——译者注

⑪ 格鲁贤（Jean-Baptiste Grosier, 1743—1823）：法国人，修道院长，一生从事文学和艺术评论。他编辑出版了冯秉正（Josoph de Mailla）的《中国通史》（*Histoire Generale de la Chine*），共13卷。此书在大众中取得了很大成功。格鲁贤作品的一个鲜明特色是立足于中国人的材料和中国人的观点。——译者注

⑫ 出自《礼记·曲礼》。——译者注

⑬ 切斯特菲尔德勋爵（Lord Chesterfield, 1694—1773）：英国著名政治家、外交家及文学家。他风流倜傥，是英国讲究礼仪的典范，有《教子书》（*Letters to His Son*）传世，内容说理透彻，辞藻华丽，在英国上流社会广为流传，被誉为"绅士教育的教科书"。——译者注

第三章　妇女和儿童的地位
Chapter Ⅲ　The Position of Women and Children

妇女的地位

民族性格很大程度上是由母亲们塑造的，所以我们可以根据妇女在社会和家庭圈子中所占的地位来判断其民族性格。中国妇女的待遇不仅因其社会地位而异，而且因居住地区而异。尽管表面上看起来没什么不同，但中国人并非同一的；人们的外貌、性格和风俗都有明显的差异。尽管表面上因循守旧，但在漫长的历史中，人们的生活习惯也发生了很大变化。

在人类社会早期，妇女似乎占据了较高的地位，并不像现今这样，与男人的地位相去甚远。到了孔子时代，妇女地位似乎已经降低至现今一样的水平。鉴于孔子

The Place of Women

The character of a people is largely formed by its mothers, and we may judge of a woman, nation's character by the place that women occupy in its social and domestic circles. The treatment of women in China varies not only with their social position, but with the parts of the country in which they live. With all its apparent sameness, China is not homogeneous; there are marked differences in personal appearance, character, and customs of the people, and with all its apparent stereotyped fixity, it has varied much in its habits during the long period of its history.

In early times women seem to have occupied a better position, and were not so far removed from equality with men as they now are. By the time of Confucius they seem to have reached much the same level as they now occupy, and from the wide influence of his writings all over the country the differences are not very material. When once the woman has attained the position of a mother of sons, she rises much in the scale of popular esteem; but if only of girls, she falls lower than ever. When once she becomes, by the death of her husband, the female head of the family, her power over sons, daughters-in-law, and grandchildren is despotic. The want of education is at once the result of the low place that woman occupies, and tends to keep her low. There have been learned ladies in China, but their number was never large, and now it is very small.

The Mother of Mencius

The praises of good and wise women are recorded in history, and illustrated by monuments in the principal streets of their cities. One of the best was the mother of one of the most distinguished philosophers of China, Mencius. She was left a widow with this one boy, and on his account twice changed her abode. In the first, which was opposite a cemetery, her little boy began to amuse himself by imitating the funeral rites; so, lest he should lose reverence for the dead and sympathy with mourners, she left the locality. The next house was opposite a butcher, whereupon

著作在全国的广泛影响，各地的妇女地位差异并不是很大。一旦妇女为家庭添丁，母凭子贵，地位就会大幅提高，备受尊崇；但是如果仅仅为家庭生育女儿，地位就会每况愈下。一旦丈夫去世，她就成为一家之主，她对儿子、儿媳和孙辈说一不二。缺乏教育既是妇女地位低下的结果，也往往是致使她地位低下的原因。中国曾有过有才华、有学问的女子，但人数从来就不多，现在就很少了。

孟　母

历史记载了对贤德、聪慧妇女的赞颂，并在其所居城市要道口用牌坊进行旌表。贤惠妇女的典型代表之一是孟母，她是中国最杰出的哲学家之一——孟子的母亲。为了有良好的环境教育孩子，孟母寡居后带着孟子三迁其居。最初他们居住在墓地对面，年幼的孟子开始模仿丧葬仪式来玩耍；为了不让他失去对死者的尊敬以及对哀悼者的同情，孟母搬离此地。新家的对面是屠户，随之孟子模仿宰杀羔羊玩具来取乐。孟母再次搬家，以免孩子变得残酷无情。第三次择邻，孟母比较幸运：家在一所学官对面，孟子开始模仿学童们上课，最终成为知名学者。

中国妇女在许多部门掌权。她们中的杰出者成为女皇或太后，其中一个突出的例子就是现今的慈禧太后。中国妇女统率军队，文采斐然，乐善好施，还有一位怒海女侠盗[①]。这些是罕见的例子，却彰显了妇女的能力，同时激发了人们对提升女性至崇高地位的希望，其实现需通过教育和男女平权，把妇女从目前低下、肮脏的苦工中解放出来。

婚　姻

中华帝国幅员辽阔，中国人的婚俗因风俗、条件和地域的不同而各异。原则上是一夫一妻制，但是也有例外。假如没有男性后裔以便将来可以披麻戴孝送终，那么娶二房不仅合法，而且被视为夫妻双方灵魂得以幸福的宗教需要。而这成为其信仰者罪恶和痛苦的根源；二房地位较低，或者只是一个小妾，几乎等于奴隶，就像亚伯拉罕家的夏甲一样。对有钱人来说，

her son took to killing toy lambs for his amusement. Again she left her house, lest her boy should become cruel. In the third choice she was more fortunate: it was opposite a school, and her son began to imitate the boys at their lessons, and became a famous scholar.

Women in China have occupied places of power in many departments. They have been distinguished as Empresses, of whom the present Dowager-Empress is a striking example. Chinese women have led armies, have been distinguished poets, and leaders in philanthropy, and one scoured the sea as a pirate. These are rare examples, but they show of what they are capable, and inspire the hope of their rising to the high position of true womanhood, when they are released from their present degradation and sordid drudgery by education and equality of privilege with the men…

Marriage

The marriage customs of the Chinese vary, with the habits, conditions and locality of the wide empire. The general rule is monogamy… There are, however, exceptions, in case of there being no son to perform the funeral rites, in which case a second marriage is not only lawful, but is looked upon as a religious necessity for the wellbeing of the souls of both husband and wife. It is then that a false religion becomes a cause of both sin and misery to its professors; the second wife occupies an inferior place, or may be only a concubine and little better than a slave, like Hagar in the family of Abraham. In the case of rich men, there is a great deal of license in adding both secondary wives and concubines to their domestic troubles. That polygamy is lawful there can be no doubt, and the example of the great Emperor Shun can be quoted. That pattern of propriety gave two of his daughters to Yu 500 years before Laban imposed his two daughters on poor Jacob. In some parts of the empire the marriage bonds are very lax, especially among the aboriginal tribes…

Prohibited Degrees

The prohibited degrees in China are peculiar. By both law and custom, no man or woman can marry anyone of the same family name, however numerous the owners of the name may be—often a large and powerful clan. The law seems to have been formed with a view to put an end to clan feuds, or to mitigate their severity. In spite of that law, these feuds are a source of much mischief, but they might have been worse had it not been in operation.

Divorce

Divorce is too costly an indulgence to be practised by the poor, and is not common among the rich. True, there are seven grounds on which a Chinaman can lawfully put away his wife;

他们在纳妾问题上是有很大自由度的，只是会增添家庭纠纷而已。毋庸置疑，一夫多妻制②是合法的，伟大的尧帝③就是一个例子。这种制度使得尧把两个女儿嫁给舜，这比《圣经》中提及拉班将两个女儿强嫁给可怜的雅各早上500年。在帝国的某些地区，婚姻契约非常松散，尤其是在原始部落中。

同姓不婚

中国同姓不婚的习俗很特别。根据法律和习俗，任何男人或女人都不能与同一姓氏之人结婚，不管该姓氏之人有多么多——通常是一个名门望族。这条法令的制定似乎是为了结束宗族争斗，或至少是为了减轻其严重性。尽管有这条法令，宗族争斗仍是许多麻烦的根源，但如果没有实施这条法令，情况可能会更糟。

离 婚

放纵自己而离婚的代价太高昂，穷人离不起，而在富人中也并不常见。诚然，古人休妻有七种合法理由，称作"七出之条"，即无子、多言、盗窃、不顺公婆、有恶疾、妒忌、淫佚。但是，这诸多的离婚礼制实际上被法律规定的仁慈条款所限制，即，若女方父母家族散亡，有所取无所归，则不得休妻。若妻子通奸淫乱，法律不仅判定罪妇死刑，而且强令丈夫将其处死。

有一个残忍的风俗，尽管不合法，但除非娘家的亲属介入，一般没人注意，即如果丈夫能得到岳母的同意，他可以在自家处死妻子。一位在华南妇女中工作多年的女士写道：

> 男人甚至可以杀死妻子；假如女方家亲戚不提起此事，就不会引起注意。我熟悉的一个女人，她现在还活着，曾差点被她丈夫处死，因为她皈依了基督教。她母亲准许丈夫和他家人处死她。他接着就动手了——把她的手脚用绳子绑上，吊在天花板上。在她将死之时，母亲心软了，让他们停手，这一要求他们不敢违抗，于是她才得以活着来讲述自己的故事。

these are barrenness, talkativeness, thievishness, disobedience to her husband's parents, leprosy, jealousy, and lust. But these many sanctions for divorce are practically nullified by the merciful condition laid down by the law, that no man can send away his wife for one or all of these seven reasons unless her parents are living to give her a home. In case of adultery, the law not only sanctions the death of the guilty wife, but compels the husband to put her to death.

There is one cruel custom which is not legal, but which is not taken notice of unless the relations of the woman interpose: a man may put his wife to death in his own house if he can get her mother's consent to do so. A lady who has worked for years among the women of Southern China writes:

> A man may even kill his wife; providing her own relations do not take the matter up, no notice is taken of it. A woman whom I know well, and who is still living, was nearly put to death by her husband because she had become a Christian. Her mother gave the husband and his family permission to put her to death. He proceeded to do so—had her hung up, hands and feet tied by a rope to the ceiling. When nearly dead, the mother's heart relented, and she bade them stop, a request they dare not disobey, so she still lives to tell the tale.

Marriage Customs

The preliminaries of marriage are tedious, and are all carried on by second parties. The go-between is an important personage, and plays the principal part. It is only through her eyes that the bridegroom sees the bride, and as the girl's parents frequently bribe her to look at their daughter through golden spectacles, the most deformed and unsightly are described in the most glowing colours. "To lie like a go-between" is a common saying in China, and yet, such is the tyranny of custom, parents and young men will trust them in the most important transactions of life, and never see the bride until she is brought home for good and aye, often leading to grievous disappointment and lifelong misery. The disappointment is frequently as great or greater on the part of the bride, and often leads to her committing suicide. Even if the husband prove all the bride could wish, she may be kept in a state of constant degradation and misery by a cruel stepmother, to whom she must yield absolute submission and pay the highest honour, whatever her character may be.

Happy Marriages

But let it not be supposed that all marriages in China are unhappy; there are fine examples of domestic happiness amongst both rich and poor. Women in

婚　俗

婚姻的前期准备很烦琐，且均由媒婆代为完成。媒婆是重要人物，并且起主要作用。新郎无法直接看到新娘，只有媒婆才能见到，因此，由于女孩父母经常贿赂媒婆，让后者美化女孩的长相，所以连残疾的、丑陋的都被描述得美若天仙。中国有句俗语，"无谎不成媒"，却也道明了说媒这种习俗的野蛮专制之处。男方在终身大事上坚信媒妁之言，直到新娘过门，木已成舟，才初见对方容貌。这往往导致他们失望至极，痛苦终生。新娘的失望情绪往往同样或更加强烈，常常导致新娘自杀。即使丈夫真成了自己的如意郎君，她也难免遭到蛮横婆婆的不断贬低，深陷痛苦之中。不管性格如何，她都要对婆婆绝对顺从、毕恭毕敬。

幸福的婚姻

但是，不要以为中国的所有婚姻都是不幸的；婚姻幸福的例子在贫寒和富有家庭里都有。中国妇女屈从了数百年，对幸福的期望值不高，并能够忍受许多足以毁掉西方家庭幸福的事情。她们不期望获得与男人平等的待遇。妻子从未想过坐下来和丈夫一起吃饭。她们甚至不反对一定量的身体摧残来取悦丈夫。缠足的中国妇女经常向来访的英国女士提出的问题之一是："你男人打你吗？"在听到斩钉截铁的回答"从不"时，她们脸上的惊异表情恰恰痛苦地表明了自己受到家暴已是家常便饭。然而，我们不必夸耀我们不受这种野蛮行径的贻害。英国男性放弃打老婆这一"特权"的时间并不长。据说，在以前，只要丈夫打老婆的棍子不粗于她的拇指，那这种行为就是合法的。沃尔特·司各特爵士④写道，即使在骑士时代，女士们还是更喜欢一个打老婆的丈夫，只要他展现勇气的方式是更彻底地打垮敌人。不幸的是，即使在现在"婚姻幸福的"英国，打老婆这一古老的恶俗也没有完全消失。

另一种在东方国家几乎普遍存在并在中国十分盛行的习俗，就是儿子婚后继续留在父系家中，于是两三代人挤在一个屋

China, from centuries of subjection, are humble in their expectations of happiness, and put up with much which would destroy the happiness of a Christian home. They do not expect to be treated as the equal of man. The wife never would think of sitting down to a meal along with her husband. They do not even object to a reasonable amount of physical correction. One of the questions constantly put by Chinawomen to English lady visitors is: "Does your husband beat you?" And the expression of amazement at the emphatic "Never!" is a painful evidence of the frequency of such chastisement among themselves. We need not, however, boast of our immunity from this relic of barbarism. It is not so long since English husbands abandoned this privilege, for we have heard the right was legal, provided the stick with which he beat his wife was not thicker than her thumb. We are told by Sir Walter Scott that ladies, even in chivalrous times, preferred a husband who beat them, provided he showed his valour by more soundly beating his enemies. Unhappily, this old vice of wife-beating has not quite died out, even in happy England.

Another evil, which is almost universal in the East, prevails in China—the custom of sons remaining after marriage in the paternal home—so that two or three generations are found huddled together under one roof, or in houses built so closely together as to form one community under the despotic government of the grandfather or grandmother.

From this arrangement of one family and one purse, with so many diverse interests, managed by even patriarchal despotism, the preservation of harmony is rare, and constantly liable to be turned to discord. The power of one evil-disposed member of such a group of discordant elements will destroy the peace of all the household, as one false note in the best of music will spoil the finest harmony. A true home, in the English sense of the word, is almost impossible.

The Redeeming of Womanhood

A redeeming feature in the position of woman in China is the respect she receives from her sons, especially after they are grown up. From the time she becomes the mother of a son her social and domestic position is secured, and as the number of sons increases, she rises higher and higher in the social scale, and receives an amount of respect which might well satisfy a European mother; and in old age, when her sons are settled around her with their families, she becomes the centre of an obedient and respectful circle of children and grandchildren. This reacts on the character of the woman, and keeps up the ideal of womanhood in both sexes. The power of such a

檐下，或住在密集建造的房子中，形成一个在祖父或祖母专制统治下的小社会。

在这样一个父权专制、统一开销安排，又有如此多的不同利益的大家庭中保持家庭和谐非常罕见，而且很容易出现不和谐分子。这群不和谐分子中的一个"邪恶分子"的力量就会破坏整个家庭的宁静和平，就像最好的音乐中一个错误的音符就会破坏最美的和声一样。从"家"的英语词义上来说，一个真正的家在这几乎是不可能存在的。

妇女的救赎

中国妇女的地位得以救赎是她从儿子们那里得到尊重，尤其是在他们长大后。从生育儿子开始，女性的社会地位和家庭地位就得到保障，而且随着儿子数量的增多，她在社会上的地位就越来越高，受到的尊重足以令一位欧洲母亲满意；年老时，儿子及其家人都住在她身边，她就成了一大群儿孙孝敬的中心。这种苦尽甘来对女性的性格产生影响，并且是两性都认同的女性的理想状态。这样的母亲权威极大，子女都不敢忤逆。按照中国习俗，她不仅可以要求儿孙对自己百般顺从，还可鞭打不顺从者加以惩处。如果有人因挨打而心生不满，甚至威胁要还手，中国法律允许她把忤逆者打死。于大家庭中拥有至高无上的权威这一点，发挥了很大作用，把妇女从屈辱中救赎出来。我们常常钦羡这些老妇人文静端庄的举止，而且谢天谢地，中国有这样的母亲，不仅是为了女人的利益，也是为了这个国家男人的利益。老年女性受人尊崇，对中国年轻女性免于沮丧或绝望大有裨益。获得崇高地位的前景为身处磨难和痛苦之中的年轻妇女带来希望。

孝 顺

中国人最引以为豪的事情是孩子对父母的孝顺，这让不期而至的观察者感到困惑。观察者们发现男孩在日常生活中很少或根本不尊重父母——事实上，他们被宠溺、惯坏了，结果自然是不听话、没礼貌；但奇怪的是，随着他们长大，他们一般的的确确变得顺从，甚至对父母关爱备至——至少表面上如此。似乎儒家思想的氛围在学校教学和日常生活交往中把几千

mother is very great. Neither sons nor daughters dare to resist her authority. She may, according to Chinese custom, not only demand obedience, but enforce it with sharp blows on the shoulders of sons or daughters or grandchildren. For one to resent, or even threaten to return, her blows would expose the offender to the penalty of death by Chinese law. This possession of supreme authority in the family circle has done much to redeem womanhood from degradation. We have often admired the quiet and dignified bearing of these old matrons, and have thanked God that China had such mothers, not only for the sake of womanhood, but for the sake of the manhood of the country. This dignified position of the old goes far to save from despondency or despair the younger women of China. The prospect of attaining to such a position inspires hope amid their many trials and sufferings in youth.

Filial Obedience

That which is China's greatest boast—the devotion of children to their parents—is a source of perplexity to casual observers. They see that boys show little or no respect to their parents in daily life—in fact, they are petted and spoiled, and as a natural consequence are disobedient and disrespectful; but the curious circumstance is that as they grow up they do become, as a rule, obedient and even affectionate—at least, in outward appearance. It seems as if the atmosphere of Confucian influence in the teaching of the schools and in the intercourse of daily life moulds them into the form of what has for thousands of years been the constitutional habit of the people, and has been the preserving salt in the moral and political life of the nation.

One of the most pleasant sights in China is the number of old and venerable men and women to be seen in the villages, the men sitting under the shade of the spreading banyan-trees, and the old women at the doors of the houses, enjoying the ease and comforts of age supplied by the industry of the children and grandchildren. It is rare for a son to neglect his duty to his parents either in old age or after death. The public sentiment on the subject is so strong that the man who would run counter to it would need to be a bold as well as a bad man. Even amongst the most lawless class the feeling is powerful. There was a striking instance of this just before we arrived in China. A local insurrection had been suppressed, but the ringleader had escaped, and was safe among a band of pirates— the most ruthless class in China. The authorities had, however, got hold of the father, who by Chinese law is responsible for the crimes of his children. They sent word to the son that if he did not give himself up to justice, which meant certain and cruel death, they would punish his father in his place. The man, rebel and pirate though he was, sent back word that he would surrender himself if they would "promise to send him to his ancestors with

年来中国人内在的固有习性塑造成型，并成为国家道德和政治生活的保鲜剂。

在中国，最令人愉悦的风景之一是在村庄里可以看到许多年迈而受人尊敬的老翁老妪，老翁坐在茂盛的榕树的树荫下，老妪坐在家门口，儿孙勤劳，供他们颐养天年。儿子很少忽视对父母的责任，无论是父母年老时的侍奉还是去世后的祭拜。公众在孝顺问题上的情绪着实强烈，若有人与之背道而驰，此人需是胆大妄为且道德败坏之徒。甚至在最无法无天的盗匪中，这种情绪同样强大。就在我们到达中国之前，发生了一个引人注目的例子。当地的一次起义被镇压了，但首领逃脱了，安然无恙地待在一群海盗——中国最残忍的人群之中。然而，朝廷抓住了他的父亲，根据中国法律，父亲应对子女的罪行负责。他们传话给儿子，如果他不来自首正法（无疑是残酷的死刑），他们将惩罚他的父亲以顶罪。尽管身为起义军首领兼海盗，这个男人却传回话来，如果朝廷"答应不斩首（中国人对斩首非常反感），并把他的全尸送回祖先安葬地"，他就会投降自首。朝廷同意了这些条件。他自首了,并被活埋。如果他拒绝以牺牲自己的生命为代价来挽救他父亲,即使在海盗中他也会成为受人蔑视的对象。

儿童教育

接受识字教育的男孩很少,而女孩几乎没有。学会读书写字的人数如此之少,以至于他们成了例外。但是,许多男孩能写字、会算数,使他们在做生意时能够自己记账或给人做账房先生。奇怪的是,尽管他们能写会算,并且算得又快又准,但他们连最简单的任何书都读不懂。

然而,在中国的教育中,有一个重要的组成部分对国民性格的养成产生了强大的影响:每个孩子都被精心训练,以履行家庭和社会责任。教学的形式和传统都含有道德元素。孔子总是把外在的形式当作内在情感的表达。但是,最重要的是,中国的教育中性格养成的影响因素是他们教科书的纯洁性。道德元素有益身心,在中国,任何一本书都不会容忍希腊文和拉丁文经典中包含的那些段落。至于在印度当

his head on" (the Chinese have a great aversion to decapitation). They agreed to the terms. He gave himself up, and was buried alive. He would have been an object of contempt even amongst pirates if he had refused to save his father's life at the expense of his own.

Education of Children

The number of boys who receive a literary education is very small, and of girls practically none. The number who are taught to read and write is so few that they only form the exception which confirms the rule. But a large number of boys get such a knowledge of writing and arithmetic as enables them to keep their own accounts when in business or to find employment as clerks. The strange thing is that, while they are ready with their pen or pencil, and quick and accurate in their calculation of sums, they cannot read the simplest book on any subject.

There is, however, one important element in Chinese education which has had a powerful influence in the formation of the character of the people: every child is carefully drilled in the performance of domestic and social duty. The forms and customs taught have a moral element. Confucius always made the outward form the expression of inner feeling. But, best of all, the influence for the formation of character in Chinese education is the purity of their school-books. The moral element is wholesome, and no book would be tolerated in China which contained such passages as are found in the Greek and Latin classics. As for the stories of the gods told in Indian native schools, and which the teachers （often priests） gloat over and present in their most realistic impurities, they would be rejected with horror by every teacher in China. This purity of Chinese school-books and classic literature has done much to preserve a fairly sound conscience and wholesome public sentiment in China.

地学校里讲述的众神的污秽不堪的故事，老师们（通常兼任祭司）津津乐道，原原本本地讲给学生听，这在中国老师那里一律会避之唯恐不及。中国教科书和经典文献的纯洁性，在很大程度上维系了中国相当健全的良知和健康的公众情绪。

【注　释】

① 应指郑一嫂（1775—1844），原姓石，乳名香姑，系广东新会籍。其丈夫因排行而俗名郑一，其因此得名郑一嫂。郑一嫂是中国最著名的女海盗之一。郑一乃红旗帮首领，多年来一直致力于把珠江口各股"疍家贼"统一成一个以他为盟主的海盗大联盟，而郑一嫂堪称贤内助，自始至终参与其事。在这个海盗大联盟签约结成的1807年，郑一却于一场强台风中坠海身亡，年仅42岁。取得合法领导地位的郑一嫂，马上通过加强舰队的组织纪律性来树立她的权威，其制定的海盗条令被严格执行，违反者严惩不贷，因此造就了一股攻则勇猛，防则顽强，即便位处劣势也会死拼到底的海上力量。——译者注

② 严格来讲，中国古代常见的是一夫一妻多妾制，也属于广义上的一夫多妻制。——译者注

③ 此处英文原文有误。原作者误将"尧帝嫁二女于舜"写成"舜帝嫁二女于禹"，即应该是尧帝把两个女儿娥皇与女英嫁给舜。——译者注

④ 沃尔特·司各特爵士（Sir Walter Scott, 1771—1832）：苏格兰小说家、诗人，确立了英国历史小说的形式，以处理乡村题材和使用方言闻名，代表小说有《威弗利》（1814）、《艾凡赫》（1819）等。——译者注

第四章　中国的历史、政府和行政管理

Chapter IV　The History, Government, and Administration of the Chinese

中国人的"历史感"

中国人表现出了罕见的大量常识和历史洞察力。在印度这样的国家，几乎不可能把历史和神话区分开；如果非要区分开，也是优先选取荒诞无稽的神话而不是平凡的历史事实。中国崇尚实事求是的历史精神，自古以来就是如此；据说公元前3300年左右的伏羲时代鼎盛一时，但中国人将伏羲时代视为传说或可疑的，表现出谨慎和批判的精神。伏羲之前很长时期的故事被历史学家视为神话，他们说这些故事是后来的哲学家们想象的产物，哲学家们构想出这些漫长的时期，以便有时间发展他们阴阳和合而生万物的理论。阴阳可以宽

Chinese "Historic Sense"

The Chinese have shown an amount of common-sense and of historical insight rare amongst Asiatics. In a country like India it is almost impossible to draw the line between history and myth; and if a line is drawn, the improbable or impossible is preferred to commonplace facts. In China the historical spirit prevails, and has prevailed from time immemorial, and the Chinese show their caution and critical spirit by treating the times of Fuh-hi, who is said to have flourished about 3300 years before Christ, as legendary or doubtful. There are stories of long periods prior to this, which are treated as myths by historical writers, who say that they are the product of the imaginations of their later philosophers, who invented these long periods to allow of time for the development of their theory of the production of all things from the principles of the Yang and Yin, which may be loosely rendered the Male and the Female, or the active and passive powers of Nature, by which all things in heaven and earth were produced. This process required endless ages for its operation, as Evolution does in modern theories.

Excess of Caution

Chinese historians seem to show an excess of caution when they treat the period subsequent to Fuh-hi as legendary, for there is good ground for accepting the accounts of his reign as authentic. He is generally said to have begun to reign 2852 B.C., but Dr. Legge gives good reason for placing it 500 years earlier, in 3322. This date is rendered the more credible from the discovery of Accadian and Egyptian records, which seem to carry authentic history back to a point about 400 years earlier. The philosophers of China, reasoning about causation, claimed time for the operations of the Yin and the Yang to construct a cosmogony, the origin of which carried things back to 45000 or 50000 years before Fuh-hi. They were modest in their demands when we consider that heaven and earth, and all things in them, had to be fashioned. Scientists of our day demand 20000000. All the heavy work seems to have fallen to Pwan-ku, who fashioned the earth, and scooped out the heavens with his great chisel and hammer. He was himself produced from chaos, and as he added six feet to his stature every day, and continued

松地表述为自然界的雌雄,或消极与积极的力量,而天地万物皆由此而生。这一过程需要无尽的时间来演进,就像现代理论中的进化论一样。

过度谨慎

中国的史学家将伏羲之后的一段时期视为传说,似乎显得过度谨慎,因为有充分的理由将关于伏羲统治的记述当作信史。人们普遍认为伏羲的统治始于公元前2852年,但理雅各①给出了充分理由,将其向前倒推约500年,即公元前3322年。阿卡德②和埃及历史记载的发现使这一日期更加可信,它们的记载似乎将信史向前回溯了大约400年。中国哲学家们对因果关系进行推理,为阴阳运转创建宇宙论找到了时间,这一理论可以追溯到伏羲之前45000年或5万年。当我们考虑到天地和其中的万物都必须被孕育创造时,他们声称的宇宙演进的时间还是适中的。我们今天的科学家判断宇宙演进需要2000万年。接下来,所有重任似乎都落在盘古身上,他用巨型斧头开天辟地。盘古生于混沌,每天长高一丈，持续长了一万八千年，直到他完成开天辟地的任务。他不用梯子伸手即可触天。

文献来源可靠的中国历史始于公元前2356年的帝尧统治时期，与古国迦勒底③和埃及的信史同时代，现在一般说这两个国家都始于约公元前2200年或前2300年，尽管有人把一些历史片段后推了1500年，就像中国学者推断中国史那样。

二十六次起义，一次大变革

有一个普遍的印象，即中国历史死气沉沉、乏味单调。若果真如此，那也是历史学家的错。中国历史的素材充满了活力和悲剧。中国从未有过那种使历史变得沉闷的一成不变的宁静。中华帝国可以吹嘘，尽管人们非常怀疑它是否会这么做，自己经历过二十六次成功的起义，导致了二十六次王朝更迭，此外失败的起义数量不详，并被血腥地镇压，流的血足以满足现代小说家低俗的趣味，更不用说历史学家了。依据中国人的观念，所有成功的起义都得到了上天的认可。在这二十六次起

his labours for 18000 years, he was able to reach high enough without a ladder before his work was finished.

Authentic documentary history in China, beginning with the reign of Yao in 2356 B.C., synchronizes with the authentic histories of Chaldaea and Egypt, both of which are now generally said to begin about 2200 or 2300 years before the Christian era, though some carry a few scraps of history 1500 years further back, as Chinese scholars do that of China.

Twenty-Six Rebellions, One Revolution

There is a general impression that Chinese history is a dead level of uninteresting monotony. If it is so, it is the fault of historians. The materials for history are full of life and tragedy; it has not enjoyed that unchanging peace which makes history dull. The Chinese Empire can make the very doubtful boast of having survived twenty-six successful rebellions, leading to as many changes of dynasty, besides an unknown number of unsuccessful ones, quenched in blood sufficient to satisfy the vulgar taste of modern novelists, not to say of historians. All the successful rebellions were, according to Chinese theory...justified by the approval of Heaven. Of these twenty-six rebellions only one could be called a revolution—that of Chi, the Napoleon of China, who reigned 250 years before Christ.

He was the first to subdue all the smaller kingdoms into which the country had formerly been divided (like our Heptarchy on a small scale), and to establish the one great empire which it has ever since remained, a monument of military genius and political sagacity. It was he who built that one great wonder of an architectural kind of which China can boast—the Great Wall—to defend the country from the invasions of the Tartar hordes on the north, and he and his successors drove the Huns from his western border, and compelled them to seek easier conquests in Europe…

Early History of China

Yao, although he reigned 2300 years before the Christian era, was not by any means the first ruler in China. His reign was that of an advanced civilization, when the people were clad in garments of wool and silk robes of varied colours, richly embroidered, and when the arts and manufactures, and even external commerce, were carried on with the petty States, but chiefly within the limits of what was then the Empire of China proper. His successor, Shun, is represented as carrying on extensive engineering works, which some pious students of Chinese history have taken to be the draining off of Noah's flood, but which is much more likely to have been a flood caused by that great river, the Hwang-ho, changing its course, as it has repeatedly done, devastating whole provinces.

义中，只有一次可以被称为大变革，即中国的拿破仑——始皇帝的变革，他于公元前250年④即位。他统一六国（英国的七王国⑤就像小一号的战国七雄），并建立了一个伟大的国家，成为军事才能和政治智慧的丰碑。正是他建造了一项中国可以夸耀的伟大建筑奇迹——长城，以保卫国家免受北方匈奴的入侵，他和后来者将匈奴赶出了西部边境，迫使他们在欧洲寻求更容易的征服地。

中国的早期历史

尧虽然是公元前2300年的君主，但绝不是中国的第一个统治者。尧的统治是一种先进文明的统治，当时人们穿着颜色各异、刺绣华丽的羊毛和丝绸长袍，与各小国进行技艺和手工业交流，甚至是对外贸易的交流，但这些交流主要仍是在当时中华帝国本土的范围内进行的。尧的继任者舜被描绘成完成了大量工程项目的首领，一些虔诚的中国史专业的学者认为舜的工程量相当于排干了诺亚时代的大洪水，但实际很有可能是那条大河——黄河因改变

福建的山涧及拱桥
Mountain Stream and Arched Bridge in Fuh Kien

第四章 中国的历史、政府和行政管理

Chapter IV The History, Government, and Administration of the Chinese

The Engineer Yu

His engineer was the great Yu, who forced the river back to its old channel and drained the flooded plains. It took him nine years to accomplish his task, during which he passed the door of his own house thrice, and never had time to enter. Shun was so pleased with the skill and devotion of his agent that he appointed him his successor on the throne instead of his own unworthy son, and the nation had no reason to regret the choice. He surveyed all the country to the north of the Yang-tsze-Kiang, and divided it into nine provinces, which formed the first Empire of China, founded in the year 2100 B.C. Yu is justly held up to the youth of the present time as the model of devotion and industry. He is said never to have lost "an inch of time" and during one meal he rose three times to give instructions to his Ministers.

A Mosaic Law Anticipated

It is characteristic of the high moral tone of these old rulers that Yu, who was the son of a man who had been executed for treason, instead of being put to death, as he would have been in the present day, was appointed to his father's post of engineer, and made

河道而引发的洪水，因为黄河总是反复改道，摧毁整个流域。

水利工程师——大禹

舜的水利工程师人称大禹，他疏导河川，使河水重回旧河道，并把平地的积水导入江河。大禹历时九年⑥方平息洪水灾祸，治水期间劳心劳力，三过家门而不入。舜举用大禹治水，对其才干和专一之心非常满意，禅位于大禹，而非自己无能之子商均。舜择大禹，天下无憾。大禹翻山越岭、蹚河过川，走遍长江以北地区，将天下划分为九州，奠定夏朝，即第一个中华帝国，建于公元前2100年⑦。大禹理所当然地被当代青年奉为敬业和勤劳的楷模。据说大禹从未浪费过一寸光阴，曾一饭三吐哺⑧，给大臣布置任务。

一条先于摩西的律法

这些古代统治者的典型特征是道德基准很高，大禹的父亲鲧治水失败而以叛国罪被处决，但大禹没有像今天律法那样被处死，而是被任命为司空，继任父亲治水

下冲式水车和上射式水车
Under-and Over-Shot Wheels

ruler of the empire. Yao had passed a law that children were not to be put to death for the sins of their parents two or three hundred years before Moses published that law for the Jews.

The Hea and Shang Dynasties

For the next 439 years after Yu, the Hea dynasty ruled in China, from 2205 to 1766 B.C. This was succeeded by the Shang dynasty, from 1766 to 1122 B.C., and that by the Chow, which lasted from 1122 to 255 B.C.—only three dynasties in 1850 years, implying a large measure of peace and prosperity in a country in which the right to depose a ruler who failed to satisfy the people was an acknowledged rule and custom. The change of dynasty was in no case a revolution. It was only an attempt to return to the ideal of all good government—that of Yao and Shun.

Its Illustrious Men

The last of these dynasties, though it dwindled away in weakness and dishonour, was made illustrious by a revival of learning, and the labours of the greatest men that China has ever produced. These were Confucius, Laotsze and Mencius. The two first flourished in the sixth, and Mencius in the fourth, century before Christ. These men exerted an influence greater far than that of any of the rulers of these long dynasties. Their

之职，最后成为夏朝的统治者。帝尧早就通过了一条律法，规定孩子不可因父母的罪过受株连而被处死，这比摩西为犹太人颁布这条律法早了两三百年。

夏商两朝

在大禹之后的439年里，从公元前2205年到前1766年，夏朝统治中国。公元前1766年至前1122年，商朝接替夏朝，而公元前1122年至前255年，周朝取代夏朝。在长达1950年间⑨仅历经3个朝代，这意味着国家的高度和平与繁荣，而且人民有权废黜一个不能让他们满意的统治者，这是一条公认的准则。朝代的更迭绝不是一场革命，而只不过是一次次试图回归天下大同的理想，即尧舜之道。

诸子百家

周朝，虽然在衰弱和耻辱中衰亡，但却因学术思想的复兴和中国有史以来最伟大的诸子百家的成果而光芒四射。诸子中有孔子、老子和孟子。孔子和老子活跃于公元前6世纪，孟子则在公元前4世纪。这些人给后世带来的影响远远超过那些漫长朝代的任何统治者。他们的笔比权杖更强大，孔子被称为中国的"素王"。

中国的一个大变革王朝

秦昭襄王⑩推翻了周朝八百年统治，他的曾孙始皇帝嬴政于公元前255年⑪建立了第五个王朝，国号为"秦"，因此西方称中国为"秦"。秦王嬴政自称"始皇帝"，他凭借军事才能和集权专制，吞并了原来附属于周天子的小诸侯国，在长江以南征服百越，天下一统，初分全国为三十六郡，任命直属于自己的郡守，中央集权，由自己掌控。这是中国有史以来的第一次，也可以说是唯一一次大变革。现在内地省份的数目已减少到十八个，但政府体制与秦始皇治下时期的体制基本相同，不过由于所设政府内阁的权力渐增，更趋向宪制。⑫秦始皇统一天下、威加海内之后，着手修建长城，保护大秦帝国免受来自外部的袭击。这项伟大的工程，花了十年的时间、强行征用百万民力完成，这也是中国唯一一项靠压迫人民来完成的工程，从此秦始皇声名狼藉。

pens were more powerful than sceptres, and Confucius has been called the "uncrowned King" of China.

China's One Revolutionary Dynasty

Chao, King of Chin, having overthrown the Chows, his son Chi established the fifth dynasty in 255 B.C., which he called after his own nation, the Chin, the name by which the country is known in the West as China, Chin, who called himself "First Emperor," by his military genius and autocratic despotism, crushed the liberties of the small States which had hitherto maintained their home rule while dependencies of the empire, conquered the nationalities south of the Yang-tsze-Kiang, and divided the empire into thirty-six provinces, appointing Governors of his own over them, and centralizing all authority in the capital, under his own control. This was the first, and we may say the only, revolution that has ever taken place in China. The number of provinces has been reduced to eighteen, but the system of government remains substantially the same as it was under Chi, but more constitutional, through the increased power of Government boards. After he had established his authority over the united empire…This great undertaking he accomplished in ten years by employing the forced labour of a million of men—the only great work in China carried on by the oppression of the people—and his name has been held in execration in the country ever since.

Slaughter of Literati

The literati and the sacred literature of Chin being all opposed to his revolutionary methods, he ordered the sacred books compiled by Confucius to be given to the flames, and 460 of the most learned men of China were burned to death, lest the books should be restored from their retentive memories. It was during this dynasty that Taoism...form rose to power, its followers being favoured by the dynasty.

The Han Dynasty

The Han dynasty, which succeeded in establishing itself by the overthrow of the Chin in 206 B.C., is that of which Chinamen are most proud, and to this day they designate themselves as the men of Han. It was distinguished by general prosperity and by the revival of literature, favoured by the internal peace secured through the union of the empire so rudely established by the despotism of Chi, and protected from external assault by the Great Wall which he had built. Taoism and Buddhism, which had both been patronized under the Chin dynasty, were discouraged, and Confucianism, which had been long under a cloud, was again restored to favour, and became more predominant and influential than ever.

It is not needful for our purpose to name each dynasty that sprang up, one after another, all alike based on the principle of reformation on the line of a return to the ideal of perfection shown in the days of Yao and Shun.

焚书坑儒

因为秦朝时的儒生和经典与他的变革方法相左，于是始皇下令将孔子编纂的经书付之一炬，并烧死460余名儒生，以免他们凭记忆恢复出书籍内容。正是在这一朝代，道教崛起，方士受到追求长生的秦始皇的青睐。

汉 朝

公元前206年⑬汉朝建立，推翻了秦朝统治，汉朝是中国人最引以为豪的王朝，直到今天，他们都称自己为汉人。汉朝以全面繁荣和文学复兴而著称，又因国内和平受人爱戴，专制的秦始皇粗暴地一统天下却造福了汉朝，而且他修建的长城又保护了汉朝免受外部袭击。道教和佛教在秦朝双双受到庇护，但在汉朝不受待见，而长期遭忌的儒家思想又重新受到青睐，并比以往任何时候都变得更为正统、强势。

鉴于本书宗旨，我们没必要把此后诞生的所有朝代都逐个提一遍，它们都本着重归尧舜时代所展现的理想之道的原则。

印刷术的发明

公元618年至905年[14]间,唐朝以诗人众多、才华横溢而璀璨生辉。唐朝初置翰林院,系文人追求的顶峰,而印刷术则发明于公元8世纪[15],比谷登堡活字印刷术早了500年。几乎没人相信,在谷登堡时代之前很长的时间里,欧洲对中国的雕版印刷术一无所知;同样不可信的是,在中文的汉字符号印刷演变成罗马字母印刷的过程中,从雕版到活字印刷的必要的技术进步是一蹴而就的。中国在很早时就有了活字印刷,但时至今日也未取代雕版印刷,只是传教士为欧洲引入了活字印刷。正是在大唐王朝,瓷器达到了完美境界,在现今的欧洲市场和中国市场上,汉代瓷器交易价格惊人。

哲学与批判的兴起

宋朝的统治时间为公元960年至1180年[16],宋朝因理学兴起而为人所知,这一哲学流派因形而上的思辨和文学批评而闻名。以才华出众、博学多识的大学问家朱熹为

Discovery of the Art of Printing

The Tang dynasty, which flourished from 618 to 905 A.D., was illustrious for the number and excellence of its poets. The Hanlin Yuan, or Imperial Academy, the highest summit of literary ambition, was established, and the art of printing was discovered in the eighth century—500 years before it was said to have been discovered by Gutenberg. It is scarcely credible that the knowledge of Chinese block-printing was unknown in Europe long before Gutenberg's time; and the advance from the block to the movable type was a simple, we may say a necessary one, when the change was made from the Chinese symbolic characters to the letters of the Roman alphabet. Movable types had been made in China at a very early period, but have never superseded the printing from blocks to this day, except where missionaries have introduced the movable type. It was under this dynasty that pottery reached its highest perfection, and specimens of the ceramic art of the Han period are now bought at fabulous prices in European and Chinese markets.

Rise of Philosophy and Criticism

The Sung dynasty, which ruled from 960 to 1180 A.D., was made famous by the rise of a school of philosophy noted for its metaphysical speculation and literary criticism. Under the guidance of its very able and learned leader, Chu-fu-tsze, it took an agnostic form, and by mythical theories worthy of a Strauss he did his best to get rid of every reference to Deity in the sacred books, and by sceptical speculation worthy of a Hume he tried to get rid of all that was supernatural…

The Grand Canal

To him China owes her only monumental work besides the Great Wall-The Grand Canal from Peking to Hang-chau, a distance of 700 miles, connecting it with the old canal from Canton, making an inland waterway from the extreme north to the south of China, open at all seasons, and to all the intermediate towns, an immense boon at a time when the passage by sea could only be carried on at long intervals with the half-yearly change of the monsoons.

The Ming Dynasty

Ming dynasty established itself in 1368, and justified its designation of the Bright dynasty by its cultivation of literature in all departments, which it embodied in the systematic form of encyclopaedias of vast dimensions, such as no other people have ever attempted, compared with which the "Encyclopaedia Britannica" is a small affair, though it includes a large field of science unknown to China. The codification of the laws

首，朱夫子以媲美施特劳斯[17]的神学理论，尽最大努力把经典中提及鬼神之处全部清除，可以比拟休谟[18]的理论，努力把一切超自然的东西清除。

大运河

除了长城之外，中国另一个不朽工程要归功于忽必烈。元朝的大运河从北京直通杭州，长达700英里，向南接续古运河与广州相连，成为贯通中国南北的一条内河水道，四季通航，并对所有沿途城镇开放。由于季风半年一变，海路运输只能间隔很久方能进行，常年可用的内陆运输可谓大有裨益。

明 朝

大明王朝于1368年建立，其后命人编修集古代典籍于大成的《永乐大典》，彰显国威，使"日月同辉"的大明国号名实相副，这体现在其涵盖广泛的百科全书式的系统性上，规模前所未见；《不列颠百科全书》与《永乐大典》相比不过是小巫见大巫，尽管前者包括大量中国未知的科学领域。明朝时开始编纂律例，尽管是在下一个王朝——清朝时才得以完成，[19]但这项工作革故鼎新、实用性强。律例的价格控制在适度的范围内，仅以几文钱的价格出售。文字表述更为简明，人人皆可理解。

在19世纪衰败的原因

在19世纪，中国的政府和人民衰败了，主要是由于西方国家的侵略和暴行，部分是由于他们自己固守着那些完全不适合人类更高文明进步要求的古老制度和惯例。毋庸置疑的是，西方国家在与中国的交往中犯下罪责，态度粗鲁、行事不公。西方借助用科学武装起来的庞大武力闯入一个民族国家，而该国政府的建立只是为了维护国内和平，不是为了对外发动侵略战争，甚至连保家卫国不受外敌入侵都不是；对外来之敌，他们一无所知，甚至大自然也没给他们提供足够的天险。

西方国家之过

当西方国家把自己和战争强加给一个政府组织有序、法律公正严明、文明更为

of China was begun during this dynasty, though completed under the succeeding one, a work of great talent and utility, the criminal code being brought within such moderate compass as to be sold for a few pence, and expressed in language so simple that anyone can understand it.

Causes of Deterioration in the Nineteenth Century

During this century the government and people of China have deteriorated, chiefly through the encroachments and excesses of Western nations, partly from their own adhesion to ancient institutions and habits totally unsuited for the progressive development of the higher civilization of the human race. That Western... nations have been guilty of much rudeness and injustice in their intercourse with China cannot be doubted. They used the tremendous forces with which science had armed them to break in upon a people whose government was framed only for the preservation of internal peace, not for aggressive wars, nor even for the defence of the country from foreign enemies, of whom there were none known to them against whom Nature had not provided a sufficient defence.

Responsibility of Civilization

Civilized nations...force themselves and their wars

on a people with an organized government, just laws, and a civilization much more ancient than their own, it is sure to lead to disorganization, if not destruction. When to an unjustifiable employment of force you add the immoral practices of many of the representatives of our modern civilization, the frauds of trade, and the unholy traffic in pernicious and poisonous drugs, the evil is increased tenfold. The present impotence and degradation of China is in a great measure due to European wars and the opium trade, for which England is so largely responsible. They have lowered the prestige of the Government, and driven it to greater corruption in raising money, besides inflicting great evils upon the people.

Limitations on Autocracy

Though the government of China is patriarchal and nominally autocratic, it is limited by important and beneficial restraints ... The following checks on absolute government may be named:

First of all, the Emperor is practically bound to rule according to the example and precepts of the early founders of the empire, especially those of Yao and Shun. These are, to the rulers of China, what the example and precepts of Moses were to the ruler of the Jews. The King was ordered to write a copy of the laws of God with his own hand.

Second, the throne is held on

古老悠久的民族时，如果这种做法没有导致亡国灭种的话，肯定也会导致混乱失序。当把我们现代文明中许多代表性的无良行径、贸易欺诈、有毒有害鸦片走私的邪恶加上滥用武力时，罪恶就如虎添翼，增加十倍。中国目前的无能和衰败，很大程度上是欧洲列强发动的战争和鸦片贸易所致，而英国对此负有极大责任。它们削弱了清政府的威信，使政府为筹集赔款而变得更加腐败，并给人民带来了巨大的灾祸。

对专制的限制

虽然中国政府是宗法制的，名义上专制，但它受许多重要而有益的限制制约。以下是对专制政府的限制：

首先，皇帝必须按照开国先皇的榜样和训诫实行统治，尤其是尧舜之道。这些榜样和训诫对于中国的统治者来说，就如同摩西十诫对犹太统治者而言。皇帝受命亲手抄写上天的旨意。

其次，坐稳皇位的前提是要正确地理解皇帝是代上天而治，而民意即为天意。这在经典中有明确的表达，书中说，皇帝被唤作"天子",并被告知"得乎丘民而为天子",以及"诸侯危社稷,则变置"。这些可以通过皇帝每年在天坛上公开祭天得以确证。

再次,人民有权利反抗和推翻任何暴虐的统治者,皇帝和人民都清楚地了解这一点。这一点在他们推崇备至的经典中有所规定,孔子曾引用中国早期最伟大帝王中的两位作为例子,他们都是在推翻前朝统治者的基础上建立了王朝。成汤因在公元前1766年[20]推翻了夏王朝而在《尚书》中被称颂,因为上天下令摧毁暴虐无道的夏王朝最后一位统治者——夏桀;周武王在公元前1112年[21]顺应天命,推翻了商朝的最后一位皇帝而同样被称颂,因为商纣王残暴地压迫人民。

复次,政府由内阁和议政会议执掌,尽管其成员是由皇帝选出,但他们受到人民的高度尊重,只有非常强势的皇帝才能推翻他们的决定。此外,还有一些品格极高尚之人被任命为御史,对任何与过去的法律或惯例有实质背离的做法,他们都敢于谏诤。在反对专制皇帝的意志时,这些

the understanding that the Emperor rules as Heaven's representative for the good of the people. This is explicitly expressed in the sacred books, in which he is called "Heaven's officer," and is told that "The real way to serve Heaven is to love the people" and that "if he fails to love the people Heaven will for the sake of the people cast him out." These truths are acknowledged by the Emperor in prayers which he offers publicly every year at the "altar of heaven."

Third, the right of the people to rebel and dethrone any oppressive ruler is distinctly understood alike by the Emperor and the people. It is laid down in their sacred books, which are held in highest honour by all, and Confucius quotes the example of two of the greatest of the early Emperors of China, who founded dynasties on the dethronement of their predecessors. Ching Tung is celebrated in the Shoo-King for having overthrown the Hea dynasty, 1766 B.C., because Heaven had decreed the destruction of its last ruler on account of his despotism, and Woo Wang, in 1112 B.C., is equally praised for carrying out the decree of Heaven for the overthrow of the last Emperor of the Shang dynasty, because he oppressed the people.

Fourth, the government is carried on by a Cabinet and Council which, though chosen by the Emperor, are held in such high esteem by the people that none but a very strong ruler could override their decision. Besides, there are certain men of the highest character who are appointed as censors, who boldly protest against any material departure from the constitutional laws or usage of former times. These men have often been faithful to the death in opposing the will of despotic Emperors.

Last of all, the power of the Emperor is checked by the limitation of his army. The only troops directly under his control are the Manchus, who are not only limited in number, but scattered throughout the vast territory, with no power of concentration or united action. All the Chinese troops are under the control of the Civil Governor of each province, and are more like a militia or an armed police force for the preservation of peace, than a regular army. This is a more effective check on despotic power than even the English control of the "sinews of war" by keeping hold of the purse-strings in the House of Commons.

There is one thing which shows that the government of China is largely dependent on the good-will of the people: that is, the regular circulation of what is generally called the Pekin Gazette—the oldest newspaper in the world, if we may call it by so modern a name. It is issued by the Government, and contains an account of all the proceedings of the Emperor and his Cabinet and Council, and of the six Boards established for the different departments of the State. It is sent to all parts of the empire for the information of the officials, and is published for the use of all, and often republished in different places for free circulation or sale. This publicity implies a necessity for ruling in a way that secures the approval and good-will of the people.

御史经常冒死进谏。

最后，皇帝的权力受制于其掌握的军队有限。皇帝直接控制的军队只有八旗兵，他们不仅人数有限，而且分散驻防在广阔的领土上，没有能力集中或采取联合行动。朝廷所有的军队都在各省督抚的控制之下，他们更像是维护和平的民兵或武装警察部队，而不是正规军。这是对专制权力的一种更有效的遏制，甚至比英国通过控制下议院的钱袋子进而控制军费更为有效。

有一样东西，即世界上最早的报纸《京报》的定期发行，表明中国政府在很大程度上以民为本。如果我们可以用现代的名字来称呼它的话，一般称作《北京公报》。该报由政府发行，载有皇帝及其内阁和议政会议大臣的所有谕旨和奏折，以及为掌管国家各个部门而设立的六部的时政记录。《京报》发行到全国各个地方，以供官员获取朝政信息，且供所有人使用，通常外地各报房予以翻印，或免费流通或出售。此等公开度意味着国家的执政方式必须获得人民的赞同和支持。

腐败的行政人员

政府管理是留给执政理念先进、实践经验丰富的贤才的,假如它能够不折不扣地执行的话。但是可惜的是,实际上腐败到了骨子里。除了少数令人尊敬的官员外,从各省督抚到基层县衙的最低级差役,所有官吏都收受贿赂,要么强行索贿,要么有人主动行贿。法律是好法律,税收也不重,但官员和收税员强行索贿,成为国家的负担和祸患之源。

《大清律例》

现在摆在我们面前的《大清律例》是正义、简约和常识的典范。《大清律例》过于随意地使用杖刑作为惩罚手段,这几乎是人们唯一反对的东西,但中国人更喜欢挨板子而不是坐牢。《大清律例》与印度教法相比,就像光明与黑暗一样。翻译《大清律例》的小斯当东爵士[22]说:"《大清律例》可与古罗马的或现代欧洲的法律相提并论。"其行文有一个特点值得一提,即律例的言辞如此清晰明了,即使

A Corrupt Executive

The administration of the government is allowed by experts to be excellent in theory, and would be good in practice, if only it were honestly carried out. But, alas! the practice is corrupt to the core. With a few honourable exceptions, from the Governors of provinces to the lowest police runners of the inferior courts of justice, the officials are influenced by bribes, which are forcibly exacted if not freely offered. The laws are good, and taxes light, but the exactions of officers and collectors are a burden and curse to the country.

The Criminal Code

The criminal code of China now lying before us is a model of justice, simplicity, and common sense. Almost the only thing one objects to is the too liberal use of the bamboo as the means of punishment, but the Chinese prefer it to imprisonment. Compared with the Gentoo code of the Hindus, it is as light to darkness. Sir George Stanton, who translated it, says: "The criminal code of China will bear comparison with the laws of Rome or of modern Europe." One feature in its composition is worthy of note. It is written in a style so clear and simple that it can be understood by the humblest of the people, if they can read at all, and can be bought for a few pence, so that everyone may know the law and the punishment due for its violation.

All Equal in the Eye of the Law

Before this law all are placed in a position of almost perfect equality—not as in the native laws of India, where the Brahman, the Sudra, and the Paria is treated each according to a different rule. Till lately even the laws of the States of Europe made a great difference between the freeman and the serf. There is in China a form of mild domestic slavery, but the law is substantially the same for slave and free man. For the murder of a free man the sentence is death by decapitation. For the murder of a slave a free man has the privilege of being hanged. This may seem a doubtful privilege to European or American tastes, but it is highly prized by Chinamen, who have a great objection to being "sent to their ancestors" with their heads off; they consider it disrespectful to their parents, who brought them into the world with their heads properly fixed on their shoulders.

是地位最卑微的人，只要识字就能看懂，而且花几文钱就可买到，于是人人都知晓了法律以及违法会受到的惩处。

法律面前人人平等

在这部法律面前，所有人都处于几乎完全平等的地位，而不像印度的本土法律那样，在印度，婆罗门、首陀罗和贱民等不同种姓是按照不同的准则对待的。甚至直到最近，欧洲各国的法律在自由人和农奴之间还有很大的区别。尽管中国有一种温和的家奴制，但法律对家奴和自由人的规定基本上是一样的。自由人谋杀一个自由人，判决斩首。自由人谋杀一个家奴，他有权选择绞刑。在欧洲人或美国人看来，绞刑选择权似乎很令人疑惑，但它却受到中国人的高度推崇。中国人极其反对把砍掉脑袋的尸体"送到祖先那里"，他们认为这是对父母的不敬，因为父母把他们带到这个世界上来的时候，脑袋可是好好地长在肩膀上的。

联结的纽带

考虑到这个统治着世界四分之一人口的伟大帝国长达四千年的历史时长，我们必须承认，在其民族的组成成分中或在其建立的制度中，有一种东西表明了他们在某些重要的品质上非凡且卓越，需要我们的尊重和研究。

中国之所以能够保持长久的统一，并不是因为武力或中国的天然边界、地理特征等外在条件。的确，中国有宽阔的河流和高高的山脉，似乎暗示并鼓励帝国分裂成几个大王国，就像历史早期那样。中国保持统一不是靠物质战胜精神，而是靠精神战胜物质。它的政府、它的法律和它的语言把人民联结在一起，形成道德的约束，外部的力量或敌对的力量无法将其打破。

日本的胜利

然而，最近这个民族被日本这样一个迄今为止无足轻重的小国超过和击败，使人很难认识到它的优越性。但这一令人伤心的事实很容易解释，其理由并未使中国

Bonds of Unity

When we take into account the duration of this great empire, ruling over a fourth part of the population of the world, and for a period of 4000 years, we must admit that there is something in the race of men of which it is composed, or the institutions which they have established, which marks them out as exceptional and superior in respect of some important qualities which demand our esteem and study.

It is not by the external conditions of either physical forces or the boundaries or features of the country that China has preserved its unity so long. There are broad rivers and high mountain chains which seem to suggest and encourage the division of the empire into several large kingdoms, as there were in early times. It is not by the triumph of matter over mind, but by the triumph of mind over matter, that China has been maintained in its unity. Its government, its laws, and its language have bound the people together in moral fetters which outward and adverse forces could not sunder.

Japanese Triumph

It is, however, difficult to recognise superiority in a race which has of late allowed itself to be out-matched and conquered by a small and hitherto insignificant country like Japan. But this sad fact is easily accounted for on grounds which reflect little discredit on the courage or patriotism of the Chinese, while they bring out features in the old maxims of government which command the respect of the lovers of peace and benevolence.

Government by Moral Force

It has always been a fundamental principle in China that the government of the country must not be by force, but by the willing subjection of the people to a beneficent ruler, and when the Emperor could not by good government secure the affections and confidence of the people, he was unfit to rule, and the people had a constitutional right to depose him. The Shoo-King, the most ancient and sacred of the Chinese classics—a book which is committed to memory by every scholar in China, including every ruler and official, from the Emperor to the lowest magistrate—contains the following words:

Heaven establishes Sovereigns merely for the sake of the people; whom the people desire for Sovereign, him will Heaven protect; whom the people dislike as Sovereign, him will Heaven reject.

It was a fundamental principle from the earliest times that the nation was to be governed by moral power rather than by physical force. For this reason the army in China has always been small, and only sufficient for the preservation of order and the defence of the country, the chief dependence being on a militia.

人的勇气或爱国精神蒙羞，反而体现出其古老治国准则的特点，值得爱好和平与仁政之人的尊重。

以德治国

一直以来，中国的一项基本原则是，国家的治理不能靠武力，而必须靠人民自愿地服从于仁慈的统治者。当皇帝不能通过仁政获得人民的爱戴和信任时，他就不适合当皇帝，人民有合法的权利废黜他。《尚书》是中国最古老、最神圣的典籍，是每一个读书人，包括每一位统治者和官员，上至皇帝下至芝麻大的县官，都要熟记于心的。其写道：

天佑下民，作之君……天矜于民，民之所欲，天必从之。……自绝于天，结怨于民……上帝弗顺，祝降时丧。

从最早的时候起，以德治国而非以武力治国，就是一项基本原则。故此，中国的军队规模一直很小，仅够维持秩序、保卫国家，而主要依赖民兵。在这里，战争得不到像在别国那样的称赞，士兵也得不到像在别国那样的崇敬。

文官占上风

文官权力得到抬高，占了上风，文官节制武将，这是欧洲列强闻所未闻的制度安排。其原理是，让最贤能之人来治国理政，民众会永远愿意顺从他们的君王，过和平的生活。为此，圣贤们制定了教育体系以及通过考试选拔各级官员的体系。他们追求对美德的纯粹之爱，但这种乐观和信心却时常被现实粗暴地破坏。这可以从孔子生前所受到的待遇以及帝国的历史中看出。

希望尚存

但这不是结束。日本带来的麻烦还在后头，且为期不远。中国在其未开发的资源中，在其人口沉着冷静的性格中蕴藏着强大的修复能力，单单一个人动起来原本就比较慢，那么如此广大的国家、如此众多的人口作为一个整体动起来就会更为缓慢，但是一旦动起来，中国就会有长足的进步，就会有丰富的资源和惊人的力量。

我们期待中国焕发新生的力量，不仅

War has not been lauded, and soldiers have not been held in honour, as in other countries.

Civil Power Predominates

The civil power was made predominant, and the highest military honours were made subordinate to those of the civil service—an arrangement unknown among the Christian Powers of Europe—the theory being that by getting the ablest and best men to rule and administer the affairs of the country, the people would always be willing to obey their rulers and live in peace. For this the sages wrought out their system of education and selection of officials of all kinds by examinations. This optimistic confidence in the pure love of virtue has frequently been rudely shaken. This might be shown by the treatment which Confucius met with at the hands of his countrymen in his lifetime, and by the history of the empire.

There Still Is Hope

But the end is not yet. The difficulties of Japan are yet to come, and are not far off. China has great recuperative force still latent in the undeveloped resources of the country and in the character of her phlegmatic population, slow of movement in the individual, and much slower in the mass of so large a country and so vast a population, but, when moved, susceptible of

一位官员视察弓箭手
A Mandarin Reviewing Archers

仅因为其历史悠久，且长期以来一直保持着统一和独立；还因为其人民的性格，他们以如此保守的坚韧精神制定并维护法律，屡屡从大灾大难中恢复如常，并且能在经历了多年的无政府状态和混乱之后，重建秩序和繁荣，而这些动荡混乱原本足以将帝国分裂成许多更为紧凑、更易于管理的小国。倘假以时日，中国很快就会自我修复，就像一艘坚固的救生艇只是被一个浪头暂时淹没一样。中国人的思想和性格中既有向上的浮力，也有不致翻船的压舱石。

灾难的原因

以下是新近导致清朝的灾难和亡国危险的原因：

1. 当中国人即将通过上天赋予他们的起义权推翻朝廷时，清朝直接或间接地得到了欧洲列强的支持。

2. 清朝通过卖官鬻爵来增加收入，侵犯了通过公平竞争获取官职的神圣权利。皇帝倒行逆施，颠覆了中国最珍贵的习俗之一，把一群卑劣贪婪之徒推上了信任与权力的高位，贪官们认为自己花钱买来了

brought into places of trust and power a lower and greedier class of men, who feel they have purchased a right to plunder the people.

3. The army, small in comparison with the extent of country and population, has been reduced and demoralized by officers not receiving their pay, and being driven to the expedient of sending home their men to earn a living, while they drew payment for them as if they were in the ranks. The subjection of the soldiers in each province to the authority of the Provincial Governor divides the army into many independent sections, and delays if it does not prevent concentration.

4. By the neglect of modern implements of warfare, as used by Western nations, who have made war a perfect science of destruction. China has neglected this from her old habit of treating all outside nations with contempt, which she could well do until Christian nations from the West came with their new implements of war, and taught her old neighbour and former dependency, Japan, to imitate their example.

5. That China has not adopted Western fashions, like Japan, is not surprising if we take into account that not only was China a peaceable nation from inclination and interest, but averse from ancient custom to make force the basis of governing. Even foreign countries, according to the theory of Confucius, were to be subdued by the example of good government at home—a theory which has been rudely exploded by the invention of gunpowder and

大肆榨取民脂民膏的权力。

3. 与国家和人口规模相比，军队本来就很小，却还被缩减，且士气低落，原因是军官领不到军饷，权宜之计是不得不把士兵打发回家去谋生，而军官则吃空饷。各省士兵分别服从各省督抚，这就将清军分成许多独立的部分，而这如果不是阻碍集中调动的话，至少也会拖延行动。

4. 忽视了现代战争工具，而西方国家借此把战争变成了一门完美的毁灭科学。中国忽视了这一点，因为它一贯轻视所有蛮夷，直到再也做不到为止，因为西方国家带着新的战争工具来了，同时教会了中国的老邻居日本效仿西方的榜样。

5. 如果考虑到中国不仅是一个本性爱好和平的国家，而且有反对以武力作为统治基础的古老习俗，那么中国没有像日本那样采用西方的模式就不足为奇了。依照孔子的理论，国内政通人和便可怀柔远人，这一理论被火药的发明和外敌来犯无情地戳穿了。要理解日本人如何效仿外国习俗并不难。他们一直都是一个效仿的民族。相反地，中国在没有借鉴任何文明的情况

foreign invasion. It is easy to understand how the Japanese should imitate foreign customs. They have been an imitative race all along… China, on the other hand, originated her own civilization without borrowing from any, and it is not easy for an old and great nation to change its time-honoured customs.

6. Japan, a small country and mercurial people, could easily adopt the new arts of destruction, and by quietly preparing while China slept in fancied security, it was easy to gain temporary advantages over the unprepared giant just awakened out of his long sleep. But for fear of European interference China exhausted the resources of Japan by passive resistance until prepared for action.

7. The exhaustion of Chinese resources, ruin of her prestige by the repeated wars and exactions of European Powers, and the injury inflicted on her people by the spread of the opium habit, for which England is so largely responsible, crippled her efforts and disheartened the defenders in a war for which they were in every way so ill prepared.

下创造了自己的文明，对这样一个古老而伟大的国家来说，要改变其悠久的习俗不是一件容易的事。

6. 日本，一个弹丸小国，有着善变的人民，可以很容易地接受战争的新破坏艺术，当中国在幻化出的安全感中沉睡时，它悄悄地准备着，很轻易地获得了暂时的优势，战胜这个刚刚从沉睡中醒来的毫无准备的巨人。但由于担心欧洲列强的干涉，中国只以消极抵抗的方式消耗日本的资源，直到准备好采取行动。

7. 中国资源的枯竭，欧洲列强连续的侵略战争和疯狂掠夺使中国威望扫地，而吸食鸦片恶习的蔓延给中国人民带来的伤害（英国对此负有主要责任），凡此种种都使中国的努力在一场毫无准备的甲午战争中被严重削弱，士气低迷。

【注 释】

① 理雅各（James Legge，1815—1897）：近代英国著名汉学家，曾任香港英华书院校长，伦敦布道会传教士。他是第一个系统研究、翻译中国古代经典的人。其《四书》《五经》译本、《法显行传》、《中国编年史》等著作在西方汉学界占有重要地位。——译者注

② 阿卡德：古代美索不达米亚的一个地区，位于巴比伦北部，在公元前3000年时达到

鼎盛时期。——译者注

③ 迦勒底：古代美索不达米亚南部的一个地区，位于现伊拉克南部。——译者注

④ 应为公元前247年。——译者注

⑤ 七王国：又称七盟邦，5—9世纪盎格鲁-撒克逊王国的非正式联盟，由肯特、南撒西克斯、西撒西克斯、东撒西克斯、诺森布里亚、东英格兰和麦西亚组成。——译者注

⑥ 此处有误。据中国传说，鲧治水九年，大禹治水十三年。此处原作者可能将大禹治水时间与其父亲鲧治水时间混淆。——译者注

⑦ 第76页提及夏朝为公元前2205年到前1766年，第112页提及禹于公元前2200年登上王位，均不一致。——译者注

⑧ 此处有误。"一饭三吐哺"的典故出自《史记·鲁周公世家》，为描述周公在一顿饭之间，多次停食，以接待宾客，比喻其求贤殷切。——译者注

⑨ 夏商周三朝的持续时间原文写作1850年，应为计算错误。依据作者推测的大致年代，从公元前2205年到前255年之间，应有1950年。根据我国新发布的夏商周断代工程报告，三代积年如下：夏（公元前2070年—前1600年）、商（公元前1600年—前1046年）、西周（公元前1046年—前771年）、东周（公元前770年—前221年）。——译者注

⑩ 秦昭襄王：嬴稷，秦惠文王之子，秦武王之弟。他攻陷东周王都洛邑，俘虏周赧王，迁九鼎于咸阳，结束周朝八百年统治。——译者注

⑪ 应为公元前221年，秦灭六国。——译者注

⑫ 清朝虽设内阁制，但内阁的权力实际上愈来愈低，尤其在军机处设立以后，皇帝的集权达到巅峰。——译者注

⑬ 公元前206年刘邦受封为汉王，公元前202年建立汉朝。——译者注

⑭ 唐朝灭亡时间为907年。——译者注

⑮ 印刷术发明于唐朝初期（7世纪）。——译者注

⑯ 宋朝灭亡时间为1279年。——译者注

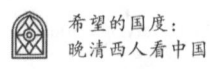

⑰ 施特劳斯（David Friedrich Strauss, 1808—1874）：德国新教哲学家、神学家、传记作家，在《圣经》研究中使用了黑格尔哲学，是最有争议的新教神学家，也是第一个对历史人物耶稣和基督教信仰中的耶稣做出了明确区分的人。——译者注

⑱ 休谟（David Hume, 1711—1776）：苏格兰哲学家、经济学家和历史学家，认为知识中不可能存在确定性，声称所有的理性材料都来自经验。——译者注

⑲ 明洪武七年（1374），《大明律例》修成，颁布天下。《大清律例》以《大明律例》为基础进行修改并颁行。——译者注

⑳ 根据夏商周断代工程报告，成汤灭夏的时间为公元前1600年。——译者注

㉑ 根据夏商周断代工程报告，武王伐纣的时间为公元前1046年。——译者注

㉒ 小斯当东爵士（1781—1859）：英格兰旅行家、东方文化研究者及政客，可能是英国最早的"中国通"。1810年，《大清律例》由他翻译并在英国出版，这是第一本直接由中文翻译为英文的书。——译者注

第五章　教育和文学
Chapter V　Education and Literature

National Education

The encouragement of education has always been considered the glory of China, and rightly so, although the extent to which it is carried on has been much exaggerated. The ideal of the Emperors of China was to have an elementary school in every village, elementary and high schools in each town, schools and a college in the cities, with a system of competitive examinations for all Government posts in the capital, so the ablest men might be secured for the government and administration of the country. But while the examinations have been kept up, the ideal of a national system of education for all the people has not been realized. Government, like the University of London, is an examining, not a teaching, body. It has encouraged the higher education of the few by dispensing the honours and employments of the State only to scholars, and that by an elaborate system of examinations, so that the poorest

国民教育

鼓励教育一直被认为是中国的荣光,且确实如此,尽管它实施的程度被夸大了很多。中国历代皇帝的理想是,乡村有蒙馆,城镇有学馆,城市有县学、府学,京城所有政府职位都是经过竞争性考试制度取得,这样才能为政府和行政管理找到最有能力的人。但是,尽管科举考试一直在进行,但全民教育的举国体系的理想并没有实现。政府,就像伦敦大学一样,是一个考试机构,而不是教学机构。①它鼓励的是少数人接受高等教育,只把朝廷的高官显职授予读书人,并通过完备的科举制度,使最贫寒之人能够升任皇帝一人之下最位高权重之人。

文职人员的最高回报

中国是世界上唯一一个重文轻武的国家，授予读书人的荣誉头衔比授予战士或祭司的头衔更高，回报更丰厚。武功最卓著的将军，其职位也低于一位翰林学士，翰林学士类似于英国的法学博士，或民法学博士。②

科举考试

授予读书人的学位头衔有四级。这些头衔不能与欧洲颁发的学位做精确比较，但大致可以分为以下几种：秀才，即"崭露头角的才之秀者"，通常被认为与英国的学士相当，但正如这个头衔所暗示的那样，它更像是儒生通过了第一次入学考试——童生试。即便是秀才这个头衔，拥有它的人在村里也很荣耀，其父也会获得一个相当于"秀才之父"的称号。秀才头衔还使他免受地方官用刑的惩罚，在中国这样一个罪过不论大小都要实施杖刑的国家，这可是一个不小的特权。童生试是在京城外的各地城镇举行。下一级学位称举人，是

can rise to the highest rank and greatest power under the Emperor.

Highest Reward in the Civil Service

China is the only country in the world in which the titles of honour for the peaceful pursuit of learning are higher and more lucrative than those conferred on warriors or priests. The most successful General takes a lower place than a scholar who bears a degree of Han Lin, similar to that of our LL.D. or D.C.L.

Examination for Office

There are four degrees conferred on scholars. They cannot be accurately compared with those given in Europe, but roughly they may be classed thus: Siu tsai, or "budding scholar," which is generally said to correspond to our B.A., but is much more like the matriculation of a youth who has passed his first examination, as the title seems to imply. Even this degree confers on its owner much distinction in his village, and confers a title on his father equivalent to that of "father of a siu tsai." It also exempts the bearer of the title from being sentenced to be beaten by the magistrate, no mean privilege in a country where all kinds of faults are punished by strokes of the bamboo. The examination takes place in provincial towns all over the country. The second is held in the capital of each of the eighteen provinces on the same days, and those who pass are called ku jin, or "promoted men," corresponding to our B.A. degree. The third title, tsin sz, or "entered scholar," is conferred by examination in the capital, and resembles our degree of M.A. The final examination entitles the successful candidate to the coveted distinction of Han Lin and membership of the Imperial Academy, with a certain allowance until he obtains an official appointment.

Talent Only Encouraged

This kind of encouragement of learning has no tendency to promote general education; it rather tends to discourage it. It is only the more promising students who have any chance of rising high enough to profit much by study, and the poor are tempted to spend all their money in the education of one member of the family or village clan in hope of his being able to confer both honours and fortune on those who have assisted him to rise. It reminds one of the ambition of Scotch families of the humbler order to have one son educated for the Church…

Doubtful Results

The theory of the Chinese Government is good, in so

在内地十八省省城于同一日举行的正式科举考试——乡试中考取的"荐举之人",与英国的文学士相当。第三级头衔为进士,是举人在京城通过会试后授予的,相当于英国的文学硕士。科举考试的最后一级是殿试,高中者可入梦寐以求的翰林院供职,以及成为国子监的一员,享受国家给予的一定津贴,直到他正式获得官职。

鼓励读书

科举制度鼓励读书,但并无促进通识教育的倾向;相反,更倾向于妨碍它。唯更有出息的读书人才有机会飞黄腾达,通过寒窗苦读升官发财,连贫寒之人也被诱惑着把他们所有的钱花在家中或家族的某个成员的教育上,希望读书之人能够帮助他出人头地。这让人想起苏格兰较卑微阶层家庭的抱负,即希望有一个儿子受教育成为牧师。

结果难料

理论上中国政府的科举制度是好的,因为其目的是让国家最有能力的人担任立法和行政职务，但像许多好的理论一样，很不幸它没有取得实际效果。最有能力的人不一定是那些通过最高级笔试的人，科举制度的教育和考试模式不可能产生最高的智力成果以及担任高官所需的最优良的道德品质。科举教育是一个耗时费力的体系，完全基于孔子传下来的一套古代典籍，用过时和无用的知识进行填鸭式学习。最有把握考取功名的人是那些将四书五经铭记在心，并能在文章中随心所欲加以引用的人。如果他学习并引用尧、舜的话语，他一定会考中。尧、舜是4000年前最好的统治者，但还达不到19世纪的要求。总的来说，科举制度有裨益，这一点不容置疑，尤其是与东方的普遍做法相比。在东方，得宠的小人居高位，君王身边围绕着无知的寄生虫，这些寄生虫往往通过怂恿主子作恶而掌权。在中国，皇帝永远不能让一个太监或一个受宠的侍从或剃头匠成为他的宰相，甚至当议政会议成员也不行。

文字起源

如今形态如此复杂、词义如此难揣测

far as it aims at getting the ablest men of the country for the posts of legislation and administration, but, like many good theories, it sadly fails in the practical results. The best men are not necessarily those who pass the highest in a written examination, and this kind of education and examination is not likely to produce the highest development of the intellect, and the best moral qualities for high office. The education is a laborious system of cramming with obsolete and useless learning, entirely based on the one set of ancient books handed down by Confucius. The man who is surest to get a degree is the man who has committed the four sacred books and the five classics to memory, and can most readily quote them in his essays. He is sure to succeed if he learns and quotes Yao and Shun, who were the best of rulers 4000 years ago, but not up to the requirements of the nineteenth century. But that the system has been, on the whole, beneficial cannot be doubted, especially if compared with the common practice in the East, where unworthy favorites are often put in places of highest trust, and rulers surround themselves with ignorant parasites, who too often rise to power by encouraging the vices of their masters. A Chinese Emperor could never make a eunuch or a favourite page or barber his Prime Minister, or even a member of his Council.

Origins of Letters

The form of Chinese letters, now so complex

and arbitrary, seems to have been originally representative of natural objects, as will be seen from the following specimen taken from Dr. Morrison's "Miscellany." The symbols are said to have been invented by Tseng-hi 2800 years before Christ:

1. The sun. 2. The sun rising—the morning. 3. The moon. 4. The light of sun and moon united; hence, morning, splendid, bright. 5. Sun and moon rising and setting, meaning to alternate; alternation, exchange. 6. The moon half seen, or evening. 7. Two evenings, or frequent occurrence; often, many. 8. Stars. 9. Clouds. 10. The symbol for flame repeated; a blaze, luminous, glorious. 11 and 11a. A human being. 12. Human being upside down; to change the state of, to transform, to convert. 13. Man with his arms and legs spread out; hence, large, great. 14. Man with head hanging on one side; mummy, weak, delicate. 15. Symbol for horned cattle of all kinds. 16. The breath issuing from the mouth of a cow; hence, to blow, to bellow, to advance, to encroach. 17. A house with three human beings within it, or a family. 18. Three united in one, or a triad. 19. One uniting three; he who rules others, a king. This etymology is attributed to Confucius, kings being in his eyes a bond of union.

的汉字，似乎最初是用来表征自然界之物，从下面摘自马礼逊③博士的《中国杂记》④中的19个汉字中可见一斑。汉字据说是在公元前2800年由仓颉创造的。

1.日：太阳。2.旦：日出地平线，指早晨。3.月：月亮。4.明：日月之光交相辉映，由此引申出早晨、灿烂、明亮。5.冒：日升月落，寓意交替、变换、交换。6.夕：月亮仅见一半，指傍晚。7.多：两个夕字，指频发，寓意故而、经常、许多。8.品：像是星星，言极多。9.云：云彩。10.炎：形从"火"上加"火"，指火焰，发光，光辉。11、11a.人。12.匕：人字上下颠倒过来，指改变的状态，转换，转变。⑤13.大：四肢伸展之人，由此引申为大、伟大。14.夭：人将头弯曲垂在一侧，指干尸，虚弱，脆弱。15.牛：象征各种有角的牛。16.牟：其音如气由牛口而出，牛鸣也，由此引申为牛吼，咆哮，牟求，攫取。17.家：三人居于屋内，指一个家庭。18.三：天地人之道合而为一，或凡三之属。19.王：一竖上下，贯通三才，指一国之王。"王"字的词源解释源于孔子，在其眼中君王是联结的纽带。

101

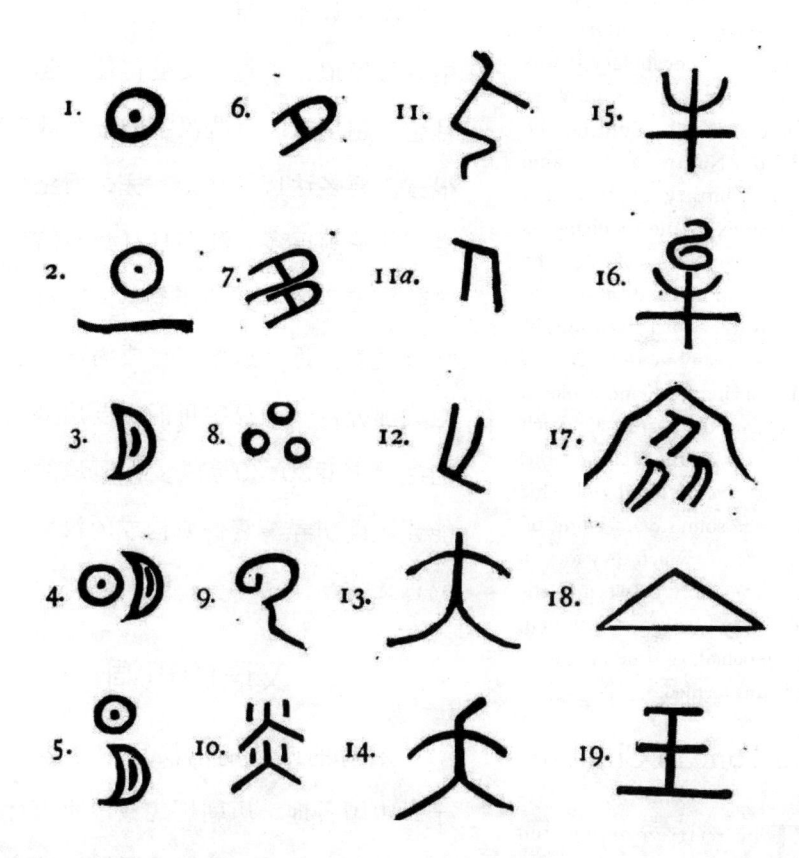

第五章　教育和文学　　　　　　　　　　　　　　　　Chapter V　Education and Literature

Complex and Inconvenient

The form of these symbols soon got changed to suit the convenience of writers; and to enlarge their vocabulary it was needful to increase the number of symbols, which could not be copied from Nature, and became altogether arbitrary, and more and more complex. Some requiring as many as seventeen strokes of the pencil to form one radical or root of a word, the word itself might have a great many more...The 214 radicals, varying from one stroke to seventeen, are the nearest approach to our letters of the alphabet. But even these give no intelligible clue to either the sound or meaning of the character of which they form a part, with possibly between twenty and thirty strokes of the pen, or rather pencil, of fine hair with which it was formed.

The Tone in Chinese

The written or printed character has the great advantage of being understood by all scholars over the length and breadth of China, with its many millions; but if read aloud it needs to be rendered in the vernacular of a great number of districts, which

复杂且不便

这些汉字符号的字形不久就被改进了,以便于书写;为了扩大词汇量,有必要增加汉字数量,而这些汉字无法从自然界中象形模拟,于是字义变得任意起来,而且越来越复杂。有些汉字的一个部首或字根就需要多达17笔才能写完,而整个字本身可能笔画更多。汉字有214个部首,从1笔到17笔不等,其功能与英文字母表中的字母最为接近。这些部首成为汉字的一个组成部分,一个汉字可能需要用毫毛制作的毛笔书写20~30笔之多,但是部首并不能让人确切弄清它们所构成的汉字的读音或意义。

汉语的声调

书写的或印刷的汉字的巨大优势在于,中国各地、历朝历代数以百万计的读书人都能读懂它;尽管不同地区的方言彼此不通,但是各地读书人只要看书页就能读懂同一本书,不过如果朗读出来,就需要用不同地区的方言来发声。因此,他们不仅有不同地区的白话，而且每个字词有不同的声调，或高或低，或升或降，或音调延长。不注意声调的话，即使字词的发音正确，也可能导致大错，表达的意思与本意刚好相反，或者荒谬无稽，以至最严肃场合的听众也忍不住捧腹大笑。例如，"zhu"读三声时是"领主"的意思，读一声时是"猪"的意思，所以一个外国人可能自以为说的是"一个高贵的领主"，但如果声调搞错，他可能会说成"一头高贵的猪"。"tang"读一声时意思是"汤"，读二声时意思是"糖"。我们认识的一位传教士对声调不太在意，随意地告诉他的厨子"买只鸡做汤"；但是他用错了声调，实际上告诉厨子的是"买只鸡做糖"。这位淳朴的或者是好恶作剧的厨子便去问另一位传教士，求证他们美国人是否有办法用鸡制作出糖来。

据说中国有上百种白话或方言，许多地方彼此差异不是很大，还不至于完全听不懂，但也有一些地区的本地人听不懂其他地区的日常白话。

cannot understand each other's spoken language, though the scholars in all of them could understand the same book by looking on the page. Not only must they give the spoken words of each district, but the tone of each word, high or low, rising, falling, or circumflex. The neglect of these tones, even when the words are otherwise correctly sounded, may cause the greatest mistakes, giving a meaning the very opposite of what was intended, or a sense so ridiculous that the listeners to the gravest discourse cannot help bursting into fits of laughter. For example, the word chu in one tone means a lord, in another tone it means a pig, so that a stranger may be, as he thinks, speaking of a noble lord, but by using the wrong tone he may call him a noble pig… The word tung in one tone means soup, and in another tone it means sugar. An honoured missionary of our acquaintance, who was careless of his tone, told his cook, as he thought, to buy a fowl and make soup; but, using the wrong tone, he really told him to buy a fowl and make sugar. The simple or waggish cook went and asked another missionary if they had a way of making sugar out of fowls in America.

There are said to be a hundred vernacular languages or local dialects in China, in which the natives of one district cannot understand the spoken language of the others, besides many more in which the differences are not so great as to be quite unintelligible.

第五章　教育和文学　　　　　　　　　　Chapter V　Education and Literature

Written and Spoken Language

The change of the written character into the spoken language is also perplexing, and far from easy even to the natives. It may be illustrated by the first four words in the first verse of John's Gospel in the Amoy vernacular, taking the Roman letters for both.

The written characters would be, Goan si eu To (In the beginning was the Word). The spoken language would be, "Khi thau u To li." Both would have the same meaning. The former would only be understood by a scholar; the second would be understood by all. Many who acquire sufficient instruction to enable them to carry on business and keep accounts never learn enough to read a book, far less to understand it. As for the women of China, not one in tens of thousands is ever taught the simplest elements of their language. It is computed that there are not more than 12000000 or 15000000 of its 400000000 who can read so as to understand an ordinary work… One great evil resulting from this difficulty in acquiring the language is, that the man who does become a scholar is regarded as a prodigy, and acquires an influence far beyond his moral and intellectual merits. The literati are the despots of China, and are the chief sources of opposition to new, and above all foreign, improvements, which would be fatal

书面语与口语

书面语向口语的转化也是一件复杂之事，即便对本地人来说也绝非易事。

这可以从厦门白话版《约翰福音》第一节的前四个字来说明，书面语和口语两个语体都用的是罗马字母。

其书面语是"Goan si eu To"（元始有道），口语则为"Khi thau u To li"（起头有道理）。两者含义相同。书面语体只有读书人才能理解，口语体所有人都能懂得。许多人获得足够用于经商和记账的教育，但他们学的知识却不足以阅读一整本书，更不用说理解它了。至于中国的妇女，不足万分之一的人被教过最简单的横竖撇捺。据计算，在其4亿人口中，能够读懂一部普通著作的人不超过1200万或1500万。汉语难学所造成的一大弊端是，一旦真的成为一个学者，他就会被当作奇才，获得的影响力远远超出了他道德和智慧可称道之处。文人是中国的专制者，也是反对新式的，尤其是外来的进步的主要力量，因为后者对他们的支配地位甚至生计来说都是致命的。

教育体制

通往精通汉语的道路上，学习文言文的困难并不是最大障碍。从教育一词的本义上讲，教育体制才是中国教育的巨大障碍。学童被要求连续多年修习汉字字形，却不解其意，这是一个极其令人沮丧和吃惊的学习过程。死记硬背确实加强了记忆力，但这是通过牺牲聪明才智来实现的，所以即使在学习的后期阶段，智力仍未得到开发。教育对思维能力的发展不做任何尝试，而思维能力的发展不仅是教育的伟大目标在词源上的，而且是在理性上的定义。强化记忆是好事，但在中国，获得它的代价太高了。上述困难导致民众中的大量文盲得不到教育。

经 典

中国古代文学是它最重要的荣耀，因为它古老悠久的书面记载超过了所有国家。最近在埃及古墓中发现的文献，以及从地底深处挖掘出的巴比伦图书馆的文献，年

The System of Education

The difficulty of acquiring a knowledge of the written character is not the worst obstacle in the way of becoming an intelligent reader of the Chinese language. The system of education is the great hindrance to education in the proper sense of the term. The pupil is required to go on learning the form of the characters for years without getting the slightest idea of their meaning—a most discouraging and stupefying process. It does strengthen the memory, but it is by the sacrifice of the intellectual powers, which are not developed even at the later stages of study. There is no attempt at drawing out the faculties of the mind, which is not only the etymological, but the rational, definition of the great object of education. The strengthening of memory is good, but in China it is purchased at too great a price. These difficulties result in the great mass of the people being uneducated.

The Sacred Books

The ancient literature of China is its chief glory; ... antiquity of written documents it excels that of all lands. Literature recently discovered in Egyptian tombs, and in Babylonian libraries dug up from the bowels of the earth, may be a little older, but that of China has continued to this day the living language of a great empire.

The sacred books of the Chinese have been a moral power in the formation of the character of the people... in the purity of thought and morality of their teaching no heathen books can be for a moment compared with them. Dr. James Legge, the highest authority on the character of the sacred books of China, which he has translated from the first to the last, told the writer that there was not an expression in any of these books which he would be ashamed to read aloud in the presence of his daughters—the strongest expression which a stanch old Puritan could use.

Genuine and Authentic

The genuineness and authenticity of these old records of the past, as collected by Confucius in the sixth century before Christ, are now placed beyond doubt. They have undergone the severest scrutiny from critics of all kinds...They have had their enemies. They were at one time almost entirely destroyed by the Emperor Chi, 200 years before Christ; every copy that could be found was burned, and the learned men who had committed them to memory were all destroyed, that

代上可能更久远一点，但中国文学延续至今，依然是中华帝国的活语言。

中国人的经典是促使民族性格形成的道德力量，就教化之思想与道德的纯洁性而言，没有任何一本世俗之书能与其相提并论。理雅各博士是研究中国经典特征的最高权威，他从第一本翻译到最后一本。他告诉笔者，在这些书中，没有一句他会羞于当着他女儿们的面大声朗读出来的——这是一个坚定老派的清教徒所能使用的最强烈的赞誉之辞。

原汁原味

这些昔日的古老记载是由孔子在公元前6世纪汇编的，原汁原味，不容置疑。它们经历了各色批评家最严苛的考辨。经典也有敌人。公元前200年⑥，经典曾一度差点被始皇帝彻底摧毁；所有能找到的抄本都被烧掉，那些将经典铭记于心的儒生都被坑杀，以便他们心中牢记不灭的记载随之一同埋进坟墓。这位暴君死后，人们尽一切努力来恢复先秦古籍，一位年老失明的博士——伏生⑦，因隐匿他乡而逃过坑杀迫害，凭着记忆口述，由专门指定的人员——晁错⑧记录下来，内容极其忠实，即《今文尚书》。尔后，曲阜孔府一座旧屋拆除时，墙壁中发现了一套完整的抄本，即《古文尚书》，人们将其与伏生的口述本进行了比照。这两个版本类似于我们现在所说的《圣经》的校订本，构成今古文经两派批评的基础，直到学者郑玄⑨博采各家之长，就两个版本中的微小差异达成妥协，今古文经之争在形式上方得平息。

四书五经

四书五经组成了中国的经典，我们不能对其一一进行分析，那样会占用太多篇幅。可以说，四书五经并不是那种主要阐述宗教或天国主题意义上的神圣之经。它们确实包含对神祇主题的提及，而且态度既不是不可知论，也不是怀疑论；但是孔子关于鬼神的观点模糊不清，他觉得他没有使命去教导人们他自己都不确切知道的东西。关于这些孔子看来十分重要的问题，他忠实地记录了古人的看法，并怀着崇敬之情叙述，正如下文对中国宗教的讨论所

the imperishable record of them in their hearts might be buried in their graves. After the death of this despot every effort was made to restore them, and one blind old scholar, who, from his obscurity, had escaped persecution, was able to repeat the whole from memory, to scribes appointed for the purpose, with wonderful fidelity. At a later time, on pulling down an old house, a complete copy was found, and compared with that taken down from the lips of the scholar. These resembled what we now call recensions of the Scriptures, and were the foundation of two schools of critics, until the common-sense of Chinese scholarship led to a compromise on the small discrepancies in the two sets of manuscripts.

The Four Books and Five Classics

We cannot give an analysis of the four books and five classics which constitute the sacred literature of China—it would occupy too much of our space. We may say it is not sacred in the sense of being chiefly taken up with religious or heavenly themes. They do contain references to sacred subjects, and are neither agnostic nor sceptical; but the views of Confucius about the invisible and eternal were vague and uncertain, and he felt that he had no mission to teach men about what he did not himself know definitely or certainly. He faithfully recorded what the ancients believed on these matters, of which he felt the importance, and writes with reverence, as we shall show when we treat of the religions of China; but he felt that his mission was to teach the people how to live in this world, and to teach their kings and statesmen how to rule, so as to promote peace, righteousness, and prosperity by imitating the ancient rulers of the country.

Their Great Influence

Confucius fulfilled his mission with fearless fidelity and unflagging zeal, and...exerted so deep and lasting an influence on so large a portion of the human race. That the influence has been on the whole beneficial to China, the unparalleled duration of so large an empire, and the general prosperity and welfare of the people, are the best proof. The Empires of Babylon and Egypt, which started in the race of civilization about the same time with that of China, perished before half the period of Chinese history had run its course. The Greek and Roman Empires, which began to flourish a thousand or fifteen hundred years later, have disappeared, while China remains the largest empire in the world under her old laws and primitive constitution.

Influence of Confucius

That the Chinese are right in attributing their dura-

展示的那般；不过，他觉得他的使命是教人们如何活在现世，教国君和大臣如何治国，以及通过效仿古代贤君以促进和平、公正和繁荣。

巨大的影响

孔子以无畏的忠诚和不倦的热情完成了他的使命，并给如此多的人民带来过如此深刻与持久的影响。最好的明证是孔子的影响总体上来说对中国有益，对庞大若此的帝国，其影响持续时间之长无与伦比，带给人民普遍的繁荣和福祉。古巴比伦和古埃及，在文明初肇的赛跑中与中国不相上下，但前两者在中国历史还没走到一半之时就消亡了。古希腊与古罗马在一千年或一千五百年后开始兴盛，现在却已经消失了，而中国仍然是世界上最大的帝国，保留着它古老的法律和最初的准则。

孔子的影响

毫无疑问，中国人把帝国的持久与繁荣归功于孔子，因为他是中国古代经典的整理者和阐释者。中国常言说："自有生民以来，未有孔子也"，"孔子之后，一无孔子"。中国人把对孔子的记忆包裹上神性光环，并以仅次于最高神昊天上帝的荣誉——至圣先师加以祭拜。他们对孔圣人的描述过于夸张，使得他的相貌在外国人眼中显得滑稽古怪，不过仍然让人觉得他是一个地道的中国人，这一事实在很大程度上解释了他对同胞的强大影响力之谜。他们甚至说孔圣人之面庞是中国地图。以下是马礼逊博士从权威的《康熙字典》中摘录的关于孔圣人的描述，绝无夸大谄媚之词：

孔子的长相

夫子之脸庞现华夏微缩之五岳四渎。高额头、突下巴、（两个）高颧骨、鹰钩鼻，代表五岳。嘴巴合不拢，牙齿外露；鼻子扭曲，鼻孔外翻；目光清澈，瞳孔凸出；大耳垂肩，引人注目，象征四条大河。身材高大，据说身高九尺六寸，双手垂下过膝。眉毛呈十二色，眼睛里流露出六十四种智

tion and prosperity to Confucius as a collator and expounder of the ancient classics of China there can be no doubt. They have a common saying, "There is no one like Confucius; before Confucius there never was a Confucius; since Confucius there has never been a Confucius." They have surrounded his memory with a halo of Divinity, and worship him with honours only inferior to that of the Supreme God. They give a description of the sage so exaggerated as to make him appear ridiculous in the eyes of foreigners, but impress one with the idea that he was a thorough Chinaman, a fact which to a large extent explains the secret of his influence on his countrymen. They go so far as to say that his face was a map of China. The following is the description of the sage, by no means flattering, taken by Dr. Morrison from the high authority, Kanghi's dictionary:

Description of Confucius

His face showed in miniature the five mountains and the four great rivers. He had a high forehead, a protruding chin, two high cheekbones, and high aquiline nose to represent the five mountains. His mouth stood open and showed his teeth. His nose was contorted so as to exhibit his nostrils. His eyes exhibited a protruding pupil, and his ears were so large as to attract notice, in this resembling the four great rivers. He was very tall, some say 9 1/2 cubits in height, and his hands hung down below his knees. His eyebrows exhibited twelve shades of colour, and from his eyes beamed sixty-four intelligences. He stood like the Fung-bird perched, and he sat like Long-tsun the dragon couchant. The highest excellences of the greatest sages of China were found in Confucius. He had the forehead of Yao and the back of Tao, and so of all the virtues of previous monarchs and great men who had shone in Chinese history.

Previous to the birth of the sage, the sacred Lin bird discharged from its stomach precious writing containing the following inscription: "A son, the pure essence of water; a successor of the fallen fortunes of Chow; a plain-robed King; one who shall rule without ever ascending a throne." On the evening of his birth two dragons wound around the house, heavenly music sounded in the ear of his mother, and when he was born an inscription appeared on his breast with these words: "The maker of a rule for settling the world." Whatever we may say of these extravagant expressions, written long after the sage had died a poor and neglected man, they show the high estimation in which this favourite of the empire has been held for 2000 years.

The "Shoo King," or History

The "Book of Records," or history, of which only fifty-eight out of a hundred sections have been preserved, is obscure from its great antiquity and incom-

慧。夫子站若凤鸟栖息，坐似虎踞龙盘。中国最伟大先贤的最突出优点都集中于孔子一身之上。他有尧之额头和皋陶之背，以及闪耀在中国历史中前代君主和伟人的所有美德。

孔圣人出生前，祥云缭绕的送子麒麟嘴吐玉书一件，上书如下文字："水精之子，继衰周而素王。"他出生那天晚上，两条苍龙绕在房子四周之上，钧天之乐在其母亲的耳中鸣响，而当孔子出生之时，其胸上显现文字："制作定世符运。"无论我们如何看待，这些溢美之词皆写于孔圣人逝去很久以后，而他离世之时穷困潦倒。这些赞美是对中华帝国尊崇两千余年的孔子的高度评价。

《尚书》

《尚书》原有100篇，现仅存58篇⑩，因其写作和编辑年代久远且篇目不齐，晦涩难懂。它以德治为核心，正如公元前2356年的尧舜及其继任者夏朝的统治者所展现的那样。德治的原则有四：美德、仁爱、庄重、真诚。这些内在的美德用他们简洁的方式来说，则是："得道则心治，失道则心乱。"尧帝身上就有体现这些美德的例子。以下是尧帝的教诲："美德、人民、领地、财货，是统治者必须关注的天道顺序，如此，昊天上帝首肯。如果顺序颠倒，将财货放在第一位、把美德放在最后，本末倒置，那么君主就会民心尽失，支持其统治的天意就会收回，还会导致上帝不悦，另择君主授予。"

起义的权利

说来也怪，这本上古之书堂而皇之地声称推翻昏庸无德之君确系天经地义，但两千多年来不仅受到民众，而且受到历朝历代帝王如此尊崇。《尚书》断言"天意即民心"，以西方谚语的方式来表达，即"民之声即神之声"。成汤发布伐夏檄文《汤誓》，起兵反叛，并推翻了残暴的夏桀，大业襄助者也受到高度赞扬。武王也因反抗前朝君主商纣王而为人所知。商汤和武王都创建了新王朝。

pleteness. It places the principles of good government in the heart, as illustrated in the lives of Yao and Shun, and their successors in the first dynasty, beginning 2356 B.C. The principles of government are four: Virtue, benevolence, gravity, sincerity. These virtues of the heart, they say, in their laconic style, "Preserved, then order; lost, then anarchy." Examples are given of these virtues in the Emperor Yao. The following is in an illustration of his teaching: "Virtue, the people, territory, revenue, is the order in which rulers are required to devote their attention to the order of Nature, which Heaven will approve, and Shang Ti (the Supreme Ruler) will regard with complacency. If this order be reversed, and revenue be made the first and virtue the last, then the people's hearts will be lost, Heaven's decree in favour of the existing ruler will be forfeited, Shang Ti's displeasure will be incurred, and the throne be given to another."

The Right of Insurrection

Strange to say, in a book held in such high honour, not only by the people, but by the Emperors of every dynasty for more than 2000 years, the right of insurrection against a bad ruler is openly declared as a law of Heaven. It is asserted that "the people's hearts and Heaven's decree are the same," the form of the Western saying, Vox populi, vox Dei. The oaths of the conspirators under the usurper Tang, who rose against and deposed the cruel tyrant Ki, are given, and the conspirator is highly praised. Wu Wang is also celebrated for rebelling against his former Sovereign, and both Tang and Wu were founders of dynasties.

The Character of Yu

The following is a description of the Emperor Yu, who ascended the throne in 2200 B.C.: "He condescended to his Ministers with easy grace; he ruled the country with generous forbearance; his punishments were limited to the criminals, and were not inflicted on their children, but his rewards were transmitted to future generations; he pardoned inadvertent faults, however great, but punished deliberate crime, however small. In cases of doubtful crimes, he dealt with them lightly, but of doubtful merit he showed the highest esteem. Rather than put to death the guiltless, he ran the risk of irregularity and laxity." Such wise and beneficent rule cannot be paralleled in the history of any other country in that early period of the world's history.

The "Shii King," or Book of Odes

The "Shi King," or "Book of Odes," is a collection of the best of the songs and poetry of different kinds illustrative of the life of the ancients. Confucius attached great importance to them, and urged kings and statesmen to study them, that they might know the habits and feelings of the people and rulers of olden times. He seems to have anticipated the familiar saying, "Give me the mak-

禹的品德

以下是对公元前2200年登上王位的禹帝的描述:"帝德罔愆,临下以简,御众以宽;罚弗及嗣,赏延于世。宥过无大,刑故无小;罪疑惟轻,功疑惟重;与其杀不辜,宁失不经。"⑪于历史早期,与他国相较,此等智慧、仁慈之治一时无两。

《诗经》

《诗经》是一部关于古人生活的歌谣、乐歌、诗赋总集。孔子非常重视《诗经》,并敦促各国君臣学习,以便了解古时劳动人民和统治阶级的风俗习惯与思想感情。他似乎早预料到那句熟语:"让我来写民族之歌,歌在民族在,管它谁来立法。"⑫理雅各博士不仅将《诗经》翻译成散文,而且在朋友的帮助下,还把它们译成朗朗上口的韵文。最精华的一些诗歌还用地道的苏格兰方言翻译。

《诗经》的内容涵盖对政治人物或褒或贬的描述,对名人的含蓄谴责,歌颂爱情,远方戍边的征夫之怨,偶尔对自然的描述,以及对许多主题的真性情流露。《诗经》所教尽皆纯洁道德，而且正如孔子所言，为正确阅读诗三百篇，需要"思无邪"，即"心思纯正"。彼时亦有诸多淫佚之歌，但编订《诗经》时，孔子都严格地将其剔除在外。在孔子看来，若不能陶冶情操，诗歌则毫无价值。

诗的概念

马礼逊博士提供了中国人关于诗歌的定义：

> 诗者，志之所之也，在心为志，发言为诗，情动于中而形于言。言之不足，故嗟叹之。嗟叹之不足，故永歌之，永歌之不足，不知手之舞之，足之蹈之也。……故正得失，动天地，感鬼神，莫近于诗。⑬

诗歌示例

我们举几首诗作为例子，皆出自公元前500年孔子编订的版本。其中一些诗采自西周，年代比孔子还早1500年或2000年。我们引用的通行版本由理雅各博士及

ing of the songs of a people, and I will leave others to make their laws." Dr. Legge has not only made a translation in prose, but, with the assistance of friends, has turned them into poetic and most readable form. Some of the most interesting are rendered in good broad Scotch.

The book contains descriptions of political characters, both laudatory and satirical, veiled censure on eminent persons, many love-songs, the complaints of soldiers serving on distant frontiers, occasional delineations of nature, and the outpouring of the feelings on many subjects. None are immoral in their teaching, and, as Confucius said, for the right perusal of the 300 odes contained in the book it was needful to have "thought not depraved," the Chinese expression for "purity of heart." There were many vicious songs of the same period, but Confucius sternly excluded them all. Poetical merit, unaccompanied by moral worth, was of no value in his estimation.

Notions of Poetry

The notions of the Chinese about poetry are thus given by Dr. Morrison:

Human feelings, when excited in the breast, become embodied in words. When words fail to express them, sighs, or inarticulate tones of admiration and other sentiments, succeed. When these sighs and aspirations are inadequate to do justice to feeling, then recourse is had to song, and when the song or hymn is still found insufficient, man naturally expresses the intensity of his feelings by the action of his hands and the motion of his feet, or, as the Chinese language expresses it, he "hands it, gesticulates it, foots it, stamps it. ...Poetry, more than anything else, moves heaven and earth, and agitates demons and gods."

Specimens of Poetry

We give a few verses as examples, all from Confucius' edition of the classics, 500 B.C. Some of them are 1500 or 2000 years before even that early date. We quote from the popular edition which Dr. Legge and his friends have turned into very literal verse.

The following is a covert allusion to King Wan's choice of the humblest to be his Ministers, if only virtuous and able—two of them were said to have been rabbit-catchers—written between 1184 and 1076 B.C.

Carefully he sets his rabbit-nets all round:
Chang-Chung his blows upon the pegs resound.
Stalwart the man and bold! His bearing all
Shows he might be his Prince's shield and wall.

War comes in for celebration. Here is a description of an officer of Ch'ing about 800 B.C.:

1.
How glossy is the lambkin's fur,
Smooth to the touch and fair to view!
In it arrayed, that officer
Rests in his lot to virtue true.

* * * * *

其朋友翻译。

以下这首诗作于公元前1184—前1076年间,暗用周文王唯贤是举、任用最卑微出身之人为大臣的典故,其中两人据说系捕兔之人⑭:

肃肃兔罝（兔网结得紧又密）,
椓之丁丁（布网打桩声声碎）。
赳赳武夫（武士气概雄赳赳）,
公侯干城（是那公侯好护卫）。

在《诗经》中,战争得到颂扬。以下是对大约公元前800年的一位郑国军官的描述⑮:

1.
羔裘如濡（身着光泽羔皮袄）,
洵直且侯（为人正直又美好）。
彼其之子（他这样一个人啊）,
舍命不渝（舍生取义守节操）。

3.
羔裘晏兮（羔羊皮袄真光鲜）,
三英粲兮（豹皮袖口更灿烂）。
彼其之子（他这样一个人啊）,
邦之彦兮（安邦治国之人选）。

《诗经》频繁提及家庭关系,夫妻间的

绵绵情意是诗歌的常见主题。下面的诗歌刻画的是丈夫们出发去从军时的无助之感[16]:

1.

击鼓其镗（战鼓擂得震天响），
踊跃用兵（士卒腾跃练刀枪）！
土国城漕（国人挑土修城壕），
我独南行（我独南行赴沙场）。

2.

从孙子仲（跟随主将孙子仲），
平陈与宋（约定联合陈与宋）。
不我以归（不知何日可还乡），
忧心有忡（忧愁痛苦心里慌）。

4.

死生契阔（同生共死在一起），
与子成说（你我誓言立心里）。
执子之手（执子之手共盟誓），
与子偕老（与子偕老不分离）。

5.

于嗟阔兮（可叹从军运多舛），
不我活兮（夫妻团圆难上难）。
于嗟洵兮（可叹山盟成空谈），
不我信兮（还乡无期再见难）。

以上见《诗经》第82页。

3.
Splendid his robe of lambkin's fur,
With its three decorations grand:
It well becomes that officer,
The pride and glory of our land.

Domestic ties are not infrequently referred to, and the mutual affection of husband and wife is often a subject of song. The following is a picture of the feelings of husbands on setting out on a desperate campaign:

1.
List to the thunder and roll of the drum;
See how we spring and brandish the dart!
Some raise Tsaou's walls, some do field work at home;
But we to the southward lonely depart.

2.
Our chief, Sun Tsze-Chung, agreement has made
Our forces to join with Chin and with Sung.
When shall we back from this service be led?
Our hearts are all sad, and our courage unstrung.

* * * * *

4.
For death as for life, at home or abroad,
We pledged to our wives our faithfullest word;
Their hands clasped in ours, together we vowed

We'd live to old age in sweetest accord.

5.
This march to the south can end but in ill.
Oh ! never again shall we our wives meet.
The word that we pledged we cannot fulfil;
Us home-returning they never will greet.

Shi King, p. 82.

A Wife deplores her Husband's Absence:

1.
Away the startled pheasant flies,
With lazy movement of his wings.
Borne was my husband from my eyes;
What pain the separation brings!

2.
The pheasant, though no more in view,
His cry above, below, forth sends.
Alas ! my princely lord, 'tis you—
Your absence—that my bosom rend?

3.
At sun and moon I sit and gaze,
In converse with my troubled heart.
Far, far from me my husband stays;
When will he come to heal its smart?

下面这首诗歌是一个妻子在哀叹丈夫的离去⑰：

1.

　　雄雉于飞（雄野鸡飞向远方），
　　泄泄其羽（缓缓扇动花翅膀）。
　　我之怀矣（我心怀念远行人），
　　自诒伊阻（阻隔独自守空房）！

2.

　　雄雉于飞（雄野鸡飞向远方），
　　下上其音（上下左右啼欢唱）。
　　展矣君子（诚实可爱的人啊），
　　实劳我心（思念悲苦我心房）。

3.

　　瞻彼日月（凝望太阳和月亮），
　　悠悠我思（思念悠悠天地长）。
　　道之云远（路途漫漫多遥远），
　　曷云能来（何时还乡诉衷肠）？

4.

　　百尔君子（君子老爷多又多），
　　不知德行（不知德行是什么）。
　　不忮不求（郎不害人不贪婪），
　　何用不臧（为何没有好结果）？

以上见《诗经》第83页。

一队省级驻军
A Sample of a Provincial Army

第五章　教育和文学　　　　　　　　　　Chapter V　Education and Literature

4.
Ye princely men who with him mate,
Say, mark ye not his virtuous way?
His rule is, Covet naught, none hate;
How can his step from goodness stray?
Shi King, p. 83.

The evils of polygamy come out in the following wail over her husband's preference for his second wife:

1.
Fierce is the wind and cold;
And such is he.
Smiling he looks, and, bold,
Speaks mockingly.

2.
As clouds of dust wind-blown,
Just such is he.
Ready he seems to own,
And come to me.
But he comes not nor goes,
Stands in his pride;
Long, long, with painful throes,
Grieved I abide.

3.
Strong blew the wind; the cloud
Hastened away;
Soon dark again, the shroud
Covers the day.
I wake, and sleep no more
Visits my eyes;
His course I, sad, deplore
With heavy sighs.

* * * * *

一夫多妻制的罪恶体现在下面一位女子哭述她丈夫对第二位妻子的偏爱上[18]：

1.

终风且暴（狂风迅疾夹寒潮），
顾我则笑（见我他就嘻嘻笑）。
谑浪笑敖（嬉笑放浪无正形），
中心是悼（让我心里真烦恼）。

2.

终风且霾（狂风席卷扬尘埃），
惠然肯来（是否他肯顺心来）。
莫往莫来（来与不来都随他），
悠悠我思（思绪悠悠心不安）。

3.

终风且曀（狂风起时云飞扬），
不日有曀（风云变幻太无常）。
寤言不寐（辗转反侧难入睡），
愿言则嚏（伤风感冒思念勤）。

以上见《诗经》第81页。

以下是一首赞美一位年轻国君的诗歌[19]：

终南何有（终南山上何所有）？
有条有梅（茂盛山楸和梅树）。
君子至止（有位君子到此地），

　　　　锦衣狐裘（锦绣衣衫狐裘服）。

　　　　颜如渥丹（脸儿红润像涂丹），

　　　　其君也哉（莫非他是我君主）！

2.

　　　　终南何有（终南山上何所有）？

　　　　有纪有堂（有棱有角地宽敞）。

　　　　君子至止（有位君子到此地），

　　　　黻衣绣裳（青黑上衣五彩裳）。

　　　　佩玉将将（身上佩玉响叮当），

　　　　寿考不亡（富贵寿考莫相忘）！

以上见《诗经》第61页。

　　一个聪明的小伙子发现自己爱慕的姑娘于东门外护城河中浸麻，于是抒发了两人感情进展、情意相投的喜悦之情[20]：

1.

　　　　东门之池（东城门外护城河），

　　　　可以沤麻（可以浸麻可泡葛）。

　　　　彼美淑姬（温柔美丽三姑娘），

　　　　可与晤歌（与她相会又唱歌）。

2.

　　　　东门之池（东城门外护城河），

　　　　可以沤纻（泡浸纻麻许许多）。

　　　　彼美淑姬（温柔美丽三姑娘），

Ibid., p. 81.

A Loyal Ode to a Young Prince:

1.
What trees grow on the Chung-nan hill?
The white fir and the plum.
In fur of fox, 'neath broidered robe,
Thither our prince is come.
His face glows with vermilion hue;
Oh, may he prove a ruler true!

2.
What find we on the Chung-nan hill?
Deep nooks and open glade.
Our prince shows there the double ke
On lower robes displayed.
His pendant holds each tinkling gent.
Long life be his, and deathless fame!

Shi King, p. 61.

A judicious lover finds the adored one engaged in home industry, but adorned with many accomplishments:

1.
To steep your hemp you seek the moat,
Where lies the pool the gate beyond;
I seek that lady good and fair
Who can to me in song respond.

2.

To steep your grass-clock plants you seek

The pool that near the east gate lies.

I seek that lady good and fair

Who can with me hold converse wise.

3.

Out to the east gate, to the moat,

To steep your rope-rush you repair.

Her pleasant converse to enjoy,

I seek that lady good and fair.

Ibid., p. 169.

The lines which follow seem to show that the lady "good and fair" had failed to keep her appointment to meet him at the eastern gate, though the poor fellow waited from sunset to sunrise:

1.

Where grow the willows at the eastern gate,

And 'neath their leafy shade we could recline,

She said at evening she would me await,

And brightly now I see the day-star shine.

2.

Here where the willows near the eastern gate

Grow, and their dense leaves make a shady gloom,

She said at evening she would

可与晤语（与她交谈情相和）。

3.

东门之池（东城门外护城河），

可以沤菅（泡浸菅草一棵棵）。

彼美淑姬（温柔美丽三姑娘），

可与晤言（与她倾诉真快活）。

以上见《诗经》第169页。

下面的诗歌似乎表明，这位"善良美丽"的姑娘失约了，没有在东门约会地点出现，而可怜的小伙子从日落一直等到日出[21]：

1.

东门之杨（依偎东门杨柳旁），

其叶牂牂（浓密叶阴透斜阳）。

昏以为期（人约黄昏老地方），

明星煌煌（苦等佳人晨星亮）。

2.

东门之杨（东城门外杨柳边），

其叶肺肺（晚霞映红密叶间）。

昏以为期（人约黄昏来相见），

明星晢晢（苦等晨星照亮天）。

以上见《诗经》第169页。

《诗经》中提到神的地方很稀少，但有

几首是写"帝"（统治者，或上帝）或"天"（上天）的。这里列出几首[22]：

> 皇矣上帝（天帝伟大又辉煌），
> 临下有赫（俯视下界眼光明）。
> 监观四方（洞察四方得与失），
> 求民之莫（唯求百姓能安宁）。
> ……
> 上帝耆之（上帝降命在邰地），
> 憎其式廓（扩展疆域助经营）。
> 乃眷西顾（于是回头向西看），
> 此维与宅（同住岐山保周兴）。

以上见《诗经》第295页。

闹饥荒时，他们这样祈祷：

> 旻天疾威（老天暴虐难提防），
> 天笃降丧（接二连三降灾荒）。
> 瘨我饥馑（饥馑遍地灾情重），
> 民卒流亡（十室九空尽流亡）。
> 我居圉卒荒（国土荒芜生榛莽）。

以上见《诗经》第348页。

提及祭祀上帝的诗很少，但以下这首很有趣。正如理雅各博士所说，文王与上帝相连，因为正是通过他，周朝得到天佑。

me await—
See now the morning-star the sky illume!
Ibid., p. 169.

References to God are few and far between, but there are a few under the name of Ti (Ruler, or God) or Thien (Heaven). We give one or two verses:

Oh ! Great is God.
His glance on earth He bent,
Scanning our regions with severe intent
For one whose rule the people would content.

He found one T'ae.
When this wise chieftain God to Chow had given,
The Kwan hordes fled away, by terror driven,
And sons came from the wife T'ae got from heaven.
Shi King, p. 295.

In time of famine they prayed:
Oh, pitying Heaven, why see we
Thee In terror thus arrayed?
Famine has come.
The people flee,
And homeless roam, dismayed.
In settled spots, and far and near,
Our regions all lie waste and drear.
Ibid., p. 348.

References to sacrifice are rare,

but the following is interesting. King Wan is associated with God, as Dr. Legge says, because through him blessings were bestowed on Chow.

1.
My offerings here are given,
A ram, a bull.
Accept them, mighty Heaven,
All bountiful.
2.
Thy statutes, O great King,
I keep, I love,
So on the realm to bring
Peace from above.
3.
From Wan comes blessing rich;
Now on the right
He owns those gifts to which
Him I invite.
4.
Do I not night and day
Revere great Heaven,
That thus its favours may
To Chow be given?
Shi King, p. 354.

Although women are sometimes referred to in terms of disparagement, we find them occupying positions which imply the happiest relations to their husbands, and even assisting in acts of worship. The following, faithfully rendered in broad Scotch, reminds us of "Tak yer auld cloak about ye":

1.
我将我享（奉上祭品献神灵），
维羊维牛（祭品有牛还有羊），
维天其右之（祈求上天佑周邦）。

2.
仪式刑文王之典（效法文王之典章），
日靖四方（日日谋求安四方）。

3.
伊嘏文王（伟大文王英名扬），
既右飨之（配祀上帝祭品享）。

4.
我其夙夜（我们早晚勤努力），
畏天之威（遵循天道畏天威），
于时保之（才能保佑我周邦）。

以上见《诗经》第354页。

尽管提及妇女时，间或带有贬低，但我们发现妇女所处的地位暗含着与丈夫的美满关系，甚至可以在丈夫祭祀时打下手。下面的这首诗[23]忠实地用苏格兰方言翻译而成，其妙处让我们想起了苏格兰民谣《好老公，穿上你的旧披风，快快找牛去》[24]：

女曰鸡鸣（妻曰：公鸡已鸣唱），
士曰昧旦（夫曰：天还没有亮）。

子兴视夜（妻曰：不信推窗看天上），
明星有烂（启明星已在闪光）。
将翱将翔（宿巢鸟雀将翱翔），
弋凫与雁（射鸭射雁去芦荡）。
弋言加之（野鸭大雁射下来），
与子宜之（为你烹肴来品尝）。
……

思妇诗经常描写妻子哀叹丈夫不在，盼望其归来的哀婉之情。以下这首诗歌描述了公元前11世纪一个高级军官妻子的相思之苦㉕：

1.
喓喓草虫（草中蝈蝈叫），
趯趯阜螽（蚱蜢蹦蹦跳）。
未见君子（忆郎郎不至），
忧心忡忡（忧愁心刀绞）。
亦既见止（想想已见着），
亦既觏止（想想已相抱），
我心则降（心安唱歌谣）。

3.
陟彼南山（南山登高瞭），
言采其薇（说是采薇苗）。
未见君子（忆郎郎不至），

Says our gudewife, "The cock is crowing."
Quoth our gudeman, "The day is dawning."
"Get up, gudeman, and tak a spy;
See gin the mornin' star be high,
Syne tak'a saunter roon' aboot,
There's rowth o' dyukes and geese to shoot;
Lat flee and bring them hame to me,
An' sic' a dish as ye shall pree."
Etc., etc., etc.

The wife is often described as lamenting the absence of her husband, and longing for his return. The following describes the feeling of the wife of a high officer about the eleventh century before Christ:

1.
Still chirp the insects in the grass,
All about the hoppers spring:
While I my husband do not see,
Sorrow must my bosom wring.
Oh, to meet him!
Oh, to greet him!
Then my heart would rest and sing.

* * * * *

3.
Ascending high that southern hill,
Spinous ferns I sought to find:
While I my husband do not see,

Rankles sorrow in my mind.
Oh, to meet him！
Oh, to greet him！
In my heart would peace be shrined.

"Filial Affection":
Father, from whose loins I sprung,
Mother, on whose breast I hung,
Tender were ye, and ye fed,
Now upheld, now gently led.
Eyes untiring watched my way,
Often in your arms I lay.
How could I repay your love,
Vast as arch of heaven above?

"Trusting God in Dark Times":
Where the forest once grew, we look, and, behold！
Fagots only and twilight are left.
To Heaven, 'mdst their perils, the people all look,
And, lo! Heaven seems of reason bereft.
But is Heaven so dark? When its purpose is fixed,
To its will opposition is vain,
And good is the rule, supreme the great God:
He hates none of the children of men?

我心伤悲（伤悲似蛇咬）。
亦既见止（想想已见着），
亦既觏止（想想已相抱），
我心则夷（我心平静了）。

《诗经·小雅·蓼莪》：
父兮生我（父母啊，你们生下了我），
母兮鞠我（父母啊，你们养育了我）。
抚我畜我（你们护我疼爱我），
长我育我（养我长大培育我），
顾我复我（想我不愿离开我），
出入腹我（出入家门怀抱我）。
欲报之德（想报父母大恩德）。
昊天罔极（怎知老天降灾祸）！

《诗经·大雅·桑柔》：
菀彼桑柔（茂密柔嫩青青桑），
其下侯旬（下有浓荫好地方）。
捋采其刘（桑叶采尽枝秃光），
瘼此下民（百姓受害难遮凉）。
不殄心忧（愁思不绝心烦忧），
仓兄填兮（失意凄凉久惆怅）。
倬彼昊天（老天光明高在上），
宁不我矜（怎不怜悯我惊惶）？

《易经》的性质

《易经》似乎试图用一系列没有人能解释的卦象来解释天地世间的变化万象。这是一个令人愉快的谜题，不同哲学体系的创始人和门徒为解谜奋斗了4000年，堪比中世纪经院神学家的精巧和精细，也堪比现代德国哲学家和神学家的深邃或晦涩。

《礼记》

《礼记》，涉及服饰、婚事、丧事、葬礼、祭祀、乡饮等方面的礼仪规范，以及与祭坛、礼器、游戏等有关的规制。孔子非常重视这些外在的礼制，而我们今天对这些不太重视。他坚持认为，外在的礼仪形式是内在情感的自然表达，而内在情感是以美德为基础的，如果人们忽视了外在的礼仪形式，很快就会失去内在情感及其赖以产生的美德。孔圣人最喜欢的一句格言是"无不敬"㉖，马礼逊博士直译为"从不失庄重"，即"永远庄重"，"不是反对快乐，而是反对轻率、轻浮和草率的举止"。

Nature of The Book of Changes

The "Yih King," or "Book of Changes," seems to be an attempt to account for the mysteries of Nature by a series of diagrams which no man has ever been able to explain. It has been a delightful puzzle, over which the founders and disciples of different systems of philosophy have fought for 4000 years, with an ingenuity and subtlety worthy of the schoolmen of the Middle Ages, and the profundity or obscurity of modern German philosophers and theologians…

The Book of Rites

The "Li Ki," or "Book of Rites," deals with the regulation of manners in dress, marriages, mourning, funerals, sacrifices, village feasts, etc.; forms relating to sacred places, utensils, games, etc. Confucius attached great importance to these outward forms, to which we in our day attach too little. He maintained that the outward form was the natural expression of inward feelings, which were based on virtue, and that if men neglected the outward, they would soon lose the inward feelings and the virtues from which they sprang. A favourite maxim of the sage was "Wu puh King," literally rendered by Dr. Morrison, "Never not grave," i.e., "always serious," "not in opposition to cheerfulness, but as opposed to lightness, frivolity, and hasty manners."

The "Chun-Tseu"

The last of the five classics, the "Chun-Tseu," or "Spring and Autumn," is a bald record of events, occurring during his lifetime, written by Confucius, the only work strictly his own. All his other writings were faithful copies from ancient records, a work for which he was specially qualified.

The "Four Books"

The Four Books have been unwisely compared to our four Gospels, to which their only resemblance consists in the fact that they are chiefly records of the sayings and doings of Confucius, by four of his favourite disciples. They contain also the sayings of Mencius, who lived 200 years after Confucius, and showed a depth of thought and originality of mind superior to that of his more renowned predecessor, to whom, however, he owed much for the matter of his discourse.

Chinese Boswells

The disciples who compiled the greater part of the Four Books bear a much greater resemblance to Boswell, in his relation to Johnson, than the four

《春秋》

《春秋》，五经中的最后一部，是孔子对当世发生之事的记录[27]，因孔子述而不作之故，它是严格意义上孔子的唯一创作。《春秋》外的所有著作皆是孔子对古代记述忠实地辑录，这一工作他做起来得心应手。

四 书

有人把四书比作《新约》前四卷的福音书[28]，其实不对，两者唯一的相似之处在于，四书主要是孔子四个最享盛誉的弟子对其言行的记录。[29]四书还包含孟子的语录，孟子比孔子晚两百余年，其表现出的思想深度和思想独创性，超过了更为知名的前者，不过孟子的言论很大程度上是对孔子的继承和发展。

中国的博斯韦尔[30]

编辑四书中大部分著作的孔门弟子，与其被比作四个福音传道者，不如比作传记作家博斯韦尔，因为弟子们与夫子的关系更似博斯韦尔与约翰逊[31]博士的朋友关系，而不是福音传道者与耶稣的关系。孔门弟子更胜一筹，使得博斯韦尔的传记看来像闲话，也胜过英国，甚至美国现代报纸的采访记者。孔门弟子及其他追随者满怀崇敬地向人们讲述孔子的言行事迹。

在前文中，我们对孔子的外貌做了详细的描述，像是其国家的缩影。他们还描述了孔子如何站立、行走和就寝，衣服的颜色和剪裁样式，以及他在下级、上级和平级之人面前的举止。尽管这些记述多是细枝末节，并且过度崇敬和狂热，但是也确实给了我们一个温文尔雅、温柔善良的伟人形象。孔子虽贫穷，不得已而渔猎糊口，但弟子们说夫子依然不用网捕鱼，也不狩猎归巢之鸟。他像一个真正的打猎爱好者，给了鱼儿和鸟儿逃跑的机会。晚年时，夫子退朝回家，发现马厩被烧毁了。人们注意到，他只问仆人是否受伤，而没有问他的马。孔子以诚待人，以诚待事，以诚敬神和祖先。孔子认为，贤德之人吃粗粮、喝白水、曲肱而枕之，乐趣也就在其中了。而缺少学识和美德的富贵之人，对于他来讲很可鄙。

Evangelists do to their Divine Master. They beat Boswell as gossips, and out-do the interviewer of the modern newspapers in England, or even of America. They and other admiring followers tell us all about their idol Confucius.

In a previous page we have given their minute description of face and outward form as an epitome of his country. They also tell how he stood and walked and slept, the colour and cut of his clothes, and his manners in presence of his inferiors, superiors, and equals. But in spite of their many littlenesses, the outcome of excessive reverence and love, they do give us the conception of a gentle, good, and great man. Though so poor that he had to fish and shoot for his food, they tell us that he would not fish with a net nor shoot a bird when sitting on its perch. Like a true sportsman, he gave to both the chance of escape. In later years, on returning from a visit to the Emperor, he found his stables had been burned: it was noticed that he only asked if the servants had been hurt, and made no inquiry about his horses. He was faithful in every relation of life, and devout in worshipping the gods and his ancestors. He held that the virtuous and learned man was happy, though he had nothing but coarse rice to eat, rugs to cover him, and his bent elbow for a pillow, while the rich man, destitute of learning and virtue, was a miserable object of contempt.

The Sayings of Confucius

The sayings of Confucius, which they have recorded with such diligence and fidelity, though often small, as the answers to trifling questions must be, are in general remarkable for common-sense and wisdom, and, with perhaps one or two doubtful cases, strictly moral and beneficent. The following are a few examples:

That which is called rectifying the motives is this: Do not deceive yourself; hate vice as you do an offensive smell; love virtue as you love beauty. This is called self-enjoyment. Hence the superior man will carefully watch over his motives.

Adorning the person with virtue depends on rectifying the heart.

The proper regulation of the family depends on the cultivation of personal virtue.

All who hold the reins of government have nine standard rules by which to act. These require them to cultivate personal virtue, honour the virtuous, love their relations, respect great officers, consider the whole of their ministers as members of their own body, view the people as their children, encourage all the trades, treat foreigners with kindness, and manifest a tender care for tributary princes.

Confucius says, if you read and do not reflect, you will lose what you learn. If you think and do not study, you are uneasy and in danger.

Confucius says, it is only the

孔子语录

弟子们如此勤勉又忠实地记录而来的孔子言论，尽管往往短小，像是对琐碎问题的回答一般，但总的来说却充满非凡的常识与智慧，而且严格来说，全部崇德贵仁，除了有一两处存疑之外。以下举几个例子：

所谓诚其意者，毋自欺也。如恶恶臭，如好好色，此之谓自谦。故君子必慎其独也。

富润屋，德润身，心广体胖。故君子必诚其意。

欲齐其家者，先修其身。

凡为天下国家有九经，曰："修身也，尊贤也，亲亲也，敬大臣也，体群臣也，子庶民也，来百工也，柔远人也，怀诸侯也。"

子曰："学而不思则罔，思而不学则殆。"

子曰："唯仁者能好人，能恶人。"

子曰："我未见好仁者，恶不仁者。好仁者，无以尚之；恶不仁者，其为仁矣，不使不仁者加乎其身。"

子曰："文，莫吾犹人也。躬行君子，则吾未之有得。"

子曰："克己复礼为仁。"

"其恕乎！己所不欲，勿施于人。"这句是孔圣人最近于金科玉律的语录。但与孔子同时代的老子更进一步，他甚至劝告追随者以善报恶。

藏书阁

中国的文学作品数量丰富，但其题材范围有限，而且由于一直渴望模仿或再现古人的风格与手法而显得单调。

《四库全书》目录计112卷，共收录3440种78000卷图书。除此之外，文渊阁[32]所藏《四库全书》目录列出了6764种93243卷图书[33]。书目依据内容分类，其中第一类是经部，包括儒家经典"四书五经"的经文及注疏。

第二类为史部，占有很大的部分，世界上没有哪个国家有比中国更好的史料以便透彻地了解历史的了。中国历代君王事迹的官方记录由史官记载保存，而每个省

virtuous that are capable of either loving or hating a man.

Confucius said, I have not seen anyone who perfectly loves virtue, nor have I seen anyone who thoroughly detests vice.

Confucius said, in learning I am equal to others; but I cannot by any means exhibit the man of perfect virtue in my own conduct.

"Confucius said, virtue consists in conquering self, and returning to propriety." And "WHAT YOU DO NOT WANT DONE TO YOURSELF, DO NOT TO OTHERS." This is the Chinese sage's nearest approach to the golden rule…We shall find that his contemporary, Lao-tse, went much further, and even counselled his followers to RENDER GOOD FOR EVIL.

Chinese Libraries

The general literature of China is plentiful, but limited in its range of subjects, and wearily monotonous from the constant desire to imitate or reproduce the style and treatment of the ancients.

The catalogue of the four libraries in Pekin consists of 112 octavo volumes, and contains 3440 separate works, consisting of 78000 volumes. Besides this, other catalogues of imperial libraries give lists of 6764 works in 93243 volumes. The catalogues are classified under different subjects, of which the first is the text and commentaries on the Five Classics and the Four Books…

Second, history occupies a

large place, and no country in the world has better materials for a good history than China. Official records are kept by competent men of the events of every reign, and every province and considerable town in China has its local hand-book or history.

The third division is historical novels, of which the people are very fond. Many of these are painfully realistic and immoral, but if openly licentious the sale is prohibited by law. The law, however, is practically a dead letter; magistrates, Government clerks, and other officials, are the chief offenders in the purchase and reading of such vile trash.

Fourth, dramatic works are numerous, but in general, like the worse class of novels, are published under fictitious names, as being a dishonourable class of works. They are called in the Amoy dialect siau swat, or small talk.

Fifth, poetry, chiefly short compositions expressing the tender and mournful feelings, or descriptive of rural scenery.

The others, as given by Morrison, are as follows:

Sixth, collectanea.

Seventh, geographical and topographical works.

Eighth, books on medicine, which are well fitted to amuse the medical faculty of Europe, though not always useless, even to modern science.

Ninth, astronomy.

Tenth, prize essays.

And last, but not least, moral and religious works, by the adherents of the three religions of China.

和有一定规模的城镇都有自己的方志。

第三类是历史小说，人们非常喜爱。其中许多小说极度地写实，不合道德，但如果公然伤风败俗，则法律会禁止销售。然而，法律实际上是一纸空文；地方官、政府职员、吏卒是购买和阅读这种作品的罪魁祸首。

第四类，戏剧作品为数众多，但一般说来就像是小说中的次品，以虚构的笔名出版，被认为是不光彩的一类作品。它们在厦门方言中被称为"小说"（Siau Swat），即琐碎的言论。

第五类是诗歌，篇幅通常很短，抒发柔情、哀伤，或描写田园风光。

其他几类由马礼逊博士提出，如下：

第六类，杂录。

第七类，地理志。

第八类，医学书籍，并非总是无用的，且大有资格吸引欧洲医学界，甚至现代科学的注意。

第九类，天文类。

第十类，文集。

第十一类，也是最后但并非最不重要

的一类，是中国儒道佛三教信徒所作的道德和宗教著作。

类书和字典

有两类书籍未被列入书目中，它们也是中国文学的一大特点。我们不知道它们该被分在哪一类。第一种是类书，四开本数百卷，比西方梦寐以求的百科全书早了几个世纪写就；第二种是字典，其中一些是在公元初年编写的。17世纪的《康熙字典》，由康熙皇帝下诏编写，由700位学者编撰而成，㉞康熙皇帝还经常亲临过问。字典有厚厚的138卷，配得上康熙皇帝的筹划并用国库之银印行。这本字典由马礼逊博士以简编本的形式翻译成英文，由东印度公司出版，四开本共6卷。马礼逊博士提到这本字典收录了43496个㉟汉字：

字典正文中收字：31214个

补遗，主要是过时或错误的：6423个；

以前无任何词典收录的字：1659个；

音义全无：4200个。

如此惊人的粗略的列表很可能会阻止任何普通学者研修汉语；但是，令人高兴

Encyclopedias and Dictionaries

There are two classes of works not named in this list which are a feature in Chinese literature. We know not under which class they are placed. The first, encyclopcedias, which are found in hundreds of quarto volumes, written centuries before such works were dreamed of in the West; and second, dictionaries, some of them composed at the commencement of the Christian era. That of Kang-hi, in the seventeenth century, was prepared at his order by 700 learned men, and superintended by himself. It consists of 138 thick volumes, and is worthy of the great monarch who planned it and published it at the expense of the Government. This dictionary, translated in an abridged form by Dr. Morrison, and published by the East India Company in six quarto volumes, contains, he tells us, 43496 characters, or, as we may say, words:

In the body of the work characters —31214

Added, principally obsolete or incorrect — 6423

Not found in any previous dictionary —1659

Without names or meaning —4200

Such a formidable list of uncouth characters might well deter any ordinary scholar from the study of such a language; but, happily, the number required for ordinary use is limited to comparatively few. The whole of the Penal Code of China is written in a simple style, so as to be understood by any scholar, and contains only 2000 different characters. The nine canonical classical works contain only 4600 different characters, although the number by repetition runs up to more than 200000 in the five classics, and the other four books would add greatly to the number. With a knowledge of 5000 characters a man would be a good scholar; with 2000 he could get on creditably.

China's Augustan Age

The Augustan age of the modern literature of China was during the Tang dynasty—the ninth and tenth centuries of the Christian era, the darkest age in European letters. It was renowned for its poets, of whom Li Tai-peh and Su Tung-pi are said to have been the most famous. If we may judge of their quality by the quantity of their productions, they will throw the poets of Europe into the shade. Li's poems fill 30 volumes, and those of Su 115. The collected poems of the Tang dynasty have been published by imperial authority in 900 volumes. The proportion of descriptive poetry in it is small compared with the sentimental. The longest poem yet turned into English is the "Hwa Tsien Ki," or "The Flower's Petal," by P. P. Thoms. Another of much greater repute among native scholars, called "Li Sao," or "Dissipation of Sorrows," dating from about 314 years be-

的是，一般用途所需的字词量相对较少。《大清律例》的文字风格简朴，任何学者都能理解，而且仅使用2000个字。四书五经等9部经典作品中只有4600个不同的汉字，而五经总字数达20多万，四书则更不止这么多。如果一个人掌握5000个字，他会是一个好学者；掌握2000字，他就可以过得很好了。

中国文学全盛时期

中国文学的全盛时期[36]是唐朝——公元9、10世纪，正值欧洲文学最黑暗的时期。唐诗享誉世界，据说以李太白和苏东坡[37]最为著名。如果以他们作品的数量来判断他们的能力，他们将使欧洲的诗人黯然失色。李白诗歌满30卷，东坡诗词115卷。《御定全唐诗》由康熙帝下旨编校刊刻，计900卷。与抒情诗相比，描述性诗歌在其中所占的比例很小。迄今为止，译成英文的最长的诗歌是彼得·佩林·汤姆斯[38]译的《花笺记》。另一个在本土文人骚客中更富声望的作品是《离骚》，可追溯到公元前314年，已由汉学家德理文[39]译成法语。下面的诗歌片段是我们从卫三畏的《中国总论》中引用过来的。

哀伤地吹起熟悉的旧曲调，何人不起故园情，此情此景令人回想起驻守印度的苏格兰高地士兵每每听到风笛时的思绪，那时音信难通，军旅漫长。思乡曲没有产生逃兵，却使人精神萎靡，不得不停止吹奏。

《四面楚歌》：

夜沉沉兮兵疲眠，
憩中嘤嗡声消渐，
哨兵默兮四方监，
防敌突袭料未然，
夜空兮楚歌绵绵：
入耳入眼入心田，
甜蜜兮柔美妙曼，
恰钟琴乐音弥散。

……

酣眠醒兮心惊颤。
此曲几度梦缠绵；
感伤时兮泪光闪，
盖诉说乡关难见。

……

fore Christ, has been rendered into French by D'Hervey-Saint-Denys. We give from the above the following specimen of poetry from Dr. W. Williams' "Middle Kingdom."

The description of the home-sickness, caused by playing plaintively some familiar old tune, recalls the effect produced by the bagpipes on Highland soldiers in India, when intercourse was rare and service long. It did not lead to desertion, but to physical prostration, and had to be discontinued.

"Chang Liang's Flute":
'Twas night: the tired soldiers were peacefully sleeping,
The low hum of voices was hushed in repose,
The sentries in silence their strict watch were keeping
'Gainst surprise, or a sudden attack of their foes,
When a low mellow note on the night-air came stealing:
So soothingly over the senses it fell,
So touchingly sweet, so soft and appealing,
Like the musical tones of an aerial bell.

* * * * *

The sleepers arouse, and with beating hearts listen.
In their dreams they had heard that weird music before;
It touches each heart, with tears their eyes glisten,
For it tells them of those they may never see more.

* * * * *

Each looked at the other, but no word was spoken,
The music insensibly tempting them on:
They must hasten home.
Ere the daylight had broken,
The enemy looked, and, behold! They were gone.
There's a magic in music, a witchery in it,
Indescribable either with tongue or with pen.
The flute of Chang Liang, in one little minute
Had stolen the courage of eight thousand men.

相望兮凝噎无言，

曲中不觉起缱绻：

归乡兮片刻不缓。

即在那破晓之前，

汉军来观，

见楚兵逃散。

歌有魔兮歌有魅兮，

皆非言词可状堪。

四面吴歌兮顷刻间，

八千子弟兵忽吹散。

【注 释】

① 此处原作者把中国古代官方主办的科举考试与伦敦大学主持的考试做了一个对比。伦敦大学位于英国首都伦敦，是由伦敦的十几所高校和研究机构组成的大学行政系统，是世界上最具影响力的公立大学联邦体，亦被称为公立联邦制大学。伦敦大学依照皇家宪章组建于1836年，起初是一个学位授予及考试委员会，专门为伦敦大学学院和伦敦国王学院以及其他因教育目的而设立的非法人机构的学生颁发学位。这一点与中国历代政府组织的科举考试在功能上相似，但是差别也很明显，科举重在国家通过考试选拔官吏，而伦敦大学的考试重在教育水平评估。——译者注

② 此处原作者把翰林学士与现代法学博士、民法学博士互相参照，做了类比，意在让西方读者大致了解翰林学士的等级之高。实际上，二者差别较大。翰林学士，中国古代官名。——译者注

③ 马礼逊（Robert Morrison，1782—1834）：英国人，西方派到中国大陆的第一位基督教新教传教士。他编辑出版了中国历史上第一部英汉字典——《华英字典》，第一个把《圣经》译成中文，并以自己的医学知识在澳门开办了第一个中西医合作的诊所。他还出版汉文期刊《察世俗每月统记传》。——译者注

④ 《中国杂记》：内容包括中文原始文献、英文译文和注解，主要讲解中国的文字、

中国的文学以及欧洲与中国交往的相关历史和相关著作。1825年于伦敦出版。——译者注

⑤ 此处原作者的解释不完全准确，形得意失。"匕"是"妣"的本字。匕，甲骨文像一个曲臂趴着或俯伏的"人"，造字本义为地位低下的妇女。有的甲骨文省去弯曲的臂的形式，简化成"人"。但是，"匕"的本义后由"妣"代替，而"匕"被错误地假借为表示餐具的刀（字形像握在手中的长柄刀），导致"匕"的义项复杂化。在存留下来的义项中，并没有原作者所说的"改变的状态，转换，转变"之意。——译者注

⑥ 应为公元前213年。——译者注

⑦ 伏生：名胜，字子贱，山东邹平人，汉代经学家。自幼嗜古好学，博览群书，对《尚书》研读尤精，为儒学博士。——译者注

⑧ 晁错：河南颍川（今河南禹州）人，西汉政治家、文学家。代表作有《言兵事疏》《守边劝农疏》《论贵粟疏》《举贤良对策》等。——译者注

⑨ 郑玄：字康成，北海郡高密县（今山东省高密市）人，东汉末年儒家学者，经学家，汉代经学的集大成者。著有《天文七政论》《尚书中候注》等书，共百万余言，世称"郑学"。——译者注

⑩ 今存《今文尚书》33篇，《古文尚书》25篇。实际上，《尚书》百篇之说乃后起。——译者注

⑪ 出自《尚书·虞书·大禹谟》。——译者注

⑫ 这句熟语出自苏格兰的安德鲁·弗莱彻（Andrew Fletcher, 1653—1716），他是当时欧洲政治秩序最敏锐的观察者之一，也是苏格兰启蒙运动的重要先驱。——译者注

⑬ 出自《毛诗序》。——译者注

⑭ 出自《诗经·周南·兔罝》。——译者注

⑮ 出自《诗经·郑风·羔裘》第六首。——译者注

⑯ 出自《诗经·邶风·击鼓》。——译者注

⑰ 出自《诗经·邶风·雄雉》。——译者注

⑱ 出自《诗经·邶风·终风》。——译者注

⑲ 出自《诗经·秦风·终南》。——译者注

⑳ 出自《诗经·陈风·东门之池》。——译者注

㉑ 出自《诗经·陈风·东门之杨》。——译者注

㉒ 以下三首分别为《诗经·大雅·皇矣》《诗经·大雅·召旻》《诗经·周颂·我将》。——译者注

㉓ 出自《诗经·齐风·鸡鸣》。——译者注

㉔ 此为亚瑟·奎勒-库奇（Arthur Quiller-Couch, 1863—1944）编辑的《牛津歌谣集》（*The Oxford Book of Ballads*）第170首。——译者注

㉕ 出自《诗经·召南·草虫》。——译者注

㉖ 出自《礼记·哀公问》："君子无不敬也，敬身为大。"——译者注

㉗ 一般认为，《春秋》从鲁隐公记述到鲁哀公，历12代君主，计244年，不止孔子一生时长。——译者注

㉘ 《新约》前四卷的福音书是对耶稣生活和传教的记录，四位作者分别为马太、马可、路加、约翰。——译者注

㉙ 实际上，四书的作者远不止这四个，包括孔子及其弟子、子思、孟子及其弟子等。其内容也不仅是对孔子言行的记录。——译者注

㉚ 博斯韦尔（James Boswell, 1740—1795）：苏格兰律师、日记作家和传记作家，著有《科西嘉岛纪实》（1785）和《约翰逊传》（1791）等。——译者注

㉛ 约翰逊（Samuel Johnson, 1709—1784）：英国辞典编纂家、作家、批评家、雄辩家。作为当时伦敦文学界的重要人物，他所编纂的《英语辞典》（1755）、《莎士比亚集》（1765）和《英国诗人传》（1781）使他闻名遐迩。博斯韦尔的《约翰逊传》详细记录了他的生平和谈话。——译者注

㉜ 文渊阁：位于北京故宫博物院东华门内文华殿后，是北京故宫中一座清代皇家藏书楼。清乾隆四十一年（1776），文渊阁建成，专贮《四库全书》。——译者注

㉝ 此处原作者提供的书籍卷册数目与现在认可的数字有微小差异。《四库全书总目》又名《钦定四库全书总目提要》，简称《四库总目》或《四库提要》，共200卷，

是清代纪昀等人编纂的一部大型解题书目，是中国古典目录学方法的集大成者，也是现有的一部最大的传统目录书。《四库全书》分为"著录书"和"存目书"两大部分，是一个创例。誊录入库的著作3461种79307卷，称"著录书"，写为定本，收入《四库全书》之内；又附录了未收入《四库全书》、仅抄存卷目的著作6793种93551卷，称"存目书"。——译者注

㉞ 《康熙字典》的编撰工作始于康熙四十九年（1710），成书于康熙五十五年（1716），因此应为18世纪而非17世纪；该字典由张玉书、陈廷敬等30多位学者合力完成，而非700位学者。——译者注

㉟ 此处原作者提供的有关数据与目前看法有所出入。其实，康熙字典字数现今也是众说纷纭。一般认为其收录汉字47035个，为汉字研究的主要参考文献之一。——译者注

㊱ 全盛时期：译自Augustan Age（奥古斯都时代）。奥古斯都是罗马帝国的第一位元首，其统治下的拉丁文学全盛时期人称"奥古斯都时代"，进而用来指英国文学的类似全盛时期（1690—1745），尤指16世纪初叶安妮女王统治下的文学全盛时期（1702—1714），或泛指任何国家的文学全盛时期。——译者注

㊲ 此处原作者误把宋朝的苏东坡当作唐朝诗人。——译者注

㊳ 彼得·佩林·汤姆斯（Peter Perring Thoms）：英国人，生卒年月、籍贯与教育程度等信息不详。长期以印刷为业，曾于1813—1825年在澳门为英国东印度公司印刷所工作；刊印过《华英词典》《中文会话及凡例》《华夏文字大观》等重要文献；曾将《三国演义》《今古奇观》《花笺记》等书译成英文。《花笺记》是明末清初广东弹词木鱼歌创作作品，全称《第八才子书花笺记》，共59回。其是粤调说唱文学唱本的佼佼者，在海内外粤语华人中极为流行。——译者注

㊴ 德理文（Hervey de Saint-Denys, 1823—1892），法国汉学家，儒莲（Stanislas Julien, 1797—1873）的学生，是为中国古诗词在法国的翻译和传播做出重要贡献的第一人。——译者注

第六章　中国的宗教
Chapter VI　The Religion of China

Primitive Religion

No form of religious worship comes so near to what we have good reason to believe was the cultus of the primitive founders of the human race, as that of the Chinese. The form of worship among the Jews was changed on their departure from Egypt from the patriarchal to the national. The religious worship of the Babylonians and Egyptians, which were as ancient as that of China, perished with these old empires long ago. The present rites of the Hindus are of comparatively recent origin, while the religious customs of the Greeks and Romans, which only existed for a few centuries during their classic supremacy, were borrowed from the East, and perished before the advancing light of Christianity. But China, in this nineteenth century of the Christian era, holds fast the same religion, and practises the same religious

原生性宗教

我们有充分的理由相信，世界上没有哪一种宗教信仰能像中国人的那样更接近人类初民的原始崇拜。在犹太人逃出埃及为奴之地后，他们的崇拜方式发生了变化，从宗法性崇拜转向了民族崇拜。古巴比伦人和古埃及人的宗教崇拜与中国人的一样古老，但很久以前就随着古老的帝国一起消亡了。印度教徒目前的仪式，起源时间相对新近，而古希腊人和古罗马人的宗教习俗，其巅峰时期仅存在了区区几个世纪，且是从东方学来的，并在基督教诞生之前消亡了。但是，在19世纪的今天，中国依然坚定地信奉并践行着与诺亚同时代的古老宗教与礼仪，如果时间上不及亚当时代的话。

同一个宗教

我们把中国宗教并为一谈或许会令许多人惊讶；普遍的习惯是将其分为三教，即儒教、道教和佛教。我们反对三教的分法和称谓。如果我们把大量中国人所接受的、得到官方批准的，甚至得到帝王庇护的各个宗教一一列举出来，教派数目至少是三的三倍。

儒学非儒教

然而，我们反对使用"儒教"一词。孔子从未自称是某一宗教的创始人，也从未宣称自己是宗教导师。他称自己为"传道者"。他的伟大功业是：于政治、道德、社会和宗教生活的方方面面之中，发现最古老的信仰与实践形式。孔子的著述作于公元前6世纪，这个世纪以东西两个半球的伟大的宗教运动而闻名，这个世纪产生了诸如印度的佛陀①、波斯的琐罗亚斯德②、巴比伦和耶路撒冷的以斯拉③以及希腊的毕

rites, as those of Noah, if not the same as those of Adam and his immediate descendants.

The One Religion of China

Many will be surprised at our speaking of the religion of China as one; the universal custom is to speak of the three religions of China, which are called Confucianism, Taoism, and Buddhism. We object to both the number and the nomenclature. If we profess to enumerate all the religions which have been accepted by a large number of the inhabitants of China, and that have received Government sanction, and some even imperial patronage, they would be at least thrice three…

Not Confucianism

We object, however, to the term "Confucian religion." Confucius never professed to be the founder of a religion; he laid no claim to the character of a religious teacher. He called himself a transmitter. His great work was to discover the most ancient form of belief and practice in all departments of political, moral, social, and religious life. He wrote in the sixth century before Christ—a century noted for its great religious movements both in the eastern and western hemispheres, a century which produced such reformers as Buddha in India, Zoroaster in Persia, Ezra in Babylon and Jerusalem, and Pythagoras in Greece—a wave of religious reform which circled the world—a Divine reformation which did much to save the world from moral and religious corruption and decay. Of all the great men of that remarkable period, none exerted so wide and lasting an influence as Confucius. Four hundred millions now own the sway of that "uncrowned king of men,"…there is no doubt that the teaching of Confucius developed a form of mental and material culture in the largest empire in the world, and has preserved it in independence and prosperity far longer than any that has ever been united in one land—speaking one language, obeying one law, and practising one form of religious worship.

Confucius' Work

Confucius, we have seen, professed to be a transmitter, but what was it he did transmit to his contemporaries and to posterity? He tells us plainly and repeatedly that his great mission —for he felt he had a mission— was to transmit the knowledge and wisdom of the great Emperors Yao and Shun, with whom he maintained authentic history began. Not that these were the first men, or even the first Emperors, of China; he knew that there were authentic traditions of a much earlier period, but his practical, matter-of-fact mind would not transmit anything for which he had not authentic documentary evidence. Traditions and myths had their own place, but they were not history, and were kept

达哥拉斯④等改革家。这是一场席卷世界的宗教改革浪潮，这场神圣改革极大地拯救了世界，使之免于道德与宗教的堕落和腐朽。在这个非凡时期的所有伟人中，没有一个像孔子那样产生如此广泛和持久的影响。今日之中国有4亿人受孔子这位"素王"的影响，孔子的教诲无疑在这个世界上最大的帝国中发展出某种形式的精神文化和物质文化，并使之保持独立与繁荣，且持续时间之久远远超过任何一个人同言、律同法、教同形的一统的国家。

孔子的功业

孔子自称传道者，但他到底给同时代之人及后人传播了什么？孔子清楚而反复地声明，他认为自己的伟大使命是传播伟大帝王尧舜的知识和智慧，孔子一直认为中华真正的历史始于尧舜。并非说尧舜时代之人是中国最古老的初民，甚或尧舜是最早的帝王；孔子知道更早的时候有可信的传统存在，但他实事求是的精神使他不会传播任何没有权威文献证据的东西。传统与神话各有其位，但它们不是历史，所以孔子将其从他的历史著作中剔除出去。

历史的开端

中国历史的开端可追溯到公元前23世纪,比摩西早600年;但是摩西和尧帝都知晓有更早的时代,无论是以口头流传的形式还是书面记载的形式存在着。很可能两种形式都有。在东亚和西亚有大量证据表明,书写艺术在很早的时代就已为人所知。巴比伦、埃及和中国大约在同一时期产生文字,即公元前3000年左右。有些人认为中国真正的历史始于伏羲的统治,其统治于公元前28世纪繁荣一时。我们更倾向于将其视为书写传说的开端,而这也是历史的原材料。

彼时之宗教

但是,有人会问,在尧舜时代信仰什么宗教?尧舜声称他们的宗教是从比繁盛的公元前23世纪更遥远的时期获得的。答案简单而确凿。它与当今中国人自然崇拜的正式教条和实践基本相同。19世纪清朝皇帝的崇拜与14世纪明朝皇帝的崇拜一般

apart from his historic works.

Commencement of History

This commencement of history in China, as we have seen, dated from the twenty-third century before Christ, 600 years before Moses; but both Moses and the Emperor Yao had knowledge, either in the form of oral or written traditions, of a much earlier period. In all probability they had both forms of tradition. There is abundant evidence in both Eastern and Western Asia that the art of writing was known from a very early period. The traditions of Babylon, Egypt, and China are substantially at one in making the discovery of letters to have taken place about the same period, and that is as early as about 3000 years before Christ. Some date the commencement of authentic history from the reign of the Emperor Fuhi, who flourished 2800 years before Christ. We prefer to regard it as the beginning of written traditions—the materials for history.

What the Religion Was

But what, we shall be asked, was the religion believed in and practised in the days of Yao and Shun, which they professed to have received from a much more remote period than the twenty-third century before Christ, in which they flourished? The answer is easy and conclusive. It was substantially the same as that which is the formal creed and practice of the Chinese of the present day in their natural worship. The worship of the Emperor of China in this nineteenth century is the same as that of the Emperors of the Ming Dynasty in the fourteenth century…

There is no doubt that the liturgy of the Ming Dynasty, founded in the fourteenth century of our era, was the same as it was in the days of Confucius in the sixth century before Christ, and Confucius made it his aim to render the worship of his time the same as it was in the days of Yao and Shun, in the twenty-third century before Christ. But these venerable sages scrupulously adhered to the religious customs handed down from a much earlier period. Thus, by well-marked stages, we can easily retrace our steps back in the footprints of history, from the present to the most primitive period of religious worship known to us—the patriarchal, when the father of the family, or head of the tribe, was the priest, and offered the sacrifice and the public prayers for all the family or tribe.

Present and Past Religion of China

What, then, is the present religion of China, which we may accept as substantially the same as that of the earliest? Before we answer that question we must

无二。

毫无疑问，创建于14世纪的明朝的祭祀仪式与公元前6世纪孔子时代的礼制是一样的。而孔子的人生目标就是使他所在时代的礼制恢复到与公元前23世纪的尧舜时代相同的地步。但这些德高望重的圣贤们一丝不苟地遵循的是从更早时期流传下来的宗教习俗。因此，通过标记分明的各个阶段，我们可以轻松地追溯历史的足迹，即从现今回溯到我们所熟知的宗教祭祀的最原始时期——宗法制时期，那时，家庭的父亲或部落的首领是祭司，代表所有家庭成员或部落成员祭祀与公开祈祷。

中国的古今宗教

那么，中国现在信奉的，且我们可以将其大体等同于最早期宗教的宗教究竟是什么？在回答此问题之前，我们必须简要说明三种普遍信奉的宗教之间的相互关系。

从最早时期到公元1世纪，中国宗教的统一是毫无疑问的。这段时间，除了从最遥远的远古时代流传下来的宗教之外，再也找不出任何一种形式的宗教。异端邪说确实出现过，但尽皆昙花一现，影响有限，且随着人民掌握经典，像基督教的路德一样，宗教改革者总是可以诉之于经典，因为人民普遍接受其权威性。经典具有权威性的观念如此强烈，以至于专制的秦始皇颠覆性地改革政体后，希望其在行政和宗教上的变革能够永续，因此下令焚书，并处死那些将经典熟记于心的儒生。但是人民对这些经典的热爱如此之深，以至于焚书坑儒也未能断绝经典，于是在秦始皇死后，中国宗教又恢复了原来的样子。

著名的"道教创始人"

老子以"道教创始人"的身份而知名，但他本人并未创立教派，⑤仅仅是传扬中国古代先贤信仰，这一点与同时代的孔子如出一辙。他从未试图创建自己的教派抑或改变祖先的信仰。他是一个虔诚的老派神秘主义者，对古老信仰的奥秘进行哲学思考，表达出精深的情感与伟大的道德之

show briefly the mutual relation of the three forms of religion which are so generally practised…

From the earliest times until the first century of the Christian era there was no doubt about the unity of the religion of China. No form of religion was recognised, except that which had been handed down from the most remote antiquity. Heresies did arise, but they were short-lived and of limited extent, and with the sacred classics in the hands of the people, reformers, like Luther, could always appeal to the universally-accepted authority of the Sacred Books. So strong was this feeling, that when the despot Chi, who revolutionised the government, wished to perpetuate his corruption in both civil and sacred things, he ordered all the ancient classics to be burned, and the scholars who had committed them to memory to be put to death. But such was the love of the people for these Sacred Books, that even he failed, and the religion of the country was restored to its old form after his death.

The Reputed Founder of Taoism

The reputed founder of Taoism, Laotsze, had no religion but that of the ancient sages of China—the same as his contemporary, Confucius. He never attempted either to form a religion of his own or to alter the ancestral religion. He was a devout old mystic, who philosophized on the mysteries of the old religion, and gave utterance to sentiments of profound depth and great moral beauty. He not only taught, as Confucius did, that "we should not do to others what we would not wish others to do to us"—the negative side of the Golden Rule as taught by Christ—but he went the full length of teaching in China the higher law, to render good for evil, 500 years before it was laid down by the Great Teacher in Judaea…

Laotsze's Speculations

While Laotsze adhered to the old religion, he introduced speculations about the doctrine of the Tao, in which the early sages had indulged centuries before, and the possibility of prolonging life indefinitely, which led his followers to superstitious rites, and to engage in the vain search after the philosopher's stone and the elixir of immortality. Laotsze sought to prolong life by a regulated moral conduct, but his followers tried to secure it by material means, and anticipated the alchemists of Europe by well-nigh 2000 years. But all this was outside of religion, and did not interfere with conformity with the old faith and ceremonials of the national religion…

Buddhism, a Foreign Religion

Buddhism was introduced from India into China in

美。他不仅像孔子那般教导"己所不欲，勿施于人"——这是耶稣所教导的金科玉律"己所欲，施于人"反过来的说法，而且一直在竭力教导更高的准则——以善报恶，这比耶稣早了500年。

老子的探索

虽然老子坚守古老信仰，但也引入了早期圣贤们在几个世纪前就沉溺其中的关于"道"的猜想，并探索长生不老的可能性，故而导致他的追随者采用迷信的仪式，并对点金石和长生不老的灵丹妙药开始了徒劳的找寻。老子试图通过规范道德行为来延长寿命，但他的追随者则试图通过物质手段来获得长寿，这先于欧洲的炼金术士近2000年。但这一切都在宗教范畴之外，并不妨碍遵守古老信仰和民族宗教的仪式。

佛教——一个外来宗教

佛教于公元66年从印度传入中国。东汉明帝遣使赴西域求法，寻找一个据说出现在西方的圣人。⑥

作为一个先验的宗教哲学体系，佛教需要一整卷书才能恰如其分地说明其真正特点，以及其创立者的美好品格。对如此美妙而又如此仁爱之人避而不谈，我们应该为此怠慢感到抱歉。

儒道佛三者的相互关系

在中国，儒道佛之间的关系最为友好。它们彼此并不对立。它们结成了联盟，因为它们相互补充。

外来的佛教改变了道教的整个体系。道教大量采纳了佛教的通行体系，并仿效其诸多仪式和惯例。借用的情形如此之多，以至于外来者很难区分一座庙到底是道观还是佛寺。两个宗教的神也差不多，而且两路神仙有家族相似性，除了名字有所改变之外，几乎没有什么区别。佛教寺庙的三位主神被称为三宝佛，道教寺庙的三位主神被称为三清尊神，两者都有许多陪祀神，而道士或僧侣在服装、礼仪和仪式上都很相似。道教的信仰和仪式显然是从佛教那里借鉴来的，而佛教又无疑受到了道教信仰和仪式的影响。

the year 66 A.D. by an imperial deputation sent in search of a sage reported to have appeared in the West....

As a system of transcendental philosophy of religion, it would require a volume to give a just account of its true character, and of the wonderful character of the man who founded it. We should be sorry to do injustice to a character so beautiful and so philanthropic...

Mutual Relations of the Three Religions

The mutual relations of the three forms of religion in China are of the most friendly character. They are not antagonistic to one another. They have formed an alliance, based...on...by their being supplementary to one another.

Buddhism—a foreign importation—altered the entire system of Taoism, which adopted much of the popular ecclesiastical system, and copied many of the rites and customs of Buddhism. So much is this the case, that it is difficult for a stranger to distinguish the temples of the one from those of the other religion. There are as many gods in those of the one as in those of the other, and they have a family likeness, with little but a change of names. The three principal gods of a Buddhist temple are called the three precious ones, those in a Taoist temple are the three pure ones, and both temples are filled with a host of subordinate deities or demons, while the priests or monks are much alike in costume, and rites, and ceremonies. Those of the Taoists are obviously borrowed from Buddhists, while there is little doubt that the Buddhists have been influenced in their turn by the beliefs and rites of the Taoists.

Preservation of the Patriarchal Religion

The marvellous circumstance is that the old patriarchal worship has been preserved almost entirely free from the influences of either Taoism or Buddhism…It is a strong proof of the powerful hold the patriarchal religion had got of the hearts of the people, and the firm root it had taken in the constitution and custom of the empire. Nothing could have given it such a hold and such a sense of its inviolable sanctity but the fact of its great antiquity, and the conviction of its sacred origin, which makes modern innovations of human origin inadmissible and profane.

The Chinese Canon

The work of Confucius in making up the Canon of sacred books must have had the same effect in securing the permanence of the religion of China that the formation of the Canon of the Old Testament in the time of Ezra had on the religion of the Jews, and which the fixing of the Canon of the New Testament had on the Creed and form of the Christian Church. In fact, the influence of the Confucian Classics and Analects has given a more fixed and unyielding form to the religion of the Chinese than the formation of the Canon of Scripture has given to the religion of Christians.

宗法性宗教的保存

令人称奇的是，古老的宗法性宗教几乎完全没有受到道教或佛教的影响而保存下来。这有力地证明了宗法性宗教在人民心中的重要地位，以及它在帝国法律和习俗中的牢固根基。能给予它如此崇高地位和不可侵犯的神圣感的，无他，唯有其伟大、古老，以及对其神圣起源的信念，这使得任何关于人类起源的现代变革都是不可接受且亵渎神灵的。

中国经典

孔子编订经典，确立准则，确保了中国宗教的持久性，其带来的效果一定与以斯拉时代《旧约》教规的形成对犹太人的宗教，以及《新约》教规的确立对基督教会的信条和礼拜形式所产生的效果一样。事实上，与《圣经》教规的形成给基督教带来的影响相比，儒家经典的影响给中国人的宗教带来了一种更加牢固、更加坚韧的形式。

中国宗教的包容性

中国宗教宽容如斯,佛道两教不仅被民众信奉,还被国家承认,甚至得到国家的支持。一个人可能既是外国人记述中通常所说的彻底的儒家,然而也是道观和佛寺里虔诚的敬拜者。就连在宗法仪式和祭祀中以大祭司身份行事的皇帝,也成为道教迷信活动的领袖,有些皇帝则是虔诚的佛教徒。至于广大民众,他们三教皆拜,在社会生活及家庭生活的一切重大事件中,自称为古老信仰信徒的人,在子女出生、葬礼或结婚庆典时,一贯都会请来道教的道士和佛教的僧侣做法事,而佛道两教的僧道也不会认为二者不同的法事相融交杂有什么不合适。孔子的教义与佛道的引入也没有不相容。

中国择一神教⑦

中国真正的宗教既没有受到外来佛教革新的影响,也没有受到道教的影响,那么,中国真正的宗教究竟是什么?答案可能不复杂。

Tolerance of Chinese Religion

It is so tolerant as to allow of their being not only practised by the people, but recognised, and even patronized, by the State. The same man may be what is commonly called by foreign writers a thorough Confucianist, and yet a devout worshipper in the temples of the Taoists and Buddhists. Even Emperors, who acted in their official capacity as high-priests in the patriarchal rites and sacrifices, have been leaders in Taoist superstitious practices, and some were devout Buddhists. As for the great mass of the people, they practise all the three forms of worship, and at all the great events of social and domestic life, the man who would call himself a follower of the old faith would think himself quite consistent in calling in the priests or monks of Taoism and Buddhism to perform their ceremonies at the birth, the burial, or marriage of his sons and daughters, and the ministers of these two different sects would see no impropriety in the union of their diverse rites. The frigid creed of Confucius is not incompatible with their introduction.

Chinese Henotheism

What, then, is the true religion of China, which we find so free from the innovation of imported Buddhism and the corruptions of Taoism? The answer must be brief.

First of all, the creed is what may be called henotheistic. The supreme object of worship is One, but he is attended by subordinate deities, or deified ancestors or heroes, who receive a lower form of worship, and are regarded as attendants on the Supreme God, who is worshipped with the highest honours. When the Emperor invites the deity to come to the altar, he summons the others as his attendants.

This supreme object of worship is known by the names or titles of Ti (Ruler), or Shang-ti (Supreme Ruler), or Thien (Heaven), the name by which God was designated in the earliest times, and found in use by Nebuchadnezzar in Babylon, and applied by Daniel to the God of Israel: "until thou know that the heavens do rule." The use of the term heaven for God as the great Ruler, is quite in harmony with the Chinese conception. The name of the dwelling-place of God is used for that of its great Occupant as not only appropriate in itself, but as more reverent than the personal name.

The Divine Attributes

The attributes of Shang-ti are summed up by Dr. Medhurst, Dr. Faber, and other competent authorities in such terms as the following: "Shang-ti made the heaven, and the earth, and man. He is the true Parent of all things. His love is over all his works. He is the great and lofty One, whose

首先，其信条可以被称为择一神论⑧。中国宗教至高无上的崇拜对象是唯一的上帝，并受到最高规格的敬拜。但它有陪祀神，或是神化了的祖先，或是英雄，这些神祇接受低一级规格的敬拜，并被视为上帝的随从。当皇帝祭天祈求上帝降临祭坛时，也召集其他神灵一道而来。

这一至高无上的敬拜对象被人们称为帝（统治者），或上帝（最高统治者），或天（上苍）。很早的时候，人们就使用天来指称上帝，古巴比伦的尼布甲尼撒王⑨便使用过，并被但以理⑩用来称呼古希伯来的神，"等你知道诸天掌权"。用"天"一词来形容上帝，这与中国人的观念非常一致。用上帝居所的名字"天"来称呼其伟大的居住者，不仅因为它本身适合，而且比直呼上帝的名讳更显尊敬。

神　性

麦都思⑪博士、花之安⑫博士和其他权威人士将上帝的特征总结如下："上帝创造了天、地和人。他是万物之父。他的爱存在于他所有的创造中。他是伟大而崇高的神，他的统治永恒不灭。他的岁月永无止境。他的善永无终结。在他的统治下，灵魂和人类一般无二。"

麦都思博士补充道："这就是中国所持有的信念，并在其最虔诚的行为中公开宣布的关于上帝的看法。"

这也许可以称为一神论，如果一神论这个词不是意味着仅崇拜一个神灵，而且完全排斥所有其他崇拜对象，甚至陪祀神的话。因此，我们更愿意称它为择一神教。在我们使用这个术语时，它意味着崇拜一个至高的上帝，但也不排除崇拜陪祀上帝的其他神。我们不知晓有哪一宗教已经真正上升到了一神崇拜，尽管有几个宗教已经产生了这个概念，或者保留了对高于所有其他神的一神崇拜的记忆。正如卫三畏所讲的，在中国国家祭典中所敬拜的一些陪祀神是天地、列祖列宗，以及土地和谷物之神。其他的神是以次级的祭品来祭祀的，且这些祭品是由皇帝的下属献祭的。

除了对上帝的信仰之外，宗法性宗教还宣扬好人有好报，但对恶人受到的惩罚却只字不提。人们用牲畜祭祀，在其最初

dominion is everlasting. His years are without end. His goodness is infinite. Spirits and men are alike under his government."

"This," Dr. Medhurst adds, "is what China holds, and, in her highest exercise of devotion, declares concerning Shang-ti…"

This might be called monotheism, were it not that the word signifies not only the worship of one God, but the entire exclusion of all other objects of worship, even of an inferior kind. We prefer to call it henotheism, which implies, in the sense in which we use the term, the worship of one Supreme God, but does not exclude the worship of other gods subordinate to the One. We do not know of any heathen religion which has risen to the true conception of monotheistic worship, though several have attained to the conception, or retained the memory of the worship of one God as supreme over all other gods. Some of the inferior deities worshipped in the great sacrifices of the national religion of China are, as given by Wells Williams, the sky and earth, the Temple of Ancestors, and the gods of land and grain. Others are honoured by medium and inferior sacrifices, but these are offered by the Emperor's subordinates.

Along with this faith in God, the patriarchal religion teaches the doctrine of a future state of rewards for good men, but says little about the punishment of the wicked. The sacrifice of animal life was, in its original significance, an acknowledgment of sin and of the forgiveness of sin through the offering of a substitute.

The Emperor, the Only Priest and Worshiper of Shang-Ti

Of this simple and comparatively pure faith, the Emperor of China is the representative head and pontiff. There is in the ancient religion of China no priestly class. The Emperor is the representative of, and the only priest of, the nation. He keeps up the form of worship designed originally for the patriarchal head of the family or tribe…The Emperor alone can approach the Supreme God by prayer and sacrifice. The officers of State and governors of the provinces worship subordinate deities, and the body of the people must worship their ancestors, but no one except the Emperor may presume to worship the Supreme God—Shang-ti or Thien.

Form of Worship

The national form of worship is most impressive and interesting as a relic of the primitive worship of the early patriarchs, so far as known from the earliest records of the Jewish Scriptures and Chinese classics. It is only once or twice in the year that the Emperor, as father and priest of the nation, approaches Shang-ti: at the spring and autumn solstices, the former being the more impor-

的意义上，是承认自身之罪，并以牺牲为替代品来获得宽恕。

皇帝，上帝唯一的祭司

在这种简单而相对纯粹的信仰中，中国的皇帝是世人的代表、首领、大祭司。中国古代宗教中没有祭司阶层。皇帝是国家的代表，也是唯一的祭司。皇帝继续保持最初为族长或部落首领设计的崇拜形式。唯有皇帝通过祈祷和祭祀才能联通至高无上的上帝。国家的官员和各省的督抚祭拜陪祀神，人民大众则一定要祭拜自己的祖先，但除了皇帝之外，任何人都不得擅自祭祀最高的神——上帝。

祭典的仪式

国家祭典的仪式最令人赞叹且有趣，它是早期宗法性原始崇拜的遗留，这一点从犹太经文和中国典籍的最早记录中可知。作为君父和祭司，皇帝一年中只有一两次接近上帝的机会：春分和秋分两祭。春分比秋分更为重要、更恒定不变，因为春分关系到一年劳作的开篇。皇帝扶犁亲耕一垄，朝臣随着等级的下降而犁地渐多，给人民做辛勤劳作的榜样；而皇后则与随侍一起去桑园养蚕，以鼓励女子纺织。丝绸产业从最早的历史时期开始就在中国蓬勃发展。

在祭祀大典之前皇帝要斋戒，独自在祭祀地点附近简陋的住处——斋宫——过夜，虔心诚意感动上天。经典说到，如果心不诚，牺牲和祈祷就不会被上天接受。

牺牲和祭坛

大典之前，祭祀用的牺牲会由礼部的高级官员省视，以确保牲畜体全、色纯，状况良好。各种牲畜，马、牛、猪、羊等皆可用于献祭。牺牲都是提前一天宰杀并制作成祭品，庖人与祭司毫无干系。在犹太人那里，也是任何人都可以宰杀献祭的牲畜。

祭 典

根据礼部的钦天监每年制定的皇历，在规定的祀日，皇帝在陪祀百官的陪同下

ant and invariable, connected as it is with the opening labours of the year, when the Emperor ploughs a furrow, and his courtiers an increasing number, according as they descend in rank, as an example of industry to the people; while the Empress goes with her attendants into the mulberry-groves to feed the silkworms, as an encouragement to females in the production of silk, which has, as a manufacture, flourished in China from the earliest historic period.

The solemn day of sacrifice is preceded by a period of fasting, and the Emperor spends the night alone in a humble dwelling near the place of sacrifice, to prepare himself for his solemn duties. The Sacred Books declare that if the heart is not purified the sacrifices and prayers will not be accepted.

The Victims and Temple

Some time before, the animals for sacrifice are carefully inspected by high officials of the Board of Sacred Rites, to see that they are perfect in form and colour, and are in good condition… and animals of all kinds are used in sacrifice: the horse as well as the ox, the sow as well as the sheep. The victims are all slain and prepared the day before by butchers with whom no idea of priesthood is associated. Among the Jews, also, anyone could kill the animals offered in sacrifice.

A Solemn Rite

On the day prescribed in the imperial almanac, which is prepared yearly by the astronomical bureau attached to the Board of Rites, the Emperor, attended by the highest officials of the Government, approaches an altar of earth, such as we find prescribed in the twentieth chapter of Exodus. It stands in the open air, under the canopy of heaven—Nature's grandest temple—with no image of any kind. Only on a table near stand the ancestral tablets of the dynasty, with the names of the Emperor's predecessors. The sacrifices, consisting of the bodies of the slain beasts, along with gifts of silks and gems, with libations of wine, are duly presented, while prayers are offered to Shang-ti, or Thien, as a living person—the hearer of prayer—and hymns are sung by a choir playing on instruments of peculiar construction and great antiquity of form. The demeanour of the Emperor is the extreme of humility. The man who will not allow the highest of his 400,000,000 of subjects to approach him without the lowest and most humiliating prostration, now prostrates himself nine times, again and again striking his forehead in the dust before this invisible but real object of his worship; and this he does as prescribed in the ritual, and after the example of the ancient Emperors Yao and Shun, who acknowledged it to be much more ancient. It may have been derived from Fuh-hi, who flourished nearly 3000 years before Christ; and by him from others of earlier date.

A Prayer Said by the Emperor

The following prayer we quote from Dr. Legge's A prayer translation in his "Notions

起驾诣圜丘坛，这与《出埃及记》第二十章中的规制中如出一辙。圜丘坛立于露天，在大自然最宏伟的庙宇——天穹的华盖之下，且不设任何神像。只有旁边的一张桌子上立着列祖列宗的牌位，上面书写历代皇帝的名号。宰杀的牲畜祭品，连同玉帛等供品，以及酒醴，要按照流程进献；司祝跪读祝文给上帝，似乎上帝如活人一般能听得到；读毕，乐歌再起，乐器结构特殊，式样庄严古朴。皇帝神态举止谦卑至极。皇帝乃九五之尊，连他四亿臣民中职位最高的大臣都必须五体投地、俯身跪拜才能接近他，现在他却三跪九叩，一次又一次地在他祭拜的这个无形但却真实的上帝面前以额头贴地叩首；他依照礼制行事，并以古代先王尧舜为榜样。尧舜认为祭天的仪式古老得很。祭天可能起源于伏羲，伏羲时代兴盛于约公元前3000年[13]；而伏羲则是从更早的先民那里继承而来。

皇帝祭天祝文

下面的祝文转引自理雅各博士的《中

国人关于神与灵的观念》。理雅各写道，"昊天上帝"一词一直使用到16世纪明朝的嘉靖皇帝，之后他改动了一个字，把"昊"（光明）改成了"皇"（君主），来指称天。甚至这种称号上的改变也被中国人视为创新。

> 仰惟玄造兮于皇昊穹，时当肇阳兮大礼钦崇。臣惟蒲柳兮蜾蚁之衷，伏承春命兮职统群工。深怀愚昧兮恐负洪德，爰遵彝典兮勉竭微衷。遥瞻天阙兮宝辇临坛，臣当稽首兮祗迓恩隆。百辟陪列兮舞拜于前，万神翊卫兮以西以东。臣俯伏迎兮敬瞻帝御，愿垂歆鉴兮拜德曷穷。

祭天颂歌

我们列出几首乐班演唱的颂歌，权当众多颂歌的示例：

> 帝皇立命兮，肇三才。中分民物兮，惟天遍该。小臣请命，用光帝陪。庶永配于皇穹哉。

我们可以大致模仿弗朗西斯·劳斯爵士翻译的《大卫诗篇》，对其进行字面化翻

of the Chinese concerning God and Spirits." He tells us it was used up to the time of the Emperor Keu-tsing in the sixteenth century, who then altered one word, changing Haou (bright) into Hwang (sovereign) as applied to the heavens. Even this is noticed by the Chinese as an innovation. "To Thee, O mysteriously-working Maker, I look up in thought. How imperial is the expansive arch (where Thou dwellest)! Now is the time when the masculine energies of Nature begin to be displayed, and with the greater ceremonies I reverently honour Thee. I, Thy servant, am but a reed or willow; my heart is but as that of an ant; yet have I received Thy favouring decree, appointing me to the government of the empire. I deeply cherish a sense of my ignorance and blindness, and am afraid lest I prove unworthy of Thy great favour. Therefore will I observe all the rules and statutes, striving, insignificant as I am, to discharge my loyal duty. Far distant here, I look up to Thy heavenly palace. Come in Thy precious chariot to the altar. Thy servant, I bow my head to the earth, reverently expecting Thine abundant grace. All my officers are here arranged along with me, joyfully worshipping Thee. All the spirits accompany Thee as guards, (filling the air) from the east to the west. Thy servant, I prostrate myself before Thee, and reverently look up for Thy coming. O Ti (Ruler), O that Thou wouldst vouchsafe to accept our offerings, and regard us, while thus we worship Thee, whose goodness is inexhaustible."

Hymns from the Chinese Liturgy

We give two or three of the hymns or psalms that are sung by the choir. They are only fair samples of many others:

When Ti (God) the Lord had so decreed, He called into existence heaven, earth, and men. Between (heaven and earth) He separately disposed men and all things, all overspread by the heavens. I, His unworthy servant, beg His (favouring) decree to enlighten me, His minister—so may I ever appear before Him in the empyrean.

This very literal rendering may be turned, with an equally literal, but very rude, imitation of Sir Francis Rouse's version of the Psalms of David, to show the resemblance between the sacred songs of China and Palestine in those early times, the Chinese being the older of the two.

When God the Lord made heaven and earth,
By His supreme decree He men and all things placed between,
Beneath heaven's canopy.
May He unto His servant grant Light for my ministry,
That I may dwell for evermore Before His face on high.

The following hymn is sung at the last offering of wine:
The precious feast is wide displayed, the generous benches are arranged, the pearly wine is presented with music and dances. The spirit of harmony is collected; men and creatures are happy. The breast of Thy servant is troubled, lest he be unable to express his obligations.

At the removal of the offerings they sing:

译，以表明早期中国颂歌和巴勒斯坦颂歌之间的相似之处，二者中中国颂歌更为古老一些。

上帝创造天地时，
乃令民物其间居，
天穹底下把身栖。
愿他赐福予仆人，
使我事工有光分，
好叫我于天国永随之。

祭天终献时，奏唱"永和之曲"：

宝宴弘。王几凭。琼液陛。乐舞翱。协气凝。民物祝。臣衷蹇蹇兮，报无能。

祭天撤馔时，奏唱"咸和之曲"：

太奏既成，微诚莫倾。皇德无京。陶此群生。巨细懞帡。刻小臣之感衷兮，罔罄愚情。实弘涵而容纳兮，曲赐生成。

这里的描述简短且不全面，但却体现了中国国家祭典的真实面貌。正如我们所见，奉老子为道祖的道教，本质上与一个思想纯洁的古老神秘主义者所设想的一般无二。老子的教诲与孔子承继的古老信仰和谐一致，就如盖恩夫人⑭、雅各布·伯曼⑮和劳威廉⑯的教导与《新约》一般和谐相融。

比较来看，有别于或相对于宗法性宗教的追随者，很少有中国人会自称为道教徒，其人数也许不超过自称为佛教徒的人，据权威人士估计，中国本土道教徒的数字低于2000万人。佛道两派都只是这个庞大帝国的一小部分，整个帝国深深浸淫在固有的古老的宗法性宗教之中。

远离血腥淫佚的典礼

让我们对中国宗教大加赞赏的是祭祀典礼温和而圣洁，没有受到血腥淫佚仪式的亵渎或玷污。即使由最敏感的人来看，典礼中也没有哪怕一句话或仪式让人惊惧得打冷战或臊得脸红。上帝无穷无尽、无形无相，没人用神像来侮辱其威严。没有任何一个性格残忍或为人卑鄙的英雄曾被提升到半神的地位。太阳神巴尔、罗马主神朱庇特或北欧雷神托尔一定对中国人对神的观念深恶痛绝。至于酒神狄俄尼索斯（巴克斯）、印度教的爱欲之神黑天，近东

The service of song is completed, but our poor sincerity cannot be expressed. Thy sovereign goodness is infinite. As a potter hast Thou made all things. Great and small are sheltered（by Thy love）. As engraven on the heart of Thy poor servant is the sense of Thy goodness, so that my feelings cannot, be fully displayed. With great kindness Thou dost bear with us, and, notwithstanding our demerit, dost grant us life and prosperity.

Such is a brief and imperfect description of the true and only religion of the Chinese as a nation. Taoism, as taught by Laotsze, was, as we have seen, essentially the same as conceived of by a pure-minded old mystic. His teaching was as much in harmony with the ancient religion handed down by Confucius as the teaching of Madame Guyon, Jacob Behmen, and William Law was in general harmony with the New Testament.

There are comparatively few Chinese who would call themselves Taoists, as distinct from, or opposed to, the followers of the patriarchal religion—perhaps not more than would call themselves Buddhists, a number which is placed by some authorities as low as 20000000 in China proper. Both are but fractions of the vast empire which is so deeply imbued with the old patriarchal religion of the country.

Free from Cruel and Licentious Rites

It adds greatly to our appreciation of the religion of China that it has never been profaned or polluted by cruel and licentious rites…There is not a word or rite to cause a shudder, or raise a blush, in the most sensitive mind… No idol ever insulted the majesty of the infinite and invisible God. No hero of cruel or immoral character was ever raised to the rank of even a demigod. A Baal, or Jupiter, or Thor would be abhorrent to Chinese ideas of deity. As for a Dionysus, a Bacchus, or a Krishna; an Astarte, an Aphrodite, or a Venus, they would not only be expelled with horror from the outer courts of a national temple: they would be excluded from the precincts of the meanest Buddhist or Taoist shrine in China.

While we find pleasure in giving expression to our high estimate of the primitive simplicity and purity of the real religion of China, and to the beauty of its ancient liturgy, we are far from being blind to its many defects and faults, which it would be easy to point out; but this is no part of our plan. These will be dealt with in another work which we hope to issue ere long, in which the religion of China will be more fully discussed, and compared with other religions. We leave it as imperfectly but truthfully portrayed, a most valuable relic of primitive religion…They are held and practised from respect for the truths handed down from remote antiquity — truths accepted on historic evidence and the authority of venerated ancestors.

In the present day, and even in the age of Confucius, the true significance of the worship of Shang-ti was unknown. Confucius himself confessed that he knew nothing of the meaning of the imperial sac-

爱神阿斯塔蒂、希腊爱神阿佛洛狄忒或罗马爱神维纳斯之流，不仅会被人满怀恐惧地驱逐出国家庙宇的外庭，还将被排除在中国最简陋的佛教寺庙或道教道观之外。

对中国原生性宗教原始、简单和纯洁的品质，以及其古代典礼之美，我们满心喜悦地表达了高度评价，但我们对它的许多缺陷和缺点也不是视而不见，指出它们很容易，但我们没有这样做，因为这不在我们的计划之中。这些问题将在不久后出版的另一部著作中讨论，其中将更充分地讨论中国的宗教，并与其他宗教进行比较。尽管此处的描述不完善，却是如实所述，我们将它留作原生性宗教最有价值的遗物。人们信奉它们，是出于对从远古流传下来的真知的尊重，这些真知是基于历史证据和最受尊崇的祖先的权威而被接受的。

在今天，甚至在孔子的时代，上帝崇拜的真正意义也未可知。孔子自己也承认，他对皇家祭祀的意义一无所知；然而，他以最大的敬意待之以礼，并严责仪式中态度倨傲轻浮之人。这些是世界原始朴素的教条与崇拜的典型化，值得我们像中国人那样去尊重。

rifices; yet he attended them with the greatest reverence, and severely censured those who attended them with an air of indifference. They are the stereotyped creed and worship of the world in its primitive simplicity, and are as deserving of our respect as they are of the reverence of the Chinese.

【注　释】

① 佛陀：对佛教的创始人乔达摩·悉达多（约前624—约前544）的尊称，他原是一个王子，后放弃家产、与家人断绝关系而成为一名苦行者，通过默想达到了大彻大悟的境界后，开始向所有前来求道的人传播思想。——译者注

② 琐罗亚斯德（约前628—约前551）：波斯先知和琐罗亚斯德教（又称拜火教）创始人，其生平鲜为人知，传说生于波斯。——译者注

③ 以斯拉：犹太教祭司和法学家，在公元前5世纪犹太教改革中起了核心作用。——译者注

④ 毕达哥拉斯（约前580—约前500）：希腊哲学家，传说他曾到古巴比伦和古埃及游历，受当地风俗、宗教影响，在意大利南部创立了"毕达哥拉斯学派"，是一个政治和宗教团体。——译者注

⑤ 实际上，老子是道家创始人，而道教的创始人为汉朝的张道陵。——译者注

⑥ 中国佛教史开始于公历纪元前后，佛教开始由古印度传入中国，经长期传播发展，而形成具有中国特色的中国佛教。据《后汉书·西域传》记载，汉明帝夜梦金人，"长大，顶有光明，以问群臣。或曰：'西方有神，名曰佛，其形长丈六尺而黄金色。'"于是汉明帝遣使西域，问佛道法。历来均以永平年间（58—75）遣使西域取回《四十二章经》为佛法传入中国之始。——译者注

⑦ 择一神教：尤指家庭、部落或其他团体在诸神中特选一神而敬奉之。此处，作者认为中国的宗教属于择一神教，即以昊天上帝为主神，同时还有陪祀神。——译者注

⑧ 我们不是在缪勒（Friedrich Max Müller）教授所归纳的意义上使用这个术语，而是在此处定义的意义上使用。——原注

⑨ 尼布甲尼撒王（Nebuchadnezzar Ⅱ，约前635—前562）：巴比伦国王，重建巴比伦城时建造了厚重的城墙、大型庙宇和金字形神塔，并把统治延伸到邻国，公元前586年攻陷并摧毁了耶路撒冷，在史称"巴比伦囚房"（Babylonian Captivity）时期驱逐并掳走了许多古希伯来人。——译者注

⑩ 但以理：希伯来先知，公元前6世纪被俘，由于其聪明才智，被选中服侍尼布甲尼撒王，在异邦朝廷历任大臣。在《圣经·但以理书》中，其曾为尼布甲尼撒王解梦。——译者注

⑪ 麦都思（Walter Henry Medhurst，1796—1857），自号墨海老人，英国传教士、汉学家。麦都思潜心研究中国的历史和文化，在《圣经》汉译、语言研究、典籍翻译等方面皆取得了不菲的成就，为中西方交流做出了卓有成效的努力和一定的贡献。——译者注

⑫ 花之安（Ernst Faber，1839—1899）：德国基督教礼贤会传教士、汉学家、植物学家。最著名的著作是《自西徂东》，这是一本在今天阅读起来依然富有启发性的文化论著，在当时希望变革的中国知识分子中间产生了广泛的影响。——译者注

⑬ 上文提及伏羲时代为公元前28世纪，与此不一致。——译者注

⑭ 盖恩夫人（Jeanne-Marie Bouvier de la Motte-Guyon，1648—1717）：法国神秘主义者，许多人认为她倡导寂静主义。罗马教会认为寂静主义是异端，盖恩夫人在出版了《简易祈祷法》一书后，于1695年至1703年被监禁。上海的俞成华医生在倪柝声的影响下，于1938年将盖恩夫人的传略译成中文，书名为《馨香的没药》。——译者注

⑮ 雅各布·伯曼（Jacob Behmen，1575—1624）：德国人，出生于一个贫穷但虔诚的路德教家庭，人称"日耳曼的神智学家"（the Teutonic Theosopher），曾被罗马教会视为异端。——译者注

⑯ 劳威廉（William Law，1686—1761）：英国人。劳威廉把盖恩夫人等饱经生命历练却显得神秘的教导，改进得非常实际，易于理解。其著作《敬虔与圣洁生活的严肃呼召》（A Serious Call to a Devout and Holy Life）首次刊发于1728年，这是一本堪称教导敬虔生活教科书的经典。——译者注

第七章　中国的未来
Chapter VII The Future of China

中国的境况

我们无意于预测中国明确的未来，或教条化地讨论现代文明对中国政治、商业和社会生活的影响。在此，我们不妨给出几条理由，来解释为何我们对这个庞大而可敬帝国的前途满怀希望，并给出一些理由来说明为什么外部国家不能通过使用武力来取得理性的、合乎道德的结果，因为这些结果只能通过智慧的、自愿的信念来实现；我们要力所能及地施以援手，终结关于欧洲某一个大国独自吞并中国或将中国在若干相互嫉妒和敌对的列强之间瓜分之类的荒谬言论。

我们对中国未来的独立、物质繁荣与

China's Position

Without attempting to predict a definite future for China, or dogmatizing on the effect of modern civilization on her political, commercial and social life, it may be well to give a few reasons for taking a hopeful view of the destiny of that vast and venerable empire, and to give some reasons why foreign nations should not attempt to use physical force to accomplish rational and moral results which can only be realized by intelligent and voluntary convictions; and to help so far as we can to put an end to the foolish talk of the absorption of China by some one European Power, or the division of the country among a number of mutually jealous and antagonistic empires.

Our reasons for hopefulness as

to the future independence and material and moral progress of China are found under the preceding chapters of our book, and we trust to the inferences being drawn by our readers; but for greater clearness and helpfulness we may briefly state our own convictions.

China Awakening

We assume that China cannot proceed on the old lines now that she has been so rudely awakened out of her long sleep. The leading minds in China are now alive to the necessity for introducing the scientific and mechanical appliances by which she has been so repeatedly humbled in recent wars; especially as this has been demonstrated in the sudden rise to power of her little old dependency, Japan.

The evidences of this awakening are manifold. The most hopeful is the establishment by the Government of a college in Peking, under the presidency of an American missionary, who has for years been on the best of terms with the leading members of the Tsungli Yamen. The introduction for some years past of questions outside the books of Confucius is a great innovation on old Chinese notions, and the premature attempt of the young Emperor to make an entire and immediate revolution in these examinations shows how the leaven

精神进步抱有希望的理由，可以在本书前面几章中找到，我们预测读者们正在得出相关推论；但为了使我们的表达更清楚、更有益，我们可以简要地阐述一下自己的主张。

中国觉醒

我们以为，既然中国已经从长眠中被如此粗鲁地唤醒，它就不能继续走老路了。清朝统治者现在切身体会到引进科学和机械设备的迫切性，因为在最近的几场战争中，它一而再地被坚船利炮彻底击溃；尤其是日本的突然崛起，更是证明了这一点。

这种觉醒的证据是多方面的。最令人鼓舞的是清政府在北京建立一所新式学堂——京师同文馆，由一位美国传教士担任总教习。多年来，丁韪良总教习与清朝总理衙门的主要成员关系良好。在过去的几年里，儒家经典之外的学说的引入是对中国旧观念的伟大革新，年轻的光绪皇帝试图对照西方进行全面和迅即的变革，虽然百日维新早早退场，却表明了发酵剂仍在发挥作用。尽管年迈的慈禧太后发动戊戌政变，囚禁光绪皇帝，但维新之势在不久的将来无可避免。在这样一个古老而又根深蒂固的体系中，与过去决裂，其重要性和意义非外国人可以理解。

教育改革

教育和科举考试改革的影响比英国公务员的竞争性考试大得多，英国公务员考试不像中国的那样包括总理大臣和政府各部门大臣的任职资格，考试的改革给全国各地的教育提供了新的动力和方向。现在中国人正在帝国的许多城市设中等学堂，学习西学，当前西式教育比旧式教育更有利可图。教育改革伴随着对科学书籍的需求，传教士协会的出版社一直忙于印刷这些被翻译成中文的著作。

甲午战争的影响

自从最近的那场战争以来，询问基督教教义和书籍的人数剧增，其学识水平也更高。因为他们觉得宗教中一定有某种东西赋予这些基督教国家此般不可抗拒的力

is working, and, though overturned by the usurpation of the old Empress, the change is inevitable in the near future. This breaking with the past in such an ancient and fundamental institution has an importance and significance which the foreigner can hardly understand.

Education Movement

This change in education and in the examinations for office is much more important than the competitive examinations in our Civil Service, which do not include in this country, as in China, admission to the office of Prime Minister and of Secretaries of State for all departments of the Government, and has given a new impulse and direction to education all over the country. The Chinese are now establishing high schools in many cities of the Empire…to be taught the learning of Europe…now more profitable than the old style. This is accompanied by a demand for books on scientific subjects, and the presses of missionary societies are kept busy printing such works as have been translated into the Chinese language.

Effect of the Japanese War

Since the recent war there has been a great increase in the number, and greater intelligence in the inquirers after Christian teaching and Christian books....because they feel that there must be something in the religion which endows these Christian nations with such resistless power, and the means of acquiring such wealth. The rapid rise of Japan has helped much to spread this spirit of inquiry. It has brought the subject before the minds of the Chinese far more forcibly. They know who and what the Japanese are, and that a paltry island, which had borrowed all its literature and art from China, and had until recently been a small dependency of the empire, should, by copying the arts and sciences of Christian nations, suddenly become more than a match in warfare and enterprise for all the power of the "Middle Kingdom" seemed a miracle...

Sleep Now Impossible

The great extension of commercial enterprise by the Chinese of late years, the increase of emigration, not merely, as of old, to the Straits of Malacca, but to distant regions and civilized countries, the opening up of the central provinces to steam navigation and foreign trade, the concession to the laying down of telegraph and railway lines, and the opening of mines, though granted reluctantly under external pressure, will make a return to the slumber of the past impossible. Even phlegmatic China cannot sleep with the click of the telegraph, the whistle of the railways, and the scream of the steamboat in her ears. The awakening may not yet be complete...A giant who has slept

量，以及获得此般财富的手段。日本的迅速崛起在很大程度上促进了这种探究精神的传播。它更有力地把这个问题呈现在中国有识之士的面前。中国人知道日本人是怎样的，也清楚一个过去从中国借鉴文学与艺术的弹丸岛国，通过模仿基督教国家的技术和科学，竟然会突然在作战能力和进取心方面超越"中央王朝"，这似乎是个奇迹。

现已无法重新沉睡

近年来，中国人的商业大规模扩张，移民增加，不仅像以前一样移民到马六甲海峡，而且移民到遥远的地区和国家，中部省份向蒸汽轮船和对外贸易开放，特许铺设电报和铁路线，以及开凿矿山等等。这一切虽然是迫于外部压力勉强同意，但将使得重归昔日的沉睡状态变得不可能。电报机滴滴答答的声音，铁路呜呜的汽笛声，蒸汽船嘟嘟的鸣笛声，让即使是沉着冷漠的中国也无法沉睡。中国可能还没完全醒过来，一个沉睡了几个世纪的巨人需要时间伸展一下筋骨，揉揉眼睛，但当它被彻底唤醒时，将走在未来亚洲进步的前沿，就像过去几千年一样。

中国的疆域和统一

我们对中国的未来充满希望，第一个理由就在于中国自身。当有人谈到瓜分中华帝国，或让欧洲任何一国对它实施征服时，他们忘记了帝国的情况。一个幅员辽阔、牢固统一的国家，拥有充足的资源来养活相当于全世界四分之一的人口，其人口是同一个种族，遵守同一部法律，信奉同一种信仰，几乎没有异见者，只有源源不断的加入者。假如欧洲列强真的同心同德，那么将这样一个国家瓜分成若干部分，以适应欧洲小国有限的同化能力，已然是一项艰巨的任务，何况列强各怀鬼胎、猜疑嫉妒，这就成了不可能的任务，还可能导致亚洲和欧洲大陆上无休止的战争；假如由某国把中国囫囵着吞下，最大的可能性是这顿饭难以消化。

英国花了一个世纪的时间征服印度，把印度划分为上百个小邦，依据许多截然不同的种族、不同的语言、不同的法律和

for centuries takes time to stretch himself and rub his eyes, but when thoroughly aroused, his march will be to the front of Asiatic progress in the future, as it has been for thousands of years in the past.

Extent and Unity of China

We find the first ground of hopefulness for the future of China in the country itself. When people speak of breaking up the Empire of China, or the conquest of it by any one nation in Europe, they forget what the empire is. A country of 1800 miles in length, and as much in breadth, a compact and solid unity, of ample resources for a population equal to the fourth part of the whole world, a population of one race, one law, one national religion, from which there is almost no dissent, only additions—to break up such a country into portions to suit the limited capacity of assimilation by the small nations of Europe would be a hard task if the nations of Europe were of one mind, but with their suspicions and jealousies, impossible, and likely to lead to endless wars, both in Asia and Europe; to swallow it whole would be found to be an indigestible meal by the largest.

It took England a century to conquer India, a country divided into a hundred petty States, separated by many distinct races, of different languages and laws and antagonistic religions, constantly at war with one another, where the maxim "Divide and conquer" was comparatively easy. China is a united nation, and though it could be overrun, it would be very difficult to subdue, as will be seen from its history. The self-satisfied exclusiveness of China is excusable in view of its vastness, compactness, and completeness of resources for all the wants of the population. Now that it is about to enter the comity of civilized empires, it will be found capable of maintaining its unity and independence if only given fair play by juvenile—one might say upstart—nationalities which have got the start in the race for civilization while China was handicapped by its unwieldy bulk and venerable prejudices.

The Past Inspires Hope

Our second ground of hopefulness is derived from a study of the history of China. Her past and present civilization is, as we have seen, all her own; she owes nothing but her misfortunes to foreign sources. A nation that could originate so much that is good in the industries and inventions, the laws, government, and administration of so vast an empire is not likely to be broken

对立的宗教把它们分隔开来，它们彼此之间战争不断。在印度，"分而治之"的格言相对容易得以验证。中国是一个统一的国家，尽管政权可能会被推翻，但很难将它征服，这从它的历史中可以看到。鉴于中国幅员辽阔、资源齐全，足以满足人民的一切需要，因此有些自满和闭关锁国情有可原。既然中国即将打开国门，进入文明国家联盟内，人们会发现，只要年轻的西方国家，也可以说是暴发户国家，给予中国公平游戏的机会，中国将有能力保持统一和独立。西方的暴发户们不过是在现代文明竞赛中抢占了先机，而中国因其庞大笨重的体量和值得尊敬的历史包袱而出师不利。

历史激起希望

我们对未来充满希望的第二个理由来自对中国历史的研究。正如我们所见，中国过去的和现在的文明都是它自己的；唯有它现今遭遇的不幸才归咎于外国。在产业及发明、法律、政府与国家行政方面能够做出许多有益创新且庞大如斯的帝国，不太可能被任何外部力量瓜分或吞并。麦考莱①在谈到西班牙人时说:"他们很容易被打败,但绝难被征服。"中国更是如此。在它四千年的历史中,中国从未被征服过。法律、社会习俗和宗教形式都没有改变。中国人是一个和平守法的民族,用一个王朝取代另一个王朝可能比较容易;但是,试图强迫他们改变,或者改变他们的律法和习俗,只会使他们更加顽强地坚守,因而这样反而是阻碍而不是加速他们的变革。

不因奢侈而萎靡

值得注意的是,中国人最近的历史和当下的习惯并没有显示出沉湎于奢侈生活而萎靡不振的迹象,而正是奢靡之风导致了古希腊和古罗马等的衰败和毁灭。诚然,他们已经远远好过第一个用象牙筷子代替木筷子的商纣王,他因沉溺于奢侈生活而被太师箕子进谏,谴责其将因此而亡国。许多富人花费大笔钱财购买宴席上的美味佳肴,但民众通常习惯于简朴、节俭,穷人并不像古希腊和古罗马衰落前的人们那样无所事事,只依靠富有公民的馈赠或被

to pieces or swallowed up by any external power. Macaulay said of the Spaniards that "they were easily defeated, but very difficult to conquer." This is much more true of China. During the 4000 years of her history China has never been conquered... not a law, nor social custom, nor form of religion, was changed....The Chinese are a peaceable and law-abiding people, and it might be comparatively easy to supplant one dynasty by another; but to attempt to force changes on the people, or to alter their laws and customs, would only make them cling to them the more tenaciously, and retard, rather than hasten, their reformation.

Not Enervated by Luxury

It is well to note that the more recent history and present habits of the Chinese do not indicate that abandonment to a life of luxury and effeminacy such as has led to the decay and ruin of empires like those of Greece and Rome. It is true they have got far beyond the Emperor who first used ivory instead of wooden chopsticks, and was denounced by the censor for the ruin of the empire by his indulging in such a luxury. Many of the rich spend large sums on dainty dishes at their feasts, but the people generally are simple and frugal in their habits, and the poor are not kept in idleness and fed on the gifts of wealthy citizens or the rations from oppressed provinces, as the Greeks and Romans were before their fall. The worst and most demoralizing vice of this kind is the indulgence in opium-smoking—a vice which has been much increased by the superior quality and scientific preparation of the drug from India, by our own country, and by the wars, which advertized it more effectively than the glaring placards of soaps or pills.

Not to multiply unduly the grounds of our confidence in the future of China, we may group two or three of the more important of them under one general head: the physical, intellectual, and religious characteristics of the people. It is on the constitution and character of a people that we must build our hopes of the stability and progress of a nation.

Physical Stamina

There are tribes and States in Asia which can boast of a physique superior to that of the Chinese, but they are few in number, and their population is limited. Taken as a whole, in average stature, weight, and muscular strength, there is no large Asiatic population to compare with them. Dr. Wells Williams says: "Their hands are small and their lower limbs better proportioned than among any Asiatics. The height is about the same as that of Europeans, and a thousand men, taken as they come in the streets of Canton, will prob-

征服地区供应的口粮为生。最糟糕也最令人沮丧的恶习是沉迷于吸食鸦片，产自印度的鸦片经过英国人的制备，以及广告效率远胜推销肥皂或药片的醒目招牌的鸦片战争，极大地助长了吸食鸦片的恶习。

为了把对中国前途充满信心的理由控制在适度的数量之内，我们不妨把其中两三个较重要的理由归入一个大标题：人民的身体素质、智慧和宗教特征。正是基于一个民族的体格与性格特征，我们才能建构对其国家稳定和进步的希望。

身体素质

亚洲有一些部落和国家可以夸耀自己的体质优于中国人，但数量很少，人口数也很有限。总的来说，在平均身高、体重和肌肉力量方面，没有多少亚洲人可以与他们相比。卫三畏博士说："中国人手很小，下肢比任何亚洲人都匀称。其身高与欧洲人差不多，假如拿广州街头的一千人来比较，他们身高和体重的数据很可能与在罗马或新奥尔良街头看到的人相当。"卫三畏博士认为他们的肌肉力量可能会弱些，但他承认，即使是在广州人中，这一结论也是存疑的，而福建人的肌肉力量会更大，到了中国北方，其身高、体重和肌肉力量明显高于普通欧洲人。在面容、脸色和肤色方面，中国人与白人无法进行审美比较，但在身体素质方面，他们与白人的平均样本相比还是占据上风的。

智　慧

在智慧方面，中国人在亚洲居首位，因为他们注重实用的特点，造就了一个又一个熟练的技工、踏实的劳动者、勤劳的店主、有进取心的商人、机敏的政治家、爱好和平的市民。这一点在今天的人民身上也可以看到，这也是我们能够解释中国作为一个帝国能长期繁荣的唯一方式。我们有理由希望，这些有益的特点成为其在未来的新环境中取得进展的保证。正是凭借着这些更朴素、更实用的特点，一个帝国才能长久稳定与真正进步，不论是在亚洲还是在欧洲，概莫能外。

ably equal in stature and weight the same number met with in the streets of Rome or New Orleans." Dr. Williams thinks their muscular power would probably be less, but this is, as he admits, doubtful, even among the Cantonese, while in Fuh Kien it would be greater, and in the North of China the stature, weight, and muscle would be decidedly above that of the average European. In face and complexion and colour they are not to be compared aesthetically with the Caucasian type, but physically they will bear favourable comparison with the average specimens of that race.

Intellectual Power

Intellectually, the Chinese take the first place in Asia, for those practical attributes which go to the formation of a skilful mechanic, a steady labourer, an industrious tradesman, an enterprising merchant, an astute statesman, and a peaceful citizen. This is seen in the people of to-day, and is the only way in which we can account for their long and prosperous existence as an empire. We have reason to hope that these useful attributes are a pledge of future progress in the new conditions by which they are environed…it is with those possessed of the more homely and useful qualities that the permanent stability and real progress of empire rests in Asia as in Europe.

Character of Their Gods

He was a wise man who said, "Tell me what their gods are, and I will tell you what the men are." As another said, "It is not the gods who have made the men, but the men who have made the gods"; and, as the Scriptures put it, "Thou thoughtest Me altogether such an one as thyself," and, "They that make them are like unto them." Judged by this test there is no heathen nation, ancient or modern, that can bear comparison with the Chinese, as we have shown in the chapter on religion, which we cannot here repeat. We admit that the superior character of the Supreme God of the Chinese, and the freedom of their inferior deities from the vices which we find in the character of the gods of all other heathen nations, has not saved the Chinese from the practice of vices as gross as those found in other lands; but we are all familiar with the expression, and too often with its practical application, "Video meliora proboque, deteriora sequor". But, though we "follow the worse course," it is a decided advantage to our moral nature that we do "see the better and approve it". It is also a proof of superiority of nature, that we do perceive and admire a moral standard higher than our practice. The superiority of the ideal to the practice of virtue is,

神的品质

一位智者曾说："告诉我他们神的样子，我就能告诉你他们的样子。"正如另一位智者所说："不是神创造了人，而是人创造了神。"也如《圣经》所说："你想我恰和你一样"，"做偶像的必和它们一样，所有倚靠它们的也必这样"。根据这一准则，无论古代还是现代，没有哪一个国家可以与中国相提并论，正如我们在关于宗教的那一章中所表明的那样，在此恕不赘述。我们承认，中国人的上帝具有优越的品质，陪祀神也没有沾染我们在所有其他国家的神的品质中所发现的邪恶，不过这并没有使中国人免于其他国家人们也有的恶习；我们都很熟悉这句话并经常这样做，"看到更好的路，却走向更坏的"。尽管我们"走的是更坏的路"，但我们确实"看到更好的并认可它"，这对我们的德性确有明显益处。这也是人类德性卓然的证明，即我们确实认识到并钦羡高于我们所作所为的道德标准。当然，理想对美德实践的优势地位对不同国家来说，正如对不同个体而言，是一个程度问题。在中国，这个程度比在当今其他国家都要高，更不用说比先前的任何时代的国家了。

道德的标准

中国人提出了比任何其他国家更高和更纯洁的上帝概念，这证明他们的道德标准更高，尽管他们的道德实践可能不比其他人高。我们在生活的各个方面都看到了这种高标准的道德情操，从皇帝的宫殿到农民的棚舍，从政府法令、法律执行、社会交往、商业买卖到一个店主的店铺。当政府欺压穷人、法官接受贿赂、商人向买主撒谎、店主欺骗顾客的时候，所有人依然口中说着正义、公平、仁慈、真理和诚实。一个肤浅的观察者可能会把这看作是在恶行的基础上平添虚伪。

与日本人比较

不要随意假设中国已经穷途末路了。这个国家拥有未来，老天在它的土壤与气候中填满了所有繁荣富足的元素，并在过去岁月中赐予了极大的祝福。日本和中国

of course, a question of degree in different nations, as in individuals. In China it is higher than in any heathen nations of our own, if not of any former age.

The Standard of Morality

That the Chinese presented, as we have seen, a higher and purer conception of God than any other heathen nation is a proof that their moral standard has been higher, though their practice is perhaps as low as that of others. We see this reference to a high standard of moral sentiment in every department of life, from the palace of the Emperor to the hut of the peasant—in Government edicts, in administration of law, in social intercourse, in commercial transactions, and in the tradesman's shop. All boast of righteousness, justice, charity, truth, and honesty, at the very time when the Government is oppressing the poor, and the judge is accepting a bribe, and the merchant is telling lies to deceive the purchaser, and the tradesman is cheating his customer. This a superficial observer may take as a proof of inferiority, adding hypocrisy to vice.

Compared with the Japanese

Do not let it be supposed that the career of China is over. There is a future for that country which God has so richly stored with all the elements of prosperity in her soil and climate, and so largely blessed in the past... In the movements of Japan and China there is all the difference between the agility of the monkey and the slow and heavy tread of the elephant; but when the elephant does set out on the march its progress will be steady and persevering.

China will not, like Japan, begin its imitation of Western customs by putting on a tile hat and a swallow-tailed coat—a kind of reform which is apt to be thrown off as quickly as it is put on. China will begin with what is important and useful, and make steady, if slow, progress. Japan's troubles are not over; in fact, they are only beginning. Internal conflicts were staved off by foreign war. That is a game which cannot well be played over again, and unjust wars, like chickens, "come home to roost."

Hope for the Future

The Chinese people have elements of character which give the hope of future prosperity for the empire. Their reverence for parents, which has always been the basis of government, gives the best foundation for the preservation of order and subjection to authority. They are peace-loving and easily governed. Their conservatism, if it retards progress, also checks useless innovations, and secures the stability of what progress is gained. They have great reverence for law and order, and have a large fund of common-sense. They

在行动上存在的差别好比猴子的敏捷与大象脚步的缓慢而沉重之间的不同；但是，当大象真的开始行进时，它的进步将是稳定和持久的。

中国不会像日本那样，从戴上高顶硬礼帽、穿上燕尾服开始模仿西方的习俗，这种改革容易被废弃，穿得快就扔得快。中国将从重要和有用的东西开始，取得稳步的进展，即便速度缓慢。日本的麻烦还没有结束；事实上，才刚刚开始。内部冲突因对外战争而得以掩盖。转嫁矛盾焦点的游戏不能总玩，非正义的战争总会让人"自食其果"。

展望未来

中国人的性格给了帝国未来繁荣的希望。他们对父母的孝顺一直是政府管理的基础，为维护秩序和服从权威打下了最好的基础。他们热爱和平，便于治理。他们因循守旧，如果说它阻碍了进步，却也会阻止无用的创新，并确保所取得的进步稳定向前。他们崇尚法律和秩序，并拥有大量的常识。他们爱好和平、崇尚勤劳、坚韧不拔、厉行节约、习惯简朴,这些都没有被吸食鸦片的恶习毁灭。他们在贸易和商业方面有天赋。在世界商业中心新加坡,各国齐聚于此展开竞争,最大的船队和修建在新加坡城周围缓坡上的最漂亮的别墅,通常属于中国人。他们在带来可怕的和有争议的成果的战争能力方面远远落后于英国,但是在优秀军官的教导下,他们是聪敏的好学生。戈登②将军不认为有比组成"常胜军"的中国人更勇敢、更精良的士兵,许多英国军官也证实了这一点。在战争后期,常胜军既没有训练,也没有军服,没有武器,没有食物。士兵对长官们没有信心,长官们对士兵也没有信心,长官们也不喜欢这位外国首领,因为戈登让他们参与到一个令人绝望的原因引发的争吵中。然而,他们中的许多人却知道如何像勇士一样在自己的岗位上以身殉职。

毫无根据的悲观主义

中国的历史证明,目前对中国现状和前景普遍所持的悲观态度是没有根据的。中华帝国尽管疆域广阔,却是一个奇妙的

are peaceable, industrious, persevering, frugal, and simple in their habits, where they have not been ruined by that vicious indulgence, opium-smoking. They have a genius for trade and commerce...In Singapore, that commercial navel of the world, where all the nations meet in competition...The largest fleets of shipping and the handsomest villas, built on the gently-rising knolls around Singapore, often belong to Chinamen...They are far behind us in the awful and questionable accomplishment of the needful art of war, but they are apt scholars under the teaching of good Christian officers. General Gordon wished for no braver and better soldiers than the Chinamen who formed his "ever-victorious army," and the same testimony has been borne by many of our British officers. In the late war they were neither drilled, nor clothed, nor armed, nor fed. They had no confidence in their leaders, and the leaders had neither confidence in them nor love for the foreign despot who sent them to fight his quarrels in a hopeless cause. Yet many of them knew how to die at their post like brave men.

Groundless Pessimism

The prevalent pessimistic view of the condition and prospects of China is not warranted by her history. The empire is a wonderful unity, notwithstanding its great extent, and has weathered worse storms and come through greater dangers than those which now threaten her…

Gordon's Mistake

His frantic attempts, with his own pistol, to shoot Li Hung Chang, by whom he had been employed and duped, was a practical admission that he had made a great mistake, though with his usual facility he soon forgave the duplicity of the man who had deceived him, butchered the Tai Pings and plundered the people. Gordon's aim was to put an end to bloodshed and cruelty; but he found that by defeating the rebels he made way for far greater cruelty and bloodshed by the Imperialists, besides binding a foreign yoke on the necks of the Chinese for at least another generation.

Compulsory Conversions

The leader of the rebels may not have been the man to found a new dynasty, or reform the Government, though the founder of the best and most enduring dynasty in China was, like him, a simple peasant. Hung would have cleared the way for others. He used rough but effectual means for putting down opium-smoking; he overthrew idolatry over a large part

统一体，它经受过比现在面临的威胁更严峻的风暴以及更严重的危险。

戈登的错误

李鸿章雇了戈登来，还欺骗了他，于是戈登拎着手枪疯狂寻找李鸿章决斗，这一举动实际上是承认自己犯下了一个大错误，尽管他很快就以一贯的灵活态度原谅了那个欺骗他、背信弃义屠杀太平军降兵降将和抢掠民众的人。戈登的目的是结束流血和残酷；但他发现，通过击败起义军，他为大清帝制拥护者实施更残酷的血腥统治铺平道路，并将洋人的枷锁套在中国人的脖子上至少又一代人的时间。

强制入拜上帝会

太平天国领袖洪秀全没能成为建立新王朝或改组政府之人，尽管中国最好的也是最持久的王朝③开创者朱元璋和他一样，都是朴实的农民。洪秀全为后来者扫清了道路。他用粗暴但有效的方法来制止吸食鸦片；他推翻了中国很大一部分地区的偶像崇拜；他消灭了许多现在阻碍进步的迷信；他以一种粗糙且错误的基督教形式宣誓入教，强迫他的追随者入拜上帝会，很像君士坦丁大帝④把基督教强加给罗马帝国一样，远没有查理曼⑤把它强加给撒克逊人那样残忍，查理曼的宗教狂热使他在一天内杀死了四千名撒克逊人，而且与使斯堪的纳维亚人皈依基督教的圣奥拉夫⑥一样始终如一；但洪秀全与热衷于改变人的信仰一样热衷于劫掠。

对立的政府理论

那个最近把中国打败并搞乱的国家，其巨大的优势主要在于近年来技术和科学上的发现，特别是学习西方国家将科学发现用于毁灭性战争，这些国家把和平的信念作为道貌岸然的理论，再把火药当作理论的实际应用。在中国，政府机构是根据先贤的理论建立的，即国内和平要靠统治者的美德和仁慈来维持，对外征服要靠一个治理良好、繁荣幸福的民族产生的吸引力来实现，只有如此，外国甚至敌国才会甘愿归附他们。所以，尽管火药最早是中国人发明的，却只是用来鸣放礼炮向朋友

of China; he put an end to many of the superstitions which now stand in the way of progress; he made a profession of a crude and corrupt form of Christianity, and compelled his followers to adopt it, in much the same way as Constantine imposed it on the Roman Empire, and with far less cruelty than Charlemagne forced it on the Saxons, of whom, in his pious zeal, he slew 4000 in one day, and with quite as much consistency as St. Olaus, who converted the Scandinavians; while he was equally zealous in proselytism and piracy...

Adverse Theories of Government

The great superiority of the nation's by which China has of late been overcome and disorganized lies mainly in mechanical and scientific discoveries of recent years, specially in their application to destructive warfare by Christian nations, who hold the Gospel of peace on earth as a pious theory, and use gunpowder as its practical application. In China the machinery of government has been set up on the theory of their sages, that peace at home is to be preserved by the virtue and beneficence of the rulers, and external conquests to be made by the attractive influence of a well-governed, prosperous, and happy people, to whom strangers, and even enemies, will voluntarily submit, or ally themselves. Hence gunpowder, which they were the first to invent, was only used for firing salutes in honour of friends, and their armies are only a badly disciplined provincial police, neither fitted nor intended for conquest, nor even for national defence. The depravity of rulers—the most of them foreign conquerors—and the cruel and unprepared-for assaults of foreign Powers, have at last opened the eyes of the present generation. Christian nations have convinced the Chinese that human nature is not so good as their old sages had represented it, and that physical, and not moral, forces are necessary for the preservation of peace and of the existence of the empire. This change will not only cause a revulsion in the feelings of the people, it will of itself go far to revolutionize the policy of the Government.

致敬的；他们的军队只是纪律松弛的地方警察，既不适合也不打算用于征服别国，甚至也不用于国防。统治者的堕落——大多数的外国征服者即如此——以及外国列强的残忍和突袭，终于让人们看清了真相。西方国家令中国人相信，人性并不像他们先贤所表述的那样"人之初，性本善"，武力，而非道德的力量，才是维护和平与中华帝国存亡所必需的。这种变化不仅会引起中国人情感上的剧变，它本身甚至会彻底改变政府的政策。

【注 释】

① 麦考莱（Thomas Babington Macaulay, 1800—1859）：英国历史学家、政治家，出生于苏格兰贵族之家。著有《自詹姆斯二世即位以来的英国史》（简称《英国史》）。——译者注

② 戈登（Charles George Gordon, 1833—1885）：维多利亚时代的英国工兵上将，由于在殖民时代异常活跃，被称为"中国的戈登""喀土穆的戈登"。他是一位管理能手，在领导常胜军时表现出一定战术技巧，清朝同治皇帝授予戈登清军最高军阶"提督"的称号。1863年12月，李鸿章在军营中招待郜永宽等八大太平天国降将。酒过三巡，李鸿章借故离开座位，然后暗示士兵动手，将八大降将处死在饭桌上。接着，李鸿章下令屠杀苏州城内4万名太平军将士（亦说2万名），是为"苏州杀降"，一时舆论哗然。李鸿章的行为使得为郜永宽等八人提供担保的戈登非常恼火。于是，他直接拿枪去淮军大营，扬言要杀了李鸿章。戈登气势汹汹，李鸿章避而不见，将大门关闭。后来中英双方为戈登和李鸿章组织了一个和解会议，希望他们化解矛盾。——译者注

③ 原作者此处应指明朝，但明朝国祚276年，少于周、商、夏、汉、宋、唐、清朝。准确地讲，明朝是中国最持久的大一统朝代。——译者注

④ 君士坦丁大帝（约274—337）：首位改信基督教的罗马皇帝，并于324年立基督教为国教。330年把首都从罗马迁至拜占庭，改城名为君士坦丁堡。——译者注

⑤ 查理曼（742—814）：亦称查理大帝，法国加洛林王朝国王（768—814年间在位），查理曼帝国建立者，因其军事征服和对罗马教廷的保护，被教皇利奥三世加冕为"罗马人的皇帝"。查理曼掌权后，试图将所有日耳曼民族统一为一个王国，并使他的臣民皈依基督教。为了完成这一使命，他在位的大部分时间都在进行军事行动。为了征服信奉异教的日耳曼部落撒克逊人，查理曼发动了血腥的、长达30年的系列战争，并赢得了冷酷无情的名声。据传，在782年的费尔登大屠杀中，查理曼下令屠杀了约4500名撒克逊人。他最终迫使撒克逊人皈依基督教，并宣布任何不接受洗礼或不遵循其他基督教传统的人都要被处死。——译者注

⑥ 圣奥拉夫（St. Olaus, 995—1030）：奥拉夫二世，挪威国王，在挪威强制推行基督教，使长期信奉北欧神灵的臣民改宗。其被后来继位的儿子马格努斯（Magnus）追认为殉道者。——译者注

附录　中国的人口
Appendix　The Population of China

We have assumed that the population of China proper is about 400 millions, on the strength of a dissertation on the subject which we appended to our work on "A Century of Christian Progress," published ten years ago, when we showed good reason for believing that at that time the population was not less than 380 millions. It is a very moderate increase to take it now at not less than 400 millions.

No Government in the world has shown such care as that of China in taking a census of the population. It is a sacred duty, and forms part of the great annual ritual when the Emperor sacrifices to Shangti. If the returns which are made officially every year show an increase, it is presented to God with joy and thankfulness. If they show a decrease, it is laid before God with profound expressions of

我们假定中国的人口大约是4亿，这是借助于我们10年前出版的《基督教百年发展史》一书中所附的一篇专题论文得出的，当时我们有充分的理由相信那时的人口不少于3.8亿。以非常温和的增长估算，现在人口不低于4亿。

在人口普查方面，世界上没有哪一个政府像中国政府那般重视。这是一项神圣的职责，是皇帝每年向上帝祭祀仪式的重要部分。如果每年官方普查报告显示人口增加，皇帝便满怀喜悦与感激地呈现给上帝；如果人口减少，皇帝在上帝面前则满怀深深的悲伤并忏悔失职之罪过。

撰文之时，我们面前有不下70份此类人口普查报告，数据参差不齐，出入很大，所以许多作者认为这些偏差证明所有数据皆不可信。但是，这些偏差有许多可以用普查时帝国所处的状况来解释，或者可以用特殊时期的普查目的来解释。

一些数字很小，其原因是当时有起义，使得一些省份无法上报普查数据。有一些数字很大，可由此前不寻常的和平与繁荣时期来解释。有些普查是按照人丁进行，目的是增加税收或摊派徭役，所以不出所料，中国百姓千方百计减少普查人数；有些普查是按照人口进行，针对的是饥荒时期要吃口粮的人口，结果数字大大增加了。

人口数的参差不一表明，每年的人口普查方法有很大缺陷，人口普查员不可靠；但并不能就此推断，一个审慎的统计学家无法从所掌握的大量材料中得出相当准确的人口估算。

我们所见过的最早的人口普查报告是公元2年的，当时西汉的户数为12233062户，人口数为59504078人。此后，人口下降了很多，波动很大。而康熙皇帝在人口普查方法上做了大量工作，使得普查过程井然有序、统一规范，从此人口普查结果

sorrow and confession of sin on the part of the ruler.

At the time we wrote we had before us no fewer than seventy of these census returns, showing great variations, which have been taken by many writers as a proof that all were unreliable. But, as we then showed, many of these inconsistencies could be explained by the state of the Empire at the time they were taken, or the object for which they were made at special times.

Some that were very low were accounted for by rebellions at the time, which prevented some provinces being returned. Some that were large were explained by previous periods of unusual peace and prosperity. Some were made as a census of heads, with a view to fresh taxes or levies of troops, and, as might be expected in China, means were taken to reduce the numbers returned; others were a census of mouths that were to be fed in times of famine, and the numbers were in consequence largely increased.

These irregularities show that the methods of taking the annual census were very defective, and the enumerators untrustworthy; but it does not follow that a fairly correct estimate may not be made from the great mass of materials at the disposal of a cautious statistician.

The earliest census that we have seen is that for the second year of the first Christian century, when the population was returned at 12233062 families, or 59504078 inhabitants. After which the numbers fell much lower, and fluctuated greatly. From the days of Kanghi, who did much to introduce order and uniformity in the method of taking the census, the returns have been much more reliable and consistent, and during the last hundred years, since foreigners have shown an interest in the subject, they seem to be substantially reliable, and where they depart from probability reasons can generally be found for apparent inconsistencies.

The following article from the *North China Herald* of July, 1887, is, we think, conclusive on the subject:

The results of an examination of these tables will be found useful for correcting opinions formed by many persons, it may be on insufficient data. The increase during the reign of Taukwang (1821 to 1848) was, according to the annual registration, 71196758; dividing this by 28, we obtain for the annual increase 2542500. This is 6.3 per cent, on 400 millions, and it amounts to an increase of 1 person to each group of 157 persons. Malthus mentions the increase annually in Sweden as 1 to 108, in Russia 1 to 63, in Prussia 1 to 62, in France 1 to 157, in England 1 to 131. Among these China most nearly approaches France. At this rate of increase the population will double

更加可靠、一致。在过去的100年中，外国人对人口问题表现出了兴趣，普查结果看起来基本上是可靠的，而每当数字偏离轨道时，通常可以找出明显不一致的原因。

下面的文章出自1887年7月的《北华捷报》①，我们认为其关于人口问题的结论无可置疑：

我们发现，人口数据表②查验的结果对纠正许多人的误解有所助益，人们的误解可能是因为数据不足。在道光皇帝统治的1821—1848年，根据每年的人口记录，人口增加了71196758人；再除以28年，我们得到每年平均增加2542500人。以4亿人为基数，人口年平均增长率为6.3%，这相当于每157人增加1人。人口学家马尔萨斯③提到瑞典人口年平均增长率为每108人增加1人，俄罗斯每63人增加1人，普鲁士每62人增加1人，法国每157人增加1人，英国每131人增加1人。其中，中国与法国最接近。按照这种增长速度，中国人口将在157年后翻一番。不过，即使如此，根据年度人口普查，中国人口的增长速度远低于许多欧洲国家。这种温和的年增长率有利于让人相信，增长率没有被夸大，反而确切地表明这些数字被低估了。马尔萨斯发现，1800年英国新增人口的估计数是每74人增加1人，增数太少了。原因是出生登记不够完善。在中国，法律要求地方官每年提交人口报告，但登记缺漏也在所难免。每年春季，里长负责报告本村人口情况。如果里长自己不会写字，他就请一个会写字的村民列出名单。村级的人口报告有时并不完全真实，有的父亲想把自家成年男丁隐瞒下来，免得将来征兵时被抓壮丁。普查登记时，只有登记家中人数，但有时来访的客人也希望自己被统计在内，以防他被当作"黑户"。然而，少报家庭人数的理由比多报家庭人数的理由强得多，影响也广得多。如果一个地方连续多年没有重新统计人口，就沿用旧的数据表。

1760年，当刘松龄④担任钦天监监正时，他从户部拿到了人口普查数

itself in 157 years. But in this case the Chinese population is increasing at a much slower rate according to the annual census than in many European countries. This moderation in the annual increase is in favour of its being accepted as not exaggerated, and rather suggests in fact that the numbers are understated. Malthus found that the estimate of population for England in 1800 was too little by 1 in 74. The registration of births was imperfect. Just so it is in China with the population returns required by law to be presented annually by local magistrates. It is the duty of the village bailiff to report the population of his village every spring. If he cannot write himself, he asks a villager who can do so to make out the list. The return is sometimes under the truth, through the desire felt by the fathers of grown-up sons to save them from conscription. Only persons at home are counted, but occasionally when some visitor is expected he is counted in, in order that suspicion may not fall on him as an unregistered person when he arrives. The reasons for understating the number of a household are, however, much stronger than those for overstating it, and are much more widely influential. The people in a locality are often not counted again for many years in succession, the old lists being used.

When Pere Allerstain was

President of the Board of Astronomy in 1760, he obtained the census from the Board of Revenue, and it gave 197 millions as the population of China for that year. The next year it was more than 198 millions. During the sixty years that elapsed from that time to the reign of Taukwang the population rose to 355 millions. The increase was 157 millions, and was made up of annual additions of about millions — the same as in the period from 1820 to 1848. Knowing this fact, we feel confidence in the correctness of the returns. The causes of increase are always at work— the thoroughness of the agriculture, the fertility of the soil, the anxiety of parents to see their sons married by the time they are eighteen, the willingness of the women to be married at seventeen or thereabouts, and become domestic drudges in their husband's home for the first few years of married life; the equality of sons as heirs to property, the thrifty habits of the people, and their adaptability to a variety of occupations requiring skill and industry. Yet with these powerful causes operating, the census is augmented at quite a moderate pace. Amyot, Malthus, Williams, accept and vindicate the Chinese numbers. It is just as well for us to follow these good examples of sober judgment on the part of men who have studied the subject. It is worth remarking that Amyot was astonished at the

据，该数据显示中国当年的人口为1.97亿。第二年超过了1.98亿。自此至道光初年的60年中，人口增加到3.55亿。人数共增加了1.57亿，每年大约有几百万的新增人口，与1820—1848年间相同。了解了这一事实，我们对普查报告的准确性充满信心。人口增长总是有起作用的诱因——农业精耕细作、土壤肥沃；家长对儿子们在18岁时结婚的期盼，女儿们在17岁左右时出嫁，并在婚后的头几年里在婆家操持家务的意愿；儿子们继承财产的平等权利，人民的节俭习惯，以及他们适应各种职业所需的技能与勤奋等。然而，尽管有这些诱因存在，人口却只是以相当温和的速度增加。阿米欧、马尔萨斯、卫三畏等人接受并证明了中国的人口数字准确无误。我们不妨听取一下研究人口问题专家的看法，他们可以冷静地判断。值得再次提及的是，阿米欧惊讶地发现四川省人口增长迅速，须缴纳人口税的家庭从144000户增加到3036342户。他补充说："家庭户数惊人的剧增无疑来自难民的涌入，在清朝入主中原时逃难之人入川寻找新家园。"他认为百年后的人口普查不会真实地反映出四川省7100万的人口状况,而事实确实如此。我们现在必须准备接受一个意想不到的结论,即这些省份没有哪一个省的人口达到了土壤肥力无法供养其居民的地步。每当发生旱灾和战争时,人们逃难到邻省,于是各省轮流变得人口稠密或稀少,只要有新的助力来应对饥荒和内战,似乎各省可以毫不费力地养活8亿人。若真如此的话,江苏省不一定比40年前人口更稠密,即便是聪明的外国旅行者也几乎不会注意到这一点。每年的人口普查结果都不完善:在许多情况下,它们可能并不是真正的新数据。但在统计人口时还是尽可能地准确,所得数字低于实际人口数。

以下的《中国人口表》,由柏百福[5]先生根据1882年的官方文件编制,不全处则由1879年官方文件的数据补充。

rapid increase of population which he noticed in Szechuen, which had risen from 144000 families, liable to the population tax, to 3036342. He adds, "this prodigious augmentation comes no doubt from the presence of refugees who sought a new home there at the time of the Manchu conquest." He did not think that the census would a century later represent the population of Szechuen as 71 millions. Yet so it is. We must now be prepared for the unexpected conclusion that the provinces are none of them populated up to the point when the fertility of the soil cannot maintain the inhabitants. When drought and war occur, the people fly to the next province, the provinces take their turns in being thickly or thinly populated, and with new aids against famines and civil war they might, it would seem, support 800 millions without much difficulty. If this were the case, Kiangsu need not be more thickly peopled than it was forty years ago, and intelligent foreign travellers would scarcely notice the difference. The census returns for each year are imperfect: they are probably not really new in a multitude of cases. But when the people are counted it is done with as much accuracy as possible, and the amount is under the actual population.

Table of Population of China, drawn up by Mr. Popoff from Official Documents of the Year 1882, supplemented where Defective by those of 1879.

省份	1842年人口数	1882年人口数	人口增减	面积（平方英里）	每平方英里人口数
山东	29529877	36247835	+6717958	65104	557
山西	17096925	12211453	-4845472*	56268	221*
河南	29069771	22115827	-6953941*	65104	340
江苏	39646924	20905171	-18741753	44500	470
江西	26513889	24534118	-1979771	72176	340
浙江	30437974	11588692	-18849282	39150	296
湖北	28584564	33365005	+4780441	70650	473
湖南	20048969	21002604	+953635	74320	822*
四川	22256964	67712897	+45455933	166800	406
广东	21152603	29706249	+8553646	79456	377*
总计		279389885*			

省份	1842年人口数	1879年人口数	人口增减	面积（平方英里）	每平方英里人口数
云南	5823670	11721576	+5897906	107969	108
贵州	5679128	7669181	+1990053	64554	118
陕西	10309769	8432193	-1877576	67400	126
甘肃	19512716	5411188	-14101528	86608	62
直隶	36879838	17937000	-18942838	58949	304
安徽	36596988	20596988	-16000000	48461	425
广西	8121327	5121327	-3000000	78250	65
福建	25799556	25799556	—	53480	482
总计⑥	413021452	382078860	-30942592	1297999*	234*

人口数从1842年的4.13亿下降到1882年的3.82亿，并未出乎人们意料之外，这正是太平天国起义的大战以及镇压者的屠杀和压迫所导致的痛苦结局；如果1882年

The fall from 413 millions in 1842 to 382 millions in 1882 is quite what one might expect, from what was suffered from the great wars of the Tai Ping rebellion and the massacres and oppression of

希望的国度：
晚清西人看中国

those who crushed it; and if it was 382 millions in 1882, it cannot be less than 400 millions in 1898.

清朝的人口是3.82亿，那么1898年的人口不可能少于4亿。

【注　释】

① 《北华捷报》：又名《华北先驱周报》或《先锋报》，上海第一家英文报刊。1850年（道光三十年）8月3日由英国拍卖行商人奚安门（Henry Shearman）在上海的英租界创办，每周六出报。主要刊载广告、行情和船期等商业性材料，同时也刊有言论、中外新闻和英国驻沪外交、商务机关的文告，并转载其他报刊的稿件，供外国侨民阅览。有关太平天国的报道甚多，是研究太平天国的重要参考资料，一定程度上反映出英国政府的观点，被视为"英国官报"。——译者注

② 我们只需从这些详尽的人口数据表中举出一例，即可见中国人口普查结果之一斑。——原注

③ 马尔萨斯（Thomas Robert Malthus, 1766—1834）：英国经济学家，著有《人口论》（1798），认为人口的增长比食物供应的增长要快，除非对人口的增长采用道德的约束或战争、饥荒和瘟疫加以抑制，否则会导致不可避免的灾难后果。——译者注

④ 刘松龄（Augustin von Hallerstein, 1703—1774）：斯洛文尼亚人，1746—1774年任钦天监监正。——译者注

⑤ 柏百福（Pavel Stepanovich Popoff, 1842—1913）：俄国外交官、汉学家，曾任驻华领事。1888年，柏百福增订并完成由鲍乃迪（Archimandrite Palladius）原著的两卷本辞典《华俄大辞典》。——译者注

⑥ 此表为中国人口数的不完全统计，仅列出内地十八省的数据。此外，此表制法在严格意义上并不严谨。表格中数字有问题处均标"*"号以注明。此处的总计包括表格上半部分的数据；1882年有记录的各省人口数总和应为279389851；人口增减一列，山西增减应为-4885472，河南省应为-6953944；面积一列，总计应为1299199；每平方英里人口数一列，山西省应为217，湖南省应为282，广东省应为274，总计应为294。——译者注

译后记
Afterword

    值此译稿杀青付梓之际，译者深怀感恩之心，回顾过去一年中所得到的无私关怀与帮助。感谢厦门市社会科学院给予立项和资金支持，感谢厦门理工学院外国语学院院长张金生教授等同事的鼓励、建议与批评，感谢集美大学苏宗文教授一如既往地给予鼓舞、关注、学术支持与无私奉献。还要感谢厦门大学出版社章木良编辑的团队，设计精美，水平专业，快速高效。章编辑既有对方向的把握，又有对细节的关注，工作井井有条，把一切都考虑得仔细周到。最后，对所有关心、关爱本书的朋友、同事，在此不具名地一并致以谢忱。

周维江
于厦门理工学院